*Strategic
Management*

Strategic Management:
A Cross-Functional Approach

Stephen J. Porth

Erivan K. Haub School of Business
Saint Joseph's University

Contributing Authors:

John B. Lord

A. J. Stagliano

Claire A. Simmers

Ravi Kathuria

Maheshkumar Joshi

Ann Mooney

Upper Saddle River, New Jersey 07458

Library of Congress Cataloging-in-Publication Data

Porth, Stephen J.
    Strategic management: a cross-functional approach/by Stephen J. Porth.
      p. cm.
    Includes bibliographical references and index.
    ISBN 0-13-042213-4
    1. Strategic planning. 2. Industrial management. I. Title.
HD30.28.P685   2002
658.4'012—dc21

                                        2001055413

Executive Editor: David Shafer
Editor-in-Chief: Jeff Shelstad
Assistant Editor: Melanie Olsen
Editorial Assistant: Kevin Glynn
Senior Marketing Manager: Shannon Moore
Marketing Assistant: Christine Genneken
Managing Editor (Production): John Roberts
Production Editor: Kelly Warsak
Permissions Coordinator: Suzanne Grappi
Associate Director, Manufacturing: Vincent Scelta
Production Manager: Arnold Vila
Manufacturing Buyer: Michelle Klein
Cover Designer: Bruce Kenselaar
Composition: BookMasters, Inc.
Full-Service Project Management: BookMasters, Inc.
Printer/Binder: Hamilton Printing Company
Cover Printer: Phoenix Color Corp.

Credits and acknowledgments borrowed from other sources and reproduced, with permission, in this textbook appear on appropriate page within text.

Pearson Education LTD.
Pearson Education Australia PTY, Limited
Pearson Education Singapore, Pte. Ltd
Pearson Education North Asia Ltd
Pearson Education, Canada, Ltd
Pearson Educación de Mexico, S.A. de C.V.
Pearson Education—Japan
Pearson Education Malaysia, Pte. Ltd

10 9 8 7 6 5 4 3 2 1
ISBN 0-13-042213-4

To Mary, Stephen, Molly, Leo, Tommy, and Conor

Brief Contents

CONTENTS

PREFACE

Welcome to the first edition of *Strategic Management: A Cross-Functional Approach.* We believe this book is the first of its kind on the market. It is a truly cross-functional perspective on strategic management, written by a professor/consultant of strategic management and enhanced by significant contributions from experts in the fields of finance, marketing, accounting, e-commerce, international business, and operations management.

The need for this cross-functional perspective first became apparent to me when a group of faculty at our university began to work on a revision of our business policy course. As we discussed our hopes for the new course, we identified a common challenge we wanted to overcome. We wanted students to see that successful strategic management requires an ability to see the organization as a whole; to step out of the functional mind-sets that students tend to acquire through previous work and academic experiences, and to see the organization in a new way. The marketers and human resources folks needed to understand the financials and how to use them, and the finance and accounting people needed to see that customer and employee relationships were the lifeblood of the organization. Good strategic managers are good general managers—they are not stuck in functional silos!

Our revised business policy course is cross-functional and integrative, emphasizing strategic concepts and tools from the fields of management, finance/accounting, international business, information systems, and marketing. As we prepared to launch the course, our review of textbooks led us to conclude that there was a gap in the market. Truly cross-functional and integrative texts that also cover the tools and theory of the strategic management field are difficult if not impossible to find. This book is an attempt to fill that gap.

Some of the special features of this book are:

- The theory and tools of strategic management are introduced, discussed, and are complemented by a cross-functional perspective. The cross-functional perspective is driven by an emphasis on *value creation* for customers, employees, and owners/stockholders. This concept, called the *customer–employee–owner cycle,* is introduced in Chapter 1 and serves as an organizing framework throughout the book.
- Each chapter includes a "focus company" used throughout the chapter as a running example of key concepts. The focus company serves as a mini-case to illustrate and embellish the material in the chapter. A box insert introduces the focus company, provides a brief description of it, identifies its Web site address, and invites the reader to go online to find out more about the company. Focus companies include organizations that students are familiar with and interested in, such as Nike, Microsoft, Wrigley, Hilton, and Southwest Airlines.

- The book is supported by a Web site that provides resources and up-to-date information on each of the focus companies, including financial statements. Discussion questions at the end of each chapter suggest ways the Web site can be used in the learning process.
- In addition to the focus company, each chapter includes vignettes about several companies as examples of text material.
- Chapters begin with an outline and a set of questions that are addressed in the chapter, and conclude with a set of key terms and concepts, discussion questions, and an experiential exercise.
- Ancillary materials include an instructor's manual with a test bank, transparency masters, a dedicated Web site, and PowerPoint disks.

ACKNOWLEDGMENTS

I have so many people to thank for their support and cooperation in writing this book, beginning with the contributing authors. John Lord has been a colleague and friend for more years than I can remember. His expertise is marketing strategy and new product development in the food industry. John was the lead author of Chapter 6 and made contributions to Chapters 1, 3, and 4. A. J. Stagliano is an accomplished researcher and teacher. His expertise in the areas of accounting and financial management has been invaluable. A. J. took the lead on Chapter 7 and also contributed to Chapter 2. Claire Simmers was the lead author of Chapter 5 and also played a part in writing Chapters 1 and 3. Claire is a terrific colleague and has been a joy to work with. Ravi Kathuria is one of the most prolific emerging scholars in the field of operations management. His work ethic is remarkable. I always enjoy working with Ravi and I thank him for taking the lead on Chapter 9. Mahesh Joshi has expertise in e-commerce and strategy implementation. He contributed the sections on e-commerce found in Chapters 1 and 2 and made a contribution on the role of middle managers in strategy implementation found in Chapter 8. Ann Mooney was an enthusiastic supporter of this project. She provided me with thorough, timely, and intelligent reviews of the book while it was in process. Ann also wrote the section on behavioral aspects of strategic choice in Chapter 6. I am indebted to my colleagues for their cooperation in writing this book, and for putting up with me throughout the process!

George Webster, Liz Davis, Ned Dunn, and Marty Meloche are faculty colleagues and friends who have supported this project from the beginning. In addition, I have had the privilege of working for two deans—Greg Dell'Omo and Joe DiAngelo—who understood the importance of this book to me and supported me each step of the way.

I have had administrative assistance for this project from some of the best. Bernice Brogan, Mary Finelli, Ann Marziani, and the MVP of all graduate assistants, Cem Coskungonul, helped to bring my dream to a reality. Thank you.

Working with Prentice Hall has been a distinct advantage for me. The Prentice Hall team has been great. I thank David Shafer, Executive Editor, for his guidance and his confidence in me. David's belief in my approach and ideas were a strong motivator for me. Thanks to Kim Marsden, David's assistant, for her responsiveness and professionalism. Read Wickham, our local sales representative, encouraged me to submit my proposal to Prentice Hall and has been enthusiastic about the project from day one. Also, I thank the team of reviewers who provided me with insightful comments and recommendations for improving this book and helped to shape its final form:

- Mike Wasserman, George Mason University
- John Cote, Baker College
- William Zierdt, Marian College of Fond du LacAnne
- D. Smith, University of New Mexico
- Brad Brown, University of Virginia
- James Shaw, University of San Francisco

It is a gift to enjoy your life's work. For that joy I thank my students—undergraduate, MBA, and executives. I look forward to my time in the classroom because of you. This book was written with you in mind.

Finally and most importantly, I want to thank my wife and children. Mary and kids—this book is dedicated to you. I am a lucky man. Thanks!

Steve Porth
Saint Joseph's University

Strategic
Management

Chapter 1

Strategic Management: An Overview

Dear Shareholders:
This year produced considerable pain. Soft markets, sagging orders,
sliding economies, operating profits down 37 percent. But, the most
painful by far was the layoff of 1,600 friends and co-workers,
people whose lives and plans were changed. It was an agony felt in
every corner of the company.[1]

This is the opening paragraph of Phil Knight's letter to shareholders in a recent Nike annual report. Phil Knight is chairman
of the board and chief executive officer (CEO) of Nike, Inc, the
$10 billion global sports and fitness company. Nike is known by
customers for its high-performance athletic shoes and apparel,
and its brash, in-your-face, "just do it" image. Investors have

known Nike for its track record of stellar growth and remarkable returns to stockholders.

But times change, even for market leaders such as Nike. At the beginning of the twenty-first century, Nike is in the unfamiliar strategic position of needing a turnaround to rebound from sub-standard performance—and Phil Knight has a lot of explaining to do. Customers aren't buying, at least not as projected, employees have been laid off, Nike has been criticized harshly for its foreign labor practices, and shareholders are not pleased.

In a general sense, Nike's strategic challenge is the same challenge faced by all organizations. Through the process of strategic management, Nike must determine a course of action that will enable the company to achieve its mission and objectives. The new course of action must address the interests of many stakeholders, especially stockholders, customers, and employees. Specifically, Nike must create and implement strategies that produce economic value for stockholders, superior products for customers, and rewarding employment experiences for Nike managers and associates, and do all this in a socially responsible way.

WHAT IS STRATEGIC MANAGEMENT?

Strategic management is a process of formulating, implementing, and evaluating **cross-functional** decisions that enable the organization to define and achieve its mission, and ultimately to create value. The process focuses on a series of fundamental questions about the organization: What is our business? What do we want to become? Who are our customers? What do our customers value?[2] By answering these types of questions the strategic management process helps to establish the future direction of the firm.

In the case of Nike, it was the strategic management process that guided managers as they created a $10 billion global success story, and it will be the strategic management process that will help Nike managers navigate through the turbulence and pain of "soft markets, sagging orders, and sliding economies."

The strategic management process is comprised of five interrelated steps:

1. Establish the vision and mission of the organization: Identify the reason for the organization and what it aspires to become.
2. Perform a situation analysis: Understand the strengths and weaknesses of the organization and scan its external environment.
3. Set objectives and craft a strategy: Determine the future direction of the organization and how it will achieve its mission and vision.
4. Implement the strategy: Execute the chosen strategy in an efficient and effective manner.
5. Assess the success of the strategy: Determine whether the strategy has created value for key stakeholders and provide feedback for corrective action if necessary.

Each step of the process focuses on one overriding purpose—to create value. The **strategic management framework,** displayed in Figure 1-1, identifies the major steps in the strategic management process and the relationships between the steps. Let's briefly examine each component of the model as an introduction to the major topics and remaining chapters of the book.

Value Creation

The essence of strategic management is the challenge of rewarding key stakeholders, especially customers, employees, and ultimately, owners. Organizations that create value for these stakeholders survive and prosper. Those that don't will inevitably

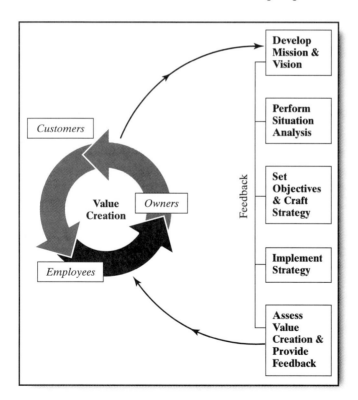

Figure 1-1
The strategic management framework

decline. Whether the organization is large or small, privately owned or public, for profit or not, the primary focus and the ultimate outcome of successful strategic management is **value creation.**

For example, Nike creates value for customers by designing and marketing high-performance athletic shoes. Value for owners is produced when Nike shoes are sold at a price that generates a profit and contributes to stockholders' interests. And value for employees is created through the financial and nonfinancial rewards and satisfaction received by employees for their efforts.

Nonprofit organizations face a similar value creation challenge. Habitat for Humanity, for example, seeks "to eliminate poverty housing from the world and to make a decent shelter a matter of conscience. By having affluent and poor work together in equal partnership, Habitat hopes to build new relationships and a sense of community as well as new houses,"[3] Habitat creates value by constructing and refurbishing houses for the poor and marginalized (the customers), within a budget that is consistent with managers' interests, by employees and volunteers who are (intrinsically) rewarded for their contributions to an important social cause. Value creation is the engine that drives Habitat for Humanity, just as it drives Nike.

Value creation is an organizational imperative, and the ultimate outcome of a successful strategic management process, but *value,* as a concept, means different things to different stakeholders. These meanings are defined and examined in Chapter 2.

Table 1-1 identifies examples of different types of value created for customers, employees, and owners by a successful strategic management process. It is important to stress that these types of value are not incompatible. To the contrary, they are interdependent. Over the long term, the organization cannot create value for its owners if it does not first create value for customers and employees. Leading companies recognize the vital link between customers, employees, and owners, and are committed to creating value for each group. That's why value creation is depicted as a dynamic cycle of interlocking pieces in Figure 1-1.

Developing a Mission and Vision

The focus of Chapter 3 is the first step in the strategic management process—developing a clear understanding of the mission and vision of the organization. The **mission** statement identifies the enduring purpose of the organization and answers questions such as Who are we? What is our business? Why do we exist? The mission statement is grounded in the present; that is, it focuses on the current markets and customers served by the organization.

Table 1-1 Examples of value creation

CUSTOMERS	EMPLOYEES	OWNERS
• Quality products and services • Perceived value in terms of price paid versus benefits received	• Rewarding jobs, in terms of both financial compensation and social and psychological benefits	• An increasing and acceptable return on financial investment

Not only do managers need to articulate the organization's current purpose and sense of identity, but also their aspirations for the future of the company. The **vision** of an organization is a statement about its future—where the firm is headed, what it aspires to become, how it hopes to be viewed by the public. The vision statement expresses a view of the future that is realistic, credible, and attractive for the organization,[4] and answers the question "What do we want to become?"

Research indicates that most organizations have a mission statement and/or a vision statement, and that these statements are becoming increasingly common. Some companies, such as Johnson & Johnson, have a credo that serves essentially the same purpose as a mission (see Table 1-2).[5] A *credo* is a statement of the organization's values, or a *philosophy* of business, and may be used instead of, or in addition to, a mission or vision.

In some organizations the conceptual distinction between mission and vision is blurred. For example, Dell's mission—"to be the most successful computer company in the world at delivering the best customer experience in the markets we serve"—is a future-oriented mission statement that reads more like a vision. Their vision is simply "There is a difference at Dell."[6] Notwithstanding the Dell example, the distinction between mission and vision is relevant for most companies. This distinction can be seen in Ford Motor's mission, vision, and values statements[7] in Table 1-3.

Mission and vision statements are meant to be important aspects of the strategic management process. They can be nothing more than words on a piece of paper in some organizations, however. When this is the case, the statement has no power; it does not influence strategic choice in any meaningful way. These types of statements are worth no more than the paper on which they are written. The true test of a mission or vision statement is the degree to which employees understand it, embrace it, and use it to guide the business decisions they make.

Performing a Situation Analysis

Before managers can define organizational objectives and choose strategies, they must understand the internal condition of the organization and its external environment. This understanding is gained through a *situation analysis,* a careful and ongoing assessment of the organization's external and internal circumstances. The situation analysis is performed in two parts: an **internal audit** to identify the organization's strengths and weaknesses (SW), and an **external audit** to determine opportunities and threats (OT). The external audit is also known as *environmental scanning.* Because of their emphasis on identifying strengths, weaknesses, opportunities and threats, the audits are often collectively referred to as a *SWOT Analysis.*

The Internal Audit

As we will discuss in Chapter 4, assessing the organization's internal environment for strengths and weaknesses is a key step in the strategic management process. This step requires an evaluation of the organization's financial condition, as well as a survey and assessment of infrastructure, human resources, technology development, procurement, inbound and outbound logistics, operations, marketing and sales, and support services, for example.[8] Essentially, the task is to critically evaluate all activities

Table 1-2 Johnson & Johnson credo

We believe our first responsibility is to the doctors, nurses and patients, to mothers and fathers and all others who use our products and services.
In meeting their needs everything we do must be of high quality.
We must constantly strive to reduce our costs in order to maintain reasonable prices.
Customers' orders must be serviced promptly and accurately.
Our suppliers and distributors must have an opportunity to make a fair profit.

We are responsible to our employees, the men and women who work with us throughout the world.
Everyone must be considered as an individual.
We must respect their dignity and recognize their merit.
They must have a sense of security in their jobs.
Compensation must be fair and adequate, and working conditions clean, orderly and safe.
We must be mindful of ways to help our employees fulfill their family responsibilities.
Employees must feel free to make suggestions and complaints.
There must be equal opportunity for employment, development and advancement for those qualified.
We must provide competent management, and their actions must be just and ethical.

We are responsible to the communities in which we live and work and to the world community as well.
We must be good citizens—support good works and charities and bear our fair share of taxes.
We must encourage civic improvements and better health and education.
We must maintain in good order the property we are privileged to use, protecting the environment and natural resources.

Our final responsibility is to our stockholders.
Business must make a sound profit.
We must experiment with new ideas.
Research must be carried on, innovative programs developed and mistakes paid for.
New equipment must be purchased, new facilities provided and new products launched.
Reserves must be created to provide for adverse times.
When we operate according to these principles, the stockholders should realize a fair return.

Source: Johnson & Johnson, Johnson & Johnson Credo, www.jnj.com, accessed July 20, 2000. Used with permission of Johnson & Johnson.

performed by the firm to identify sources of strength or weakness. Some of the critical questions to be answered in the internal audit include:

- What are the firm's financial strengths and weaknesses?
- Are employees competent and committed to the organization's mission? How well does the organization recruit, retain, and reward qualified employees?
- How well does the firm manage customer relationships? What does the firm do or not do that creates or loses value for customers?
- What are the firm's core competencies? That is, what are the firm's special skills, abilities, and resources relative to competitors? What core competencies will be needed in the future to compete successfully?

Table 1-3 Ford Motor Company—Vision, mission, and values statements

- Our **Vision** is to become the world's leading consumer company for automotive products and services.
- Our **Mission:** We are a global family with a proud heritage, passionately committed to providing personal mobility for people around the world. We anticipate consumer needs and deliver outstanding products and services that improve people's lives.
- Our **Values:** The customer is Job 1. We do the right thing for our customers, our people, our environment and our society. By improving everything we do, we provide superior returns to our shareholders.

Source: Ford Motor Company, "Vision, Mission, Values," www.mycareer.ford.com/OurCompany.asp, accessed September 29, 2000. Used with permission of Ford Motor Company.

Accomplishing the internal audit is a matter of extensive research and analysis, and includes examining financial statements, staffing and productivity standards, information resources, organization charts, customer and employee surveys, and interviewing internal stakeholders (e.g., managers and staff) and external stakeholders (suppliers, distributors, customers).[9]

Turning to the example of Nike, it is clear that their declining performance is due not only to external forces but also to internal factors. Boring ads, management resignations, and a major layoff all reflect or result from internal weaknesses. In addition, Nike has been sharply criticized for its foreign labor practices, especially for working conditions and wages in Asian factories. In response, Nike contends that it pays more than the prevailing average local wage and that it does not own the foreign production plants where its products are made. Nevertheless, Nike has suffered from poor public relations. Protests on college campuses have been held and "anti-Nike" Web sites have even been created. Nike's response to its public relations woes is discussed at the end of this chapter in the section on Ethics and Social Responsibility.

The External Audit

In his letter to shareholders, Nike's CEO Phil Knight attributed the company's unacceptable performance to several factors, including "soft markets, sagging futures orders, and sliding economies." Each of these factors is an *external force*—a trend, event, or issue outside the company that affects Nike's ability to create value. Soft markets and sagging futures orders reflect a change in buying habits of Nike's consumers. Teenagers and young adults, one of Nike's primary target markets, were shifting away from buying Nike shoes for casual wear in favor of boots and "brown shoes." To compound the customer problem, "sliding economies," especially Asian economies, have meant reduced demand for Nike shoes, apparel, and sports equipment outside the United States.

External forces create opportunities and/or threats for organizations. During the situation analysis, the external environment is monitored and emerging or potential strategic opportunities and threats are identified. This process is described in Chapter 5.

The external environment of any organization includes both a *macro environment* made up of broad forces such as technology, economic and social conditions, demographic trends, and political and international forces, and a *task environment* consisting of customers, competitors, suppliers, creditors, government agencies and regulators, and perhaps unions and other groups. Each component of the external environment may have a critical influence, either positive (opportunity) or negative (threat), on the organization and its ability to create value. Thus, each needs to be monitored and evaluated for its impact on the organization. The external audit not only informs strategic choice, but through a feedback mechanism, may also suggest the need to revise the firm's vision and mission.

In Nike's case, changes in the external environment have created new threats and an urgent need to reconsider certain strategies. In other cases, the same environmental changes create opportunities for some organizations and threats for others. For example, technology has transformed the music industry by allowing consumers to download, store, and play music on their home computers. The impact on music sales has been dramatic as shown in Figure 1-2. Sales of mail-order record clubs have plummeted, sales in music stores have also dropped, but online music sales are expected to skyrocket. To take advantage of the trend, Columbia House (a joint venture of Time Warner and Sony) and CDNow Inc. have merged to compete in the high growth online music market.[10] The merger links the pioneer in the digital music world (CDNow) with two of the world's largest record companies (Warner Music and Sony Music).

Setting Objectives and Crafting Strategy

In Chapter 6 we turn our attention to the process of setting objectives and making strategic choices. Objectives are set during the strategic management process so that the organization can specify its intended results and track its progress toward achieving its mission and vision. **Objectives** are specific, measurable standards of performance that the organization seeks to achieve. At this stage of the process, the objectives that are set are long term, meaning that they extend beyond the current year. Annual, short-term objectives are set as part of the implementation phase of the process. Examples of long-term objectives are shown in Table 1-4.

Strategy is the organization's means to achieve its vision, mission, and objectives. While the mission addresses "who we are," and the objectives indicate "what we want to achieve," the strategy states "how we will achieve our mission and objectives."

Figure 1-2
Technology and music sales

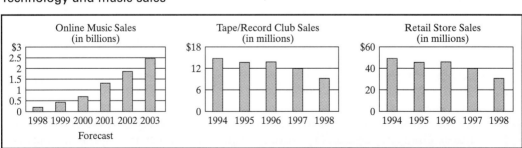

Source: "Wedding March for CDNow, Columbia House," *The Wall Street Journal,* July 14, 1999, B1.

Choosing or crafting a strategy involves generating feasible alternative strategies, evaluating the alternatives, and selecting a strategy that will create value. Strategies are crafted and not merely selected in the sense that strategic choice is a mixture of both intuition and analysis. Strategies are subjective decisions based on both objective information and behavioral considerations. Objectively, the strategy is based on the firm's vision, mission, and situation analysis, and how well the strategy is expected to contribute to the achievement of long-term goals. Strategic choice is influenced by the firm's SWOT analysis, as well as other analytical tools described later in the book. But strategic choice is not strictly the result of analytical thinking. The behavioral aspects of strategic choice are the result of human nature and our inability to obtain and process all relevant information. Strategies are also influenced by factors such as the firm's culture, the characteristics of the senior management team, politics in the company, ethical considerations, and social responsibility. In addition, corporate boards of directors are exercising more control over strategic choice in today's organizations.

Levels of Strategy

Strategic choices are made and implemented at different levels of the organization. Specifically, strategic decisions are made at three levels, although for smaller and very focused companies with only one business, the first two levels are the same. The three levels of strategy are (1) corporate or organizational, (2) business unit, and (3) functional.

Corporate Level Strategy.   Corporate or organizational level strategy focuses on two major issues: (1) determining the organization's *business scope,* that is, in what businesses the organization will compete, and (2) how organizational resources are allocated to these businesses. For example, in the 1960s Nike started as a running shoe company. Since then Nike has evolved and expanded its business scope and now competes in several different industries, including athletic apparel, equipment, and event management as well as marketing a full line of athletic footwear. These forays into new industries are examples of changes in corporate strategy.

PepsiCo is best known as a leading manufacturer and marketer of carbonated soft drinks. As shown in Figure 1-3, however, PepsiCo is more than a beverage company. In fact, PepsiCo generates more revenue from snack foods than soft drinks. PepsiCo's business scope also includes Tropicana orange juice. These three business units differ in terms of markets and customers, competitors, suppliers, and so on. Until the late 1990s, PepsiCo also competed in the fast food industry through their ownership of Pizza Hut, Taco Bell, and KFC (formerly known as Kentucky Fried

Table 1-4   Examples of long-term objectives

- Increase unit sales by at least 10 percent per year for the next 3 years.
- Build market share in Mexico by 5 percent within 18 months.
- Maintain return on equity (ROE) at 15 percent over the next 5 years.
- Establish a joint venture in China before any of our direct competitors.

Chicken). Their decision to spin off or divest these units and thereby change their business scope represented a corporate level strategic decision. Similarly, when Hershey Foods sold its pasta division and then acquired Leaf, Inc., another candy company, Hershey was making a corporate strategy decision to focus on its core business—confections—and at the same time expand its position in that business.

Portfolio analysis and other tools for analyzing corporate strategy decisions, are discussed in Chapter 6. Portfolio theory suggests that the most attractive business units with the greatest growth potential and the most significant business strengths are candidates for aggressive investment designed to grow the business. Alternatively, weaker business units receive that level of investment necessary to maintain position, harvest revenues or, in extreme cases, exit the industry.

Business Level Strategy. At the business unit level, strategic decisions are made about how to compete within the industry and how to gain a competitive advantage. At PepsiCo, for example, beverage division managers must decide how to compete with Coca-Cola, Snapple, and others. Can PepsiCo build and sustain an advantage by creating a unique and valuable position in the market?[11] In addition, managers need to decide how to allocate the resources of the business unit across product lines and functional areas.

For example, Campbell Soup Company is one of Pepsico's competitors in the juice market. Campbell's V8 brand languished as new fruit beverages from Tropicana, Very Fine, Ocean Spray, and others, plus new age beverages such as Clearly Canadian and Nantucket Nectars drew the attention of the juice consumer. In an attempt to build on the interest in wellness but at the same time to appeal to kids' taste buds, Campbell introduced V8 Splash Tropical Blend. The main ingredient of V8 Splash is carrot juice, which offers both Vitamin A and beta-carotene to health-conscious consumers. Most people, especially kids, do not find the flavor of carrot juice appealing, so Campbell disguised the carrot juice in different blends of fruit flavors, including mango, pineapple, orange, and others. By so doing, V8 Splash offered moms "stealth health" for their kids. V8 Splash has become one of the most successful product launches in the history of Campbell and its success has revitalized the V8 franchise.

Functional Level Strategy. Strategic decisions are also made within the major functions of the organization such as marketing, finance, information systems, human

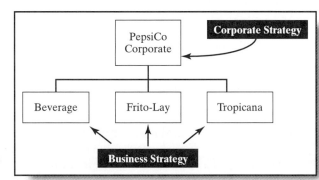

Figure 1-3
PepsiCo and levels
of strategy

resources, logistics, research and development, and operations and production. Functional strategies may also attempt to integrate activities (linking strategies) to create internal capabilities across functions (for example, quality initiatives or reducing cycle times).

Production managers typically focus on competitive priorities such as product and process quality, cost containment, reliability of delivery, and flexibility of the manufacturing process.[12]

Functional decisions in the marketing area may include product or service positioning, branding, packaging, promotion, and distribution. At the product line level, the major decisions involve which specific items in the line should be carried, how broad or narrow and how deep or shallow the line should be, and how marketing dollars should be distributed among the different items. Product line decisions involve adding, modifying, and deleting items from the line. Tide from Procter & Gamble, for example, has been reformulated more than 40 times since World War II to clean more effectively, more gently, and more safely, and to accommodate new fabrics and new washing machine technology. Nike frequently launches "new and improved" athletic shoes to enhance consumer satisfaction.

Brand decisions such as positioning are another important aspect of marketing strategy. *Positioning* means creating a meaning for the brand to the consumer, so that the consumer makes mental associations between the brand name and certain characteristics or benefits. The other brand decisions—advertising and promotion, pricing, packaging and labeling, and distribution—are designed to create the intended position in the customer's mind. For example, Dean Foods launched Milk Chugs in 1998 in response to declining milk consumption among teens and research that suggested that milk was viewed by teens as "uncool." Dean developed resealable plastic bottles in the shape of classic milk bottles of old. The new milk bottles fit in automobile cup holders and featured bright colors for different flavors. The packaging plus the brand name, "Chugs," has helped to change consumer perceptions and to make milk more competitive with bottled tea and fruit beverages among teens. Chugs was heavily advertised and promoted, and emerged as one of Dean's most successful product launches of the decade. Its success is based on identifying, creating, and delivering value to a specifically targeted set of customers.

The three levels of strategy should be coordinated. Functional level strategies support the business strategy, which in turn is aligned with corporate strategies. Organizational performance tends to suffer when different levels of strategies clash.

Implementing Strategy

The next step in the Strategic Management Framework shown in Figure 1-1 is **strategy implementation,** which includes all the steps and decisions necessary to carry out or execute the strategy. Implementation is a complex process. It requires that managers set short-term objectives, reexamine the organization's structure and corporate culture in light of the new strategy, make the right resource decisions in support of the strategy, and manage the human side of the change process. Implementation also depends on a coordination of functions and activities across the organization and between the corporate, business, and functional levels. These topics are covered in Chapters 8 and 9.

To carry out strategic choices, managers must make three types of resource decisions:

- Financing: What resources are needed for the strategy? How much will the strategy cost and how will it be financed?
- Investing/Resourcing: How will the available resources be allocated?
- Operations: How will the allocated resources be used? What changes in operations are necessary to support the new strategy?

The Role of FIO Decisions. Most management decisions and all financial decisions may be classified as financing, investing, or operating (FIO) decisions. Successful implementation depends in large part on FIO decisions that fit and support the strategic choices of the organization. FIO decisions are the choices made by managers to achieve the organization's mission, strategies, and long-term objectives. Examples of FIO decisions are given in Table 1-5. Clearly, these are cross-functional decisions. They involve finance, information technology, accounting, human resources, marketing, sales, distribution, and operations, for example. Thus, each functional area must support the strategy if implementation is to succeed.

Figure 1-4 shows that the relationship between the components of strategy formulation and FIO is circular. The long-term strategic choices made by managers (i.e., vision, mission, objectives, strategies) inform and drive FIO decisions, and the quality of FIO decisions in turn affect the ability of the firm to create value and achieve its long-term objectives. Another way of stating this is that FIO decisions are keys to successful implementation.

Cross-functional decisions and actions, especially FIO decisions, are part of the foundation of the strategic management process. These decisions are emphasized throughout the book.

Table 1-5 Examples of FIO decisions

FINANCING DECISIONS	INVESTING DECISIONS	OPERATING DECISIONS
Issuing additional shares of common stock	Building a production plant	Introducing a new discount pricing program
Borrowing from banks	Hiring a new sales force for international markets	Increasing advertising
Tapping into retained earnings		Paying employee incentives
Acquiring funds from venture capitalists	Purchasing a distribution center	Receiving payments from customers
Buying back stock	Acquiring technology to develop e-commerce	Deciding how much to produce

Figure 1-4
Strategy formulation and FIO decisions

Assessing Value Creation and Providing Feedback

The final chapter of the book focuses on the last step in the strategic management process—evaluating results and providing feedback. An effective strategic management process requires accountability. Not only does the organization need to know where it is going (formulation) and how it will get there (implementation), but whether it is making progress toward its destination. Measuring and evaluating strategic progress is the purpose of the *assessment of value creation* phase of the strategic management framework. Providing feedback by communicating the results of the assessment is an equally important task so that corrective action may be taken if necessary.

A popular notion in management is "if you can't measure it, you can't manage it."[13] Thus, a critical aspect of the strategic management process is to establish benchmarks or standards of performance for value creation, and measure and compare desired results with actual outcomes.

Another popular management notion is "what you measure is what you get."[14] This speaks to the importance of measuring the right things. The traditional approach to strategy evaluation and control has been to focus exclusively on financial measures of performance such as return on investment and earnings per share. These measures continue to be critical indicators of the health of an institution. However, an overly narrow focus on financial indicators tends to emphasize value creation for the owners without considering employees and customers. It may also place too much emphasis on short-term financial performance at the expense of the organization's overall strategic health and future prospects for value creation. A narrow focus on owners can undermine the firm's ability to create value in the long term. In place of strictly financial measures, the notion of a *balanced scorecard* has been emphasized as a tool for evaluating organizational performance.[15]

The balanced scorecard focuses on value creation for customers, employees, and owners by emphasizing both financial and nonfinancial standards of performance. This approach encourages managers to assess performance in several areas simultaneously, a requirement for managing in an increasingly complex and competitive era. The scorecard concept is discussed in Chapter 10.

Phil Knight's letter to Nike shareholders reflects his chagrin for failing to pass the test of value creation. It also reflects his disappointment in not achieving the performance standards of a balanced scorecard. The financial expectations of owners were not met, as reflected in disappointing sales and declining rates of profitability. Nike's share of the footwear market declined, suggesting a lack of value creation for customers. Moreover, resignations and layoffs indicate unacceptable results for employees.

In short, Nike failed to create sufficient value for owners, customers, and employees. The assessment stage of the process monitors the firm's ability to create value, provides feedback for corrective actions, if necessary, and reinforces the earlier point that value creation is both the primary objective and the ultimate outcome of an effective strategic management process.

THE NATURE OF THE STRATEGIC PROCESS

Is strategy long term and deliberately planned or is it opportunistic and emergent? What makes a decision strategic? These are questions that have occupied researchers in the strategy field. Consider the following example:[16]

> The largest airline in the United States is turning to the Internet in search of growth opportunities. United Airlines (UAL Corp.) has announced that it intends to form a joint venture with Buy.com Inc. to create an online travel service, which will be known as BuyTravel.com. This new strategy is the result of United's expectation that online ticket sales will grow rapidly. At the time of the announcement, United was selling about 3 percent of its tickets online, and projected that within 4 years 20 percent of sales would be booked via its own Web site and other Internet-booking services. Table 1-6 shows the growth of airlines bookings via the Internet.

This example illustrates that strategy is both deliberate and emergent. United's long-term strategy is based in part on its objective to remain the nation's largest airline. Originally, United planned to compete on the Internet through its own corporate Web site and established computer-reservation systems. Over time, however, United discovered that emerging Internet middlemen, such as priceline.com and Travelocity.com, were not only formidable competitors but also potential partners. United's strategy was then adjusted to counteract the threat of Internet intermediaries and convert the threat into an opportunity for more sales. The final or realized strategy included the joint venture, BuyTravel.com, and the commitment to compete through Internet intermediaries.

Thus, strategy is based on research and analysis as well as on ingenuity and opportunism. It is both proactive and reactive. As we have already stated, it is based on both analysis and intuition. It includes both a rational, logical left-brain orientation and creative and spontaneous right-brain thinking.

Henry Mintzberg has developed a model to capture these dynamics of the strategic process.[17] The model, shown in Figure 1-5, reflects both sides of the strategic process.

Table 1-6 Airlines bookings and the Internet

Internet airline bookings are increasing, as is viewership of travel and airline Web sites. Numbers of unduplicated viewers, in thousands.

COMPANY SITES	JUNE 1999	JUNE 1998	% INCREASE
Expedia.com	4,203	2,145	+ 95.9
Travelocity.com	4,118	2,093	+ 96.8
priceline.com	2,012	896	+124.6
American Airlines	1,530	1,304	+ 17.3
United Airlines	1,250	640	+ 95.3
Delta Air Lines	1,152	1,093	+ 5.4
Southwest Airlines	1,151	315	+265.4

Source: Media Metrix (Siemers, E., and E. Harris, "Airlines Begin to Click with Internet-Booking Services," *The Wall Street Journal,* August 2, 1999, B4.)

The process begins with a clearly defined **intended strategy,** the result of a formal and structured planning process. In response to changing conditions inside and outside of the organization, some of the original intended strategy is discarded and some of it is retained. The retained or *deliberate strategy* combines with a new emergent strategy to produce the **realized strategy.** Realized strategy is a combination of both deliberate, rational planning and more spontaneous, opportunistic thinking. This is precisely the type of thinking that United used to create BuyTravel.com.

The concept of realized strategy harks back to the discussion of financing, investing, and operating (FIO) decisions. FIO decisions are the means by which strategy is realized. FIO decisions are made in light of intended strategies and, at the same time, are the true test of realized strategy. An organization may espouse any strategy it

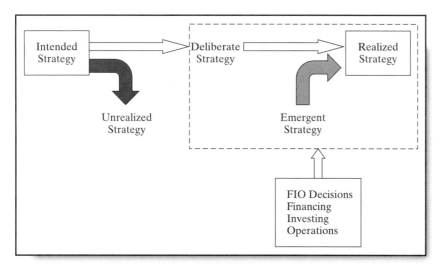

Figure 1-5
Intended and realized strategies and FIO

Source: Adapted from Mintzberg, H., and A. McGugh, "Strategy Formation in an Adhocracy," *Administrative Science Quarterly,* 30, 2, June 1985, p. 160–197.

wishes, but its true or realized strategy is the result of the FIO decisions it actually makes. This is shown in Figure 1-5.

The focus of this book is strategy at the business and corporate levels. These types of strategic decisions have the following characteristics:

1. *Directive.* Strategic decisions set or influence the future direction of the organization.
2. *Cross-functional.* Strategic decisions require the cooperation and coordination of multiple functions and activities across the organization.
3. *Resource-dependent.* Strategic decisions require resource commitments by the organization. Strategies must be financed (internally or externally), investments are made, and operations are changed in some way.

Who Are the Players in the Strategic Process?

The **senior management team** (SMT) and especially the chief executive officer (CEO) or senior manager of the organization are ultimately responsible for the strategy and performance of the organization, but that does not necessarily mean that they are the only ones responsible for strategy. As we have seen, there are different levels of strategy and different managers and employees involved in making those strategic decisions.

No universal approach to the strategy process exists. In most large corporations though, the CEO and senior corporate executives have primary responsibility for corporate strategy decisions. Senior managers in the business units develop and implement business level strategies. Functional strategies are typically the domain of the vice presidents of the functional areas (manufacturing, marketing, R&D, human resources, etc.) in cooperation with operating managers who report to the vice presidents.

In addition to ultimate responsibility for strategy, another important issue is participation in the process. The traditional approach to planning is top-down and suggests that strategy formulation is the sole and exclusive domain of the senior management team. The SMT makes the strategic choices, and then relies on other managers and employees to implement strategy. As organizations grow and become more diverse in the products or services they provide and the global markets they serve, the traditional approach becomes increasingly difficult to manage. Senior executives may be too isolated from customers and operations to be adequately informed. A more inclusive approach to strategic management becomes important.

One such practice is *high-involvement strategic planning,* also known as the **direct participation** (DP) **planning** approach.[18] This more inclusive planning approach is discussed in Chapter 8. It is achieved by moving away from the top-down, control-oriented traditional model of planning to a process that invites and nurtures the innovative ideas of managers at all levels, as well as front-line employees such as sales representatives, engineers, and operating employees. As we shall discuss later in the book, broad participation has important advantages for managing strategic change.

Corporate Governance

Another group that plays a critical role in the strategic management process is the organization's board of directors, the corporate governors of the organization. The board is usually comprised of the organization's CEO and other senior executives and a larger number of **outside directors** (people who are not employed by the firm). Boards will typically meet at least on a quarterly basis to review, discuss, and evaluate the organization's plans and performance.

A common practice is for the board to form committees that are responsible for getting the work done between the quarterly meetings. Regular committees, often called *standing committees,* are permanent committees with duties and responsibilities outlined in the organization's charter or bylaws. Temporary or *ad hoc committees* can also be formed to oversee special tasks as needed. Typical standing committees are the executive, compensation, audit, nominating, and finance committees. The executive committee acts for the entire board between meetings. The audit committee reviews the financial operations of the organization. The nominating committee recruits new board members and the compensation committee evaluates compensation packages, especially of senior executives. More organizations are also forming a corporate governance or board committee to manage board processes like training, evaluation, and compensation.

The board of directors has a legal obligation to represent the owners in the affairs of the organization. In the case of nonprofit organizations, each board member has a legal responsibility to the organization's donors (corporate, foundation, individual, and government) and the public interest/public trust. Directors also have the responsibility to ensure that the organization operates within the parameters of the law. The summary term for these duties is **corporate governance.**

Laws and standards defining the responsibilities and obligations of corporate governance are different from country to country. For example, in the United States, corporations disclose much more information, especially financial, than in other countries, so board actions are open to more scrutiny. Corporate governance in France focuses more on workers and the environment than it does in the United States.[19]

Even within the United States, specific requirements of directors vary, depending on the state in which the corporate charter is issued. There is, however, general agreement on the following common responsibilities of corporate governance:

- Monitoring the overall direction of the organization
- Hiring, firing, and compensating the CEO
- Controlling, monitoring, or supervising top management
- Reviewing and approving the use of resources
- Caring for shareholder or public interests[20]

Thus, the role of the board in the strategic management process is primarily oversight and approval of strategies and major resource commitments, as well as supervision of the CEO rather than direct participation in developing strategies.

Several trends are influencing corporate governance. The power of *institutional investors,* those shareholders representing large institutions like pension funds or mutual funds, is increasing. Institutional investors hold over half of all listed corporate stock in the United States and are at the forefront of efforts to increase board accountability, especially in the area of corporate financial performance.[21] Recent lawsuits against boards have underscored this by finding board members legally liable for the performance of the organization.

Shareholder social activism is expanding the range of issues that boards consider. Beginning in the 1970s, peace and social justice issues were put forward as shareholder proposals, requiring action at the annual shareholders meetings. Today, shareholder resolutions have increased and cover a range of social justice issues. Nike has been the target of shareholder social activism for its overseas operations, particularly on issues such as sweatshops, child labor, and wages.

Improving board structures and processes is a third trend in corporate governance. Increasingly, boards are seen as active partners in the strategic management process and as such, are exercising tighter oversight and control on the organization. Good boardroom practices include having a majority of outside directors, formal evaluations of director performance, responsiveness to investors, open communications with the CEO and other board members, and attention to details, including asking tough questions about the future direction of the organization as well as its past performance.[22]

ETHICS AND SOCIAL RESPONSIBILITY

Firms are under increasing scrutiny by the media, regulators, environmental groups, and the general public. The pressure to operate based on sound ethical principles and a concern for social responsibility has never been stronger, and rightly so. Good business ethics are an absolute requirement for good strategic management. Business strategies have ethical consequences and managers must identify and carefully consider what they are. Managers who choose to bury their heads in the sand and ignore the social consequences of their strategic choices are no less culpable than those who knowingly and willingly make unethical decisions.

Cases of unethical business conduct are reported in the press on a daily basis. Insider trading, product safety, truth in advertising, Internet privacy, sexual harassment, racial discrimination, environmental protection, and employee health concerns are just some of the issues that require firms to clarify and communicate their ethical standards. To do so, organizations are increasingly developing a **code of ethics,** a formal and official document that describes the standards that all employees of an organization are expected to know and follow.

A code of ethics is an important and necessary step but most firms find that it is not sufficient. Workshops, training sessions, simulations, and even board games are other ways that firms try to instill an understanding of and commitment to ethical principles. Perhaps the most important issue, however, is the behavior and decisions of the senior management team. Managers at the top set the tone in the organization and others learn from their example. To create an organizational culture based on sound ethics, senior managers must lead the way.

The Natural Environment

One of the most pressing issues of corporate social responsibility in the twenty-first century will be the natural environment. Firms will be increasingly scrutinized for their treatment of the environment. More stringent environmental regulations are likely to be enacted, especially if businesses are not willing or able to regulate themselves.

Proactive businesses have taken the initiative to go beyond the minimum regulatory requirements to address environmental issues by setting environmental goals and tracking progress toward those goals. For example, J. Sainsbury plc, a supermarket chain based in the United Kingdom, has set environmental goals in areas such as waste management, energy consumption, refrigerants used, and carbon dioxide emissions from transporting products. Sainsbury publishes an annual **environment report** that highlights the goals, accomplishments and new targets of the company. These environmental report cards will become more common in the future. Some firms are already using their proactive stance toward the environment as a way to position themselves as environmentally friendly companies.

Let's return to our example of Nike, a company that has been criticized for its environmental performance and its foreign labor practices. In response to the former, Nike has initiated new environmental standards and policies for its foreign manufacturing partners. In addition, Nike developed an environmental mission statement.[23]

> Through the adoption of sustainable business practices Nike is committed to securing intergenerational quality of life, restoring the environment, and increasing value for our customers, shareholders, and business partners.

The use of Nike products by college athletics programs has been a topic of heated debate on many campuses. Some critics have called for universities to dump Nike and to refuse to wear any officially licensed Nike merchandise. Allegations against Nike and/or Nike's foreign manufacturing partners include unsafe working conditions, low wages, and child labor. Nike has taken these criticisms seriously and responded, in part, by disclosing information about their foreign partners, publicizing their labor policies, and creating a program with their partners to promote best labor practices and to achieve continuous improvement. Nike's Code of Conduct is shown in Table 1-7.

According to its CEO Phil Knight, "Nike has zero tolerance for under-age labor." The company recently increased the minimum age of footwear factory workers to 18 years of age, and the minimum age for all other light-manufacturing workers (apparel, accessories, and equipment) to 16 years. These new minimum age requirements exceed those mandated by most governments.

THE BENEFITS OF STRATEGIC MANAGEMENT

Research has shown that organizations that use a strategic planning process tend to perform better than similar organizations that do not. That is not to suggest that all successful firms follow a highly formal, structured, and detail-oriented strategic process. Studies indicate that the formality of the process tends to increase as the size

Table 1-7 Nike Code of Conduct

NIKE Inc. was founded on a handshake. Implicit in that act was the determination that we would build our business with all of our partners based on trust, teamwork, honesty and mutual respect. We expect all of our business partners to operate on the same principles.

At the core of the Nike corporate ethic is the belief that we are a company comprised of many different kinds of people, appreciating individual diversity, and dedicated to equal opportunity for each individual.

Nike designs, manufactures and markets products for sports and fitness consumers. At every step in that process, we are driven to achieve not only what is required, but also what is expected of a leader. We expect our business partners to do the same. Specifically, Nike seeks partners that share our commitment to the promotion of best practices and continuous improvement in:

1. Occupational safety and health, compensation, hours of work and benefits standards.
2. Minimizing our impact on the environment.
3. Management practices that recognize the dignity of the individual, the rights of free association and collective bargaining, and the right to a work place free of harassment, abuse or corporal punishment.
4. The principle that decisions on hiring, salary, benefits, advancement, termination or retirement are based solely on the ability of an individual to do the job. There shall be no discrimination based on race, creed, gender, marital or maternity status, religious or political beliefs, age or sexual orientation.

Wherever Nike operates around the globe, we are guided by this Code of Conduct. We bind our manufacturing partners to these principles. Our manufacturing partners must post this Code in all major workspaces, translated into the language of the worker, and must endeavor to train workers on their rights and obligations as defined by this Code and applicable labor laws.

While these principles establish the spirit of our partnerships, we also bind these partners to specific standards of conduct. These standards are set forth below.

1. Forced Labor: The manufacturer does not use forced labor in any form—prison, indentured, bonded or otherwise.
2. Child labor: The manufacturer does not employ any person below the age of 18 to produce footwear. The manufacturer does not employ any person below the age of 16 to produce apparel, accessories or equipment. Where local standards are higher, no person under the legal minimum age will be employed.
3. Compensation: The manufacturer provides each employee at least the minimum wage, or the prevailing industry wage, whichever is higher; provides each employee a clear, written accounting for every pay period; and does not deduct from worker pay for disciplinary infractions, in accordance with the Nike Manufacturing Leadership Standard on financial penalties.
4. Benefits: The manufacturer provides each employee all legally mandated benefits. Benefits vary by country, but may include meals or meal subsidies; transportation or transportation subsidies; other cash allowances; health care; child care; emergency, pregnancy or sick leave; vacation, religious, bereavement or holiday leave; and contributions for social security and other insurance, including life, health and worker's compensation.
5. Hours of Work/Overtime: The manufacturer complies with legally mandated work hours; uses overtime only when each employee is fully compensated according to local law; informs each employee at the time of hiring if mandatory overtime is a condition of employment; and, on a regularly scheduled basis, provides one day off in seven, and requires no more than 60 hours of work per week, or complies with local limits if they are lower.

(continued)

Table 1-7 (cont.)

6. Management of Environment, Safety and Health (MESH): The manufacturer has written health and safety guidelines, including those applying to employee residential facilities, where applicable; has a factory safety committee; complies with Nike's environmental, safety and health standards; limits organic vapor concentrations at or below the Permissible Exposure Limits mandated by the U.S. Occupational Safety and Health Administration (OSHA); provides Personal Protective Equipment (PPE) free of charge, and mandates its use; and complies with all applicable local environmental, safety and health regulation.

7. Documentation and Inspection: The manufacturer maintains on file all documentation needed to demonstrate compliance with this Code of Conduct; agrees to make these documents available for Nike or its designated auditor to inspect upon request; and agrees to submit to labor practices audits or inspections with or without prior notice.

Source: Nike, Code of Conduct, www.nikebiz.com, accessed July 19, 2000. Used with permission of NIKE Inc.

of the organization increases, and as the turbulence and complexity of the firm's external environment increase. In any case, strategic thinking is important for the success of all organizations for both financial and nonfinancial reasons. Some of the most important benefits of a strategic management process include:

1. More forward-looking, future-oriented thinking results in more effective strategies and better financial performance. Value creation is enhanced.
2. Better internal communication is fostered when managers from different functional areas listen and discuss their views in strategic management meetings. This interaction yields learning and understanding among managers who otherwise may not interact on a frequent basis.[24]
3. Firms become more proactive and less reactive and are better able to anticipate, influence, or initiate changes in the external environment.

CONCLUSION

Value creation is ultimately what the strategic management process is all about. Successful organizations are adept at rewarding their customers, employees, and owners. But to create value, organizations must adapt to change. As markets become more globally competitive and technology more advanced, the need for strategic flexibility and responsiveness grows. Strategies, both intended and realized, are the engines that produce value and allow the organization to adapt to its changing circumstances. A firm's realized strategy is largely the result of the financing, investing, and operating decisions it makes.

The chapters that follow describe each aspect of the strategic management process in more detail. The essential need to create value for customers, employees, and owners is emphasized throughout the book. By viewing strategy through the lens of value creation, the cross-functional nature of strategic management is emphasized. These themes are critical for strategic management at the beginning of the twenty-first century.

KEY TERMS AND CONCEPTS

After reading this chapter you should understand each of the following terms.

- Code of ethics
- Corporate governance
- Cross-functional
- Direct participation planning
- Environmental reports
- External audit
- Intended strategy
- Internal audit
- Mission

- Objectives
- Outside directors
- Realized strategy
- Senior management team
- Strategic management
- Strategic management framework
- Strategy implementation
- Value creation
- Vision

DISCUSSION QUESTIONS

1. What are the five major steps of the strategic management process?
2. What is value creation? Review Johnson & Johnson's credo (see Table 1-2). For whom does Johnson & Johnson attempt to create value? How?
3. How are the concepts of vision, mission, long-term objectives, and strategy related? How are they different?
4. What role do financing, investing, and operating decisions (FIO) play in the strategic management process?
5. In what way is the fundamental purpose of a business organization the same as a not-for-profit social agency such as Habitat for Humanity?
6. Use the textbook's Web site to learn more about the current condition of Nike. How well is Nike creating value for customers, employees, and owners?

EXPERIENTIAL EXERCISE

Social Responsibility. Nike's track record in the area of social responsibility has been the subject of heated debate. Research Nike and its manufacturing partners. In what ways has Nike been a good corporate citizen? How has Nike not met its social obligations? Do you agree or disagree with the following statement: Nike strives to be a socially responsible organization. Explain.

ENDNOTES

1. Nike, *1998 Annual Report,* www.nikebiz.com, accessed June 2, 2000.
2. Magretta, J., and N. Stone, "The Original Management Guru," *The Wall Street Journal,* November 11, 1999, A20.
3. Notre Dame chapter of Habitat for Humanity, www.nd.edu/~habitat, accessed April 17, 2000.
4. Bennis, W., and B. Nanus. *Leaders: The Strategies for Taking Charge.* New York: Harper & Row Publishers, 1985, 89.
5. Johnson & Johnson, Johnson & Johnson Credo, www.jnj.com, accessed July 20, 2000.

6. Dell, "Dell Vision," www.dell.com/us/en/gen/corporate/ vision.htm, accessed October 20, 2000.

7. Ford Motor Company, "Vision, Mission, Values," www.mycareer.ford.com/OurCompany.asp, accessed September 29, 2000.

8. Duncan, W. J., P. M. Ginter, and L. E. Swayne, "Competitive Advantage and Internal Organizational Assessment," *Academy of Management Executive* 12, no. 3 (1998): 6–16.

9. Duncan, W. J., P. M. Ginter, and L. E. Swayne, "Competitive Advantage and Internal Organizational Assessment," *Academy of Management Executive* 12, no. 3 (1998): 7.

10. "Wedding March for CDNow, Columbia House," *The Wall Street Journal,* July 14, 1999, B1 and B4.

11. Porter, M. E., "What Is Strategy?" *Harvard Business Review* (November–December 1996): 61–77.

12. Porth, S. J., R. Kathuria, and M. P. Joshi, "Performance Impact of the Fit Between Manufacturing Priorities of General Managers and Manufacturing Managers," *Journal of Business and Economic Studies* 4, no. 1 (1996): 13–35.

13. Garvin, D. A., "Building a Learning Organization," *Harvard Business Review* (July–August 1993): 89.

14. Kaplan, Robert S., and D. P. Norton, "The Balanced Scorecard—Measures That Drive Performance," *Harvard Business Review* (January–February 1992): 71–79.

15. Kaplan, Robert S., and D. P. Norton, "The Balanced Scorecard—Measures That Drive Performance," *Harvard Business Review* (January–February 1992): 71.

16. Siemers, E., and E. Harris, "Airlines Begin to Click with Internet-Booking Services," *The Wall Street Journal,* August 2, 1999, B4.

17. Mintzberg, H., and A. McGugh, "Strategy Formulation in an Adhocracy," *Administrative Science Quarterly* 30, no. 2 (June 1985), 160–197.

18. Ellis, C. M., and E. M. Norman, "Real Change in Real Time," *Management Review* (February 1999): 33–38.

19. "Foreign Companies Lag U.S. Model," *Investor Relations Business* 5, no. 16 (August 14, 2000): 14.

20. Demb, A., and F. F. Neubauer, "The Corporate Board: Confronting the Paradoxes," *Long Range Planning* 25, no. 3 (1992): 9–20.

21. McRitchie, J., ed. Corporate Governance, www.corpgov.net/, 2000, accessed February 11, 2001.

22. Coombes, P., and M. Watson, "Three Surveys on Corporate Governance," *The McKinsey Quarterly 2000,* no. 4 (2000): 74–77; Steinberg, R. M., "A Roadmap to Board Effectiveness," *Corporate Board* 21, no. 125 (2000): 9–16.

23. Nike, *Annual Report,* www.nikebiz.com, accessed October 20, 2000.

24. David, F. *Strategic Management Concepts.* 7th ed., Upper Saddle River, NJ: Prentice Hall (1999): 18.

Chapter 2

Creating Value:
A Strategic Imperative

Chapter Outline
The Importance of Value Creation
Customers and Value Creation
Value Disciplines as Paths to Market Leadership
Employees and Value Creation
Owners and Value Creation
Emerging Technologies and Value Creation
Conclusion
Key Terms and Concepts
Discussion Questions
Experiential Exercise
Endnotes

THE IMPORTANCE OF VALUE CREATION

Organizations and senior managers in particular are under relentless pressure to satisfy stockholders' demands for profit and growth. The pressure is especially strong in the United States because of a financial system that expects results on a short-term, often quarterly, basis. Financial goals must be met, at least over the long term.

The implications of not meeting financial goals can be dire. In the first 10 months of the twenty-first century, 38 of the largest 200 U.S. companies had replaced their CEOs, including Gillette, Lucent Technologies, Campbell Soup, Aetna, Procter & Gamble, and Mattel.[1] Stockholders and corporate boards are putting unprecedented pressure for results on senior managers.

Employees are not immune from the pressure to produce profits. Chrysler, maker of cars, minivans, Jeeps, and the PT Cruiser and now a division of DaimlerChrysler AG, recently announced it would eliminate the jobs of 25,800 salaried and hourly employees—about 20 percent of its workforce—over 3 years. This action was taken in light of a slowing U.S. economy and a huge loss reported by Chrysler. Other companies have suffered similar massive employee reductions in the wake of poor financial results. Polaroid cut 35 percent of its workforce from the start of 2001, after being hit hard by the growth of new technologies in digital photography.[2] Lucent Technologies Inc. plans to layoff 16,000 employees, Xerox Corp. is eliminating 4,000 jobs, and Hewlett-Packard said that it will be cutting 1,700 jobs.[3]

These examples highlight the importance of creating financial or economic value for stockholders, but a successful strategic management process focuses not just on satisfying stockholders or owners. Effective organizations understand that the financial performance of the company is an outcome that depends on pleasing customers, and that employees play a pivotal role in doing so. Satisfied employees create delighted and loyal customers, which in turn creates economic value in the form of cash flow for owners and stockholders. A short-term and exclusive focus on value for stockholders can be counterproductive.

The strategic management framework shown in Figure 2-1 emphasizes the pre-eminent role of value creation and identifies key questions addressed in this chapter. The figure shows that value creation is both the beginning and end of strategic management; it is the goal of the process and the standard by which it is ultimately judged. The purpose of this chapter is to examine the concept of value creation, and to discuss its role in strategic management. As we will see, the success of the organization, and its strategic planning process in particular, are judged with respect to its ability to satisfy key stakeholders, especially customers, employees, and owners.

Customer-Employee-Owner Linkages

Chevron is an example of a company that understands that value creation is the key to strategic management, and that customers, employees, and owners are closely linked in the value creation process. The company strives "to exceed the financial performance of our strongest competitors. Our goal is to be No. 1 among our competitors in Total Stockholder Return" (over a 5-year period).[4] Chevron recognizes

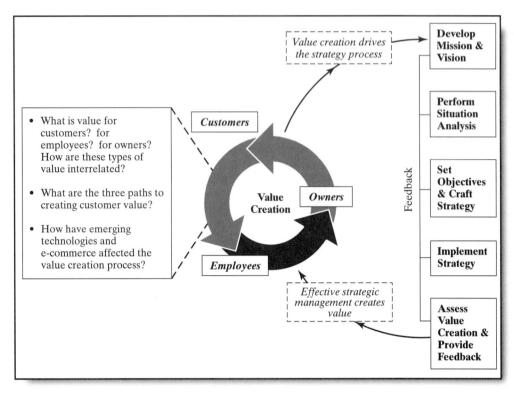

Figure 2-1
The strategic management framework

that its ability to create value for stockholders and its overall financial success, however, depend first on developing loyal and productive employees and satisfied customers.

Chevron has developed a model for value creation that depicts these key relationships in the strategic management process (see Figure 2-2). The model begins with a committed team of employees. The employee team is responsible for creating customer satisfaction and productive and efficient operations. Delighted customers and efficient operations contribute to superior financial performance and stockholder returns. Operating in a socially responsible way (public favorability in Figure 2-2) and with a committed team, while pleasing customers and stockholders, also contributes to a favorable public image. Chevron believes that these are the ingredients for its success: "We are an international company providing energy and chemical products vital to the growth of the world's economies. Our mission is to create superior value for our stockholders, our customers and our employees."[5]

This series of interdependent relationships between customers, employees, and owners is known as the **customer-employee-owner cycle,** or the **C-E-O cycle.** The C-E-O cycle is a dynamic force that drives any business. Each component of the cycle is like a link in a chain. The organization can be no stronger than its weakest link. Value creation depends on cultivating and strengthening these links in the customer-employee-owner cycle. A mismanaged and disgruntled workforce doesn't serve customers well, poorly served customers translate into declining sales, and sagging

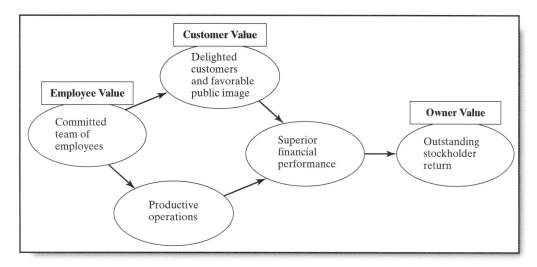

Figure 2-2
Chevron and value creation
Source: Adapted from Chevron, About Chevron, www.chevron.com, accessed January 20, 2000.

sales don't create shareholder value. As we have seen above, failure to create financial value often leads to employee layoffs.

Like Chevron, many organizations formalize and codify their commitment to customers, employees, and shareholders in statements to the public. As shown in Table 2-1, for example, The Chase Manhattan Corporation strives to create "solutions for our customers, opportunities for our employees and superior returns for our shareholders."[6] Table 2-1 also shows that Coca-Cola,[7] US Airways,[8] and the Great Atlantic & Pacific Tea Company (A&P)[9] explicitly identify the need to create value for customers, employees, and shareholders in their corporate statements. A&P, for example, acknowledges that to become "the supermarket of choice" for customers, it must become an employer of choice, a rewarding place for people to work. This in turn will position A&P to become a dynamic and profitable corporation and an attractive investment choice for shareholders.

Businesses are increasingly searching for ways to solidify and strengthen the customer-employee-owner cycle relationships by aligning the interests of these key stakeholders. One example is the trend toward introducing employee incentive programs. Stock options and employee stock ownership programs have always been important forms of compensation for senior executives. The trend now is to make all employees, regardless of level, eligible for these stock programs. The effect is to directly link the interests of employees and owners. Value created for owners becomes value shared by employees.

CUSTOMERS AND VALUE CREATION

We know an essential purpose of any business organization is to create and deliver customer value, and do so at a profit. An analogous statement for nonprofits would

Table 2-1 Examples of corporate statements of value creation

Chase Manhattan:
"We provide financial services that contribute to the success of individuals, businesses, communities, and countries around the world. By creating solutions for our customers, opportunities for our employees and superior returns for our shareholders, we help each to achieve their goals."

Coca-Cola:
"Our mission is to maximize share-owner value over time. In order to achieve this mission, we must create value for all the constituents we serve, including our consumers, our customers, our bottlers, and our communities."

US Airways:
"To provide shareholders with a suitable return on equity; to provide customers with quality service and value for their money; to provide employees with secure, rewarding careers; to be a responsible neighbor and good corporate citizen in the communities we serve."

A&P:
"To become the supermarket of choice; the place where people choose to work, choose to shop, and choose to invest."

Source: J. P. Morgan Chase, www.chase.com; The Coca-Cola Company, www.cocacola.com; US Airways, www.usairways.com; The Great Atlantic and Pacific Tea Company (A&P), "Becoming the Supermarket of Choice: Issue 3," February 1999.

be that organizations must understand and satisfy client needs and wants, and do so within the financial constraints they face, but what exactly is customer value and who in the organization is responsible for creating it?

What Is Value for Customers?

Customer decisions to buy products and services are based on the anticipation of value. Customer value is a function of benefits received relative to price paid. To be more precise, **customer value** is the degree of satisfaction derived by the customer relative to the total price paid for the product or service. *Satisfaction* is defined in terms of benefits received by the customer from possession and use of the product, including how well the product solves specific customer problems relative to customer expectations. The *total price* includes out-of-pocket cost plus everything else the customer must do (search activities, travel, activities such as carrying and setting up) to accomplish the acquisition and use of the product. These concepts are illustrated in Figure 2-3.

Customer Satisfaction

Customer satisfaction may be broadly classified as *value-in-use* (derived from consuming or using the product) and/or *possession value* (derived by having the product).[10] For example, customers can derive value-in-use from driving a car or derive possession value merely by owning a status car, such as a Mercedes Benz. Products create value through the delivery of consequences or outcomes experienced by the customer.

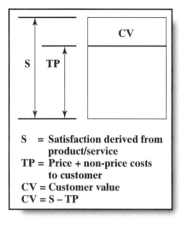

S   = Satisfaction derived from
      product/service
TP = Price + non-price costs
      to customer
CV = Customer value
CV = S – TP

Figure 2-3
The concept of customer
value

These notions of customer value are somewhat illusory. Let's consider an example. Suppose you stop at a convenience store at 7:00 A.M. and purchase a bagel and cup of coffee to provide quick, convenient, and tasty appetite satisfaction on the way to work or school. Or you might purchase a cellular phone and calling plan to provide reliable telecommunications access to coworkers, friends, and family at virtually any time or place. In a sense, you are not really buying the bagel and coffee, but convenient appetite satisfaction. You are not really buying the cell phone and calling plan, but access to others at virtually any place, any time. Your perceived customer value is a function of how well these products deliver the benefits you seek relative to the costs you incurred in acquiring them.

Providing Customer Value. Goods and services provide value in a number of ways. Delivering a product with a radical new technology that significantly improves product performance, like the Gillette Mach3, creates value and makes all other products in the category seem outmoded. Providing add-ons, such as frequent-shopper points, helps airlines, hotels, CD clubs, food retailers and many other firms to create added value for the customer. Branding can add value through both physical and psychological attributes. In fact, branding a category that has historically been a commodity, for example, what Frank Perdue did with chicken, is a path to creating added perceived value for customers. Along with added value comes the ability to charge higher prices and generate higher margins, provided that consumers associate added value with the branded item.

Campbell Soup Company has recently instituted a "focus on icons" strategy, innovating by extending brand equity in soup and Prego sauces to provide value for both customers and consumers by meeting consumer demand for easy meals and retail demand for products that compete with restaurant takeout. For example, a promotional program called "Souper Solutions Across the Store" includes recipes for quick meals assembled from Campbell's grocery ingredients grouped in a point-of-purchase display. Campbell also has a program whereby a consumer can go into Campbell's Web site and subscribe to a service called "Campbell's Meal-Mail." Every day, subscribers receive an e-mail with a recipe that gives not only suggestions regarding what to have for dinner, but the instructions for making a quick and easy meal, using Campbell's products, of course. By helping to solve the consumer's "what's for dinner?" dilemma, Campbell is providing value for consumers.

Perceptions of Value Depend on the Usage Situation. Customers' value judgments are influenced by the usage situation. At McDonald's, one expects food that is filling and tasty (and safe) but not of what might be termed gourmet quality. There is also the expectation that the order will be filled accurately and very quickly, and that the food will be served at the correct temperature. You might pay $5 for a value meal, including specialty hamburger, French fries, and soft drink. If expectations for a quick, satisfying meal are met, the customer will be satisfied, and given the relatively low cost in money, time, and effort, this transaction may generate high perceived value. The same person on a different occasion might pay $60 or substantially more for a dinner for two in a fine restaurant with food and service that is of significantly higher quality than that available at the McDonald's. However, if that meal does not meet the substantially higher expectations in terms of service, ambience, and other elements unique to a fine dining experience, the customer may be left less than satisfied and perceive a low level of value.

Who Is Responsible for Creating Customer Value?

Creating value for customers is a cross-functional responsibility. That is, all functions of the firm are expected to contribute to the effort. Indeed, if a function does not add value one must question whether it is necessary. Because it is so closely tied to the customer, however, the marketing function plays a particularly important role in creating customer value.

The focus on customer value represents a significant shift in the way marketing is carried out by organizations. Rather than thinking of marketing as something that must be accomplished to sell products, marketing is now conceived of as a set of activities that identifies, creates, and delivers value to the customer. The emphasis has shifted from pursuing individual sales to creating customers, and from an emphasis on transactions to an emphasis on relationships, given the recognition that profitability is ultimately a function of the number, types, and quality of customer relationships the firm maintains.

Providing customer value is the key to creating and sustaining customer relationships. The efficient creation and delivery of customer value requires cross-functional cooperation within the firm and cooperation of partners in the supply chain and distribution channel, with an emphasis on developing mutually profitable relationships with supply and distribution partners.

Consider the example of car buying. For some consumers, buying a new car is seen as a real hassle. Sparring with salespeople, spending countless hours in dealerships, and never feeling confident about being treated fairly and getting the best deal have been characteristic of automobile shopping. Recently, however, Internet technology has created a completely different approach to new car shopping. Internet sites such as Autobytel.com and AutoWeb.com have allowed consumers to efficiently search for the best car deals, providing buyers with more information about alternatives and prices, and allowing them to cut better deals. Internet sites for auto shopping act as referral services. They provide shoppers with detailed information about prices, models, and options. Revenues come from member auto dealers who do the actual car selling. By serving as matchmaker between dealer and shopper, these Internet auto-buying services have enhanced customer value by both facilitating the shopping experience and by lowering the prices consumers must pay.

Thus, marketing is more than a series of activities; marketing is a company-wide philosophy with the recognition that a fundamental purpose of the organization is to create and sustain profitable customer relationships. Customer relationships are viewed as assets of the organization. Strategy involves defining which customers and customer segments the company can profitably serve, based on an understanding of the firm's capabilities, and developing ways to serve them more effectively and more efficiently than competitors.

VALUE DISCIPLINES AS PATHS TO MARKET LEADERSHIP

Companies like Dell Computer, Home Depot, and Nike redefined value for their customers, created business systems that could deliver more of that value than competitors, and ultimately raised the expectations of customers beyond the reach of the competition. Each of these companies, and many other successful organizations, took leadership positions in their respective industries by narrowing their business focus to delivering superior customer value via one of three value disciplines. These value disciplines, or paths to market leadership, are: (1) **operational excellence,** (2) **customer intimacy,** and (3) **product leadership.**[11] Each discipline creates a different kind of value for customers by relying on superior performance in different functional areas. The value disciplines and their functional requirements are shown in Table 2-2.

Operational Excellence

Operational excellence means "providing customers with reliable products or services at competitive prices and delivered with minimal difficulty or inconvenience."[12] Chevron is an example of a company that seeks operational excellence by striving for "industry-leading performance in cost reduction and capital stewardship . . . and a decentralized organization that enhances speed of execution and customer responsiveness."[13]

Companies such as Dell Computer, UPS, and Wal-Mart have invested in supply chain, production, and distribution technologies, and processes and systems that generate reliable delivery at low cost. Wal-Mart has been so successful in driving down costs and prices, and gaining market share in both mass merchandise and food retailing, that the traditional supermarket industry had to respond. Supermarkets did so in the early 1990s with the Efficient Consumer Response (ECR) initiative, designed to drive cost out of the food supply chain so that traditional food retailers could compete with Wal-Mart.

Rapid response to customer demands has become more and more necessary as the speed of change accelerates. Developments in communications technology and greater emphasis on supply chain partnering have lowered mean response times for almost all competitors. Firms that want to compete on the basis of operational excellence are challenged to stay on the leading edge both in terms of technology and processes.

Table 2-2 Value Disciplines

Type of Value Emphasis	Description	Functional Excellence Required
Operational excellence	Providing customers with reliable products or services at competitive prices and delivered with minimal difficulty or inconvenience	Efficiency of operations, Distribution/logistics
Customer intimacy	Segmenting and targeting markets precisely and then tailoring these offerings to match exactly the demands of those niches	Marketing, sales, Flexibility of operations
Product leadership	Offering customers leading- edge products and services that consistently enhance the customer's use or application in the market, thereby making rivals' goods obsolete	Research and development

Source: Descriptions from Treacy, M., and F. Wiersema, "Customer Intimacy and Other Value Disciplines," *Harvard Business Review* (January–February 1993): 84–93.

Firms competing on the basis of operational excellence often strive for flat and flexible organizations. In addition, they must maintain tightly focused organizations to maintain the simple and efficient structure necessary to be truly "lean and mean." Thus, operationally excellent firms define core operations fairly narrowly and may rely on outsourcing and partnering to perform non-core functions. Finally, operationally excellent firms must have a culture that "abhors waste and rewards efficiency."[14]

The FedEx Corporation virtually created the overnight delivery business. Lately, however, FedEx has struggled with the shipping opportunities created by Internet shopping. Rival UPS has captured 55 percent of the e-commerce delivery market, with the U.S. Postal Service running second at 32 percent while FedEx has only a 10 percent share. The problem has been the failure of FedEx to integrate separate operating units offering ground and air shipping services, which were creating problems for corporate customers who wanted to ship both on the ground and overnight, forcing them to engage in two totally separate transactions with different people. By comparison, UPS offers one-stop shopping, allowing customers to contract for services ranging from same-day and overnight delivery to shipping that takes a full week, with the same UPS truck picking up parcels and the same customer representative handling problems. This added convenience has attracted many clients to UPS, including e-commerce giants like Amazon.com, and left FedEx in a distant third place in the e-commerce shipping business.[15]

Customer Intimacy

Customer intimacy means "segmenting and targeting markets precisely and then tailoring these offerings to match exactly the demands of those niches."[16] Companies such as Home Depot, Nordstrom's, Ritz-Carlton Hotels, and Amazon.com combine detailed knowledge about customers with operational flexibility to enable them to respond rapidly to emerging and changing customer demands, to customize offerings for specific customers, and to fulfill special requests. In turn, this creates tremendous customer loyalty.

One important aspect of customer intimacy as a path to market leadership is the recognition that customers have a lifetime value to the supplier and that emphasis must be placed on a long-term relationship, not short-term, individual transactions. Another important aspect of customer intimacy as a value discipline is that not all customers are equally important to a company in terms of profitability or value creation for owners. Successful companies pick and choose the customers they want to cultivate. Finally, computer technology has enabled true customization, both of goods and services, meaning that successful companies cannot rest on their laurels; there must be a constant push to become more and more responsive to customers.

After years of strong growth, athletic shoe companies including Nike, Reebok, Adidas, and Converse experienced significant sales slippage in 1998 and 1999 as consumer tastes changed and power brands such as Nike lost their "coolness." Nike's condition was described in Chapter 1. Branded sneaker sales in the United States rose 11.3 percent to $8 billion in 1997, which followed a 9.8 percent jump in 1996.[17] However, as we know from Chapter 1, athletic shoes were becoming less popular with teens and young adults, who became tired of the same old styles and shifted emphasis to "brown shoes" including hiking boots and other styles that look better with khaki, the hot new clothing style. Reacting to steep sales declines, major manufacturers suddenly became more customer focused by moving from white to colors, especially in shoes priced under $65, which account for the lion's share of athletic shoe sales.

Ford is trying to get closer to its customers through ConsumerConnect, an e-business effort that crosses company lines. Because Ford lacks the capabilities and competencies to carry on an e-business venture of its own, Ford has partnered with companies such as Oracle, Cisco, Microsoft, Hewlett-Packard, Yahoo!, and Priceline.com. These leading technology firms have linked in various ways with Ford to provide the necessary competencies. These include networking, database management, communications, hardware and software, and specialized systems that deliver highly personalized warranty, loan, repair, and customized services based on more detailed knowledge of driver lifestyles and buying habits.

Product Leadership

Product leadership means "offering customers leading-edge products and services that consistently enhance the customer's use or application in the market, thereby making rivals' goods obsolete."[18] Firms such as Nike, Intel, Merck, and 3M have demonstrated product leadership through significant investment in research and development plus corporate cultures designed to encourage and reward innovation and creativity. Product leaders provide customer value via innovative solutions to important customer problems. These companies are successful at discovering and nurturing new ideas that not only solve customer problems but do so in ways much different, and more effective, than those solutions currently available. They do a great job of monitoring the external environment and reacting quickly as windows of opportunity open, albeit for a brief time.

Product leaders are also willing to compete with themselves. Intel has been noted for creating new generations of computer processors that render existing items in their product line obsolete for their customers—computer manufacturers. Intel is willing to do this in order to preempt competition. Like most companies, Intel prefers that Intel products, not other manufacturer's products, are Intel's chief competition. When Intel realized in late 1997 that competitors were taking away significant share of the microprocessor business at the low end of the market, Intel became much more aggressive in developing and promoting the Celeron chip, even at the risk of cannibalizing sales of higher-priced chips.[19]

Achieving a Customer Value Discipline

To gain an advantage over competitors, a firm must "push the boundaries of one value discipline while meeting industry standards in the other two."[20] This entails a clear focus and a strong commitment to one specific value discipline. This sharp focus starts with a lucid description and a vivid understanding of the firm's mission and vision. As shown in the strategic management framework (see Figure 2-1), value creation rests on this clarity of focus. Only then does a value discipline become a path to market leadership.

The value discipline chosen as a company's strategic focus must be supported by its culture, competencies, and competitive situation. Once a value discipline is chosen and a path to market leadership has been achieved, the firm must continue to invest heavily in enabling technology, disciplined processes, and the right people to sustain that leadership.

Faced with the realities of strong and dynamic competitive conditions—market changes, technological advances, regulatory changes, and economic policy decisions—maintaining this focus on a single value discipline is a challenge. This is especially difficult for publicly held companies beholden to shareholders and subject to the vagaries and instability of financial markets. The temptation to generate revenues or cost efficiencies quickly, to meet the quarterly (or monthly or even weekly) numbers can lead a company away from their value discipline. For instance, despite the fact that Procter & Gamble's strategic approach to marketing in the late 1990s was to simplify, that is, reduce items in the line, cut back on dealer-loading promotions, and so on, they were forced by market pressure to reinstitute certain retail promotions to build short-term sales.

EMPLOYEES AND VALUE CREATION

Before the mid-1800s, when farming and agriculture were the driving forces behind national economies, land was the key to creating value. With the advent of the Industrial Revolution in the late 1800s, when machines and industry flourished, access to capital became perhaps the most critical factor for value creation. In the Information Age of today, however, the key to creating value for customers and owners and gaining a competitive advantage is no longer land or capital but employees. According to Pfeffer and Veiga, authors of *The Human Equation: Building Profits by Putting People First*, "An irrefutable business case can be made that the culture and capabilities of an organization—derived from the way it manages its people—are the real and enduring sources of competitive advantage. Managers today must begin to take seriously the often heard, yet frequently ignored, adage that 'people are our most important asset'."[21]

An organization's ability to create financial value is linked to its capacity to build a committed team of employees,[22] unified by a shared vision of the future,[23] and adept at innovation and organizational learning.[24] This combination of factors—commitment, vision and innovation—helps organizations to adapt, change, and grow in a dynamic and competitive era. Building high-performance teams, creating shared vision, and achieving innovation require a fundamentally different approach to managing employees than the centralized, control-oriented approach of Frederick Taylor.[25] They require human resource (HR) practices that view employees not as costs to be minimized, but as strategic assets whose energy, initiative, and creativity shape the future of the organization.

Creating Value by Putting People First

A substantial and growing body of research speaks to the strong connection between how firms manage their people and the financial success they achieve. This evidence is drawn from a variety of samples and industries, and "shows that substantial gains, on the order of 40 percent, can be obtained by implementing high performance management practices,"[26] such as self-managed teams, information sharing, extensive training, and pay tied to organizational performance.

One compelling study looked at the survival rates of a sample of 136 companies that went public in 1988. Five years later only 60 percent of those companies were still in existence. Analyses of the sample showed that the value firms placed on employees and how they rewarded their people were strongly related to survival. Specifically, firms that placed a higher emphasis on employees were 20 percent more likely to survive than those that placed a low emphasis on employees.[27] Furthermore, the difference in survival rates was even more pronounced depending on how firms scored on rewarding employees. Those that used rewards effectively were 42 percent more likely to survive. Another study based on a sample of 702 firms found that high-performance HR practices were associated with an increase in shareholder wealth of $41,000 per employee.[28]

Valuing employees is a common sense principle not only because it contributes to better organizational performance, but because it is the right thing to do. Unfortunately, common sense is not necessarily common practice. In the end, the key to managing people in ways that lead to profits and innovation, according to Pfeffer and Veiga, is the manager's perspective. When managers look at their people do they see costs to be reduced or assets to be nurtured? Do they see recalcitrant employees who can't be trusted and who need to be closely controlled or do they see intelligent, motivated, trustworthy individuals?*

The Chevron model of value creation (Figure 2-2) emphasizes the importance of employees in the value creation process. Kenneth Derr, chairman of the board and chief executive officer (CEO) of Chevron, states that building a committed team of employees "is our first strategic intent" because it is their dedication, hard work, and entrepreneurial spirit that make it possible for Chevron to accomplish its other strategic intents. "It is their creativity, willingness to try new things and to adapt to change that will enable us to continue to cut costs and find ever-more-effective ways to do business. Employees help make Chevron a strong, lean and nimble company able to successfully compete in today's tough global environment."[29]

At Chevron, as in all organizations, value creation begins with employees. It is their commitment, energy, and creative spirit that provides the fuel that powers the customer-employee-owner cycle. Employees are responsible for creating enthusiastic and loyal customers, customers who are willing to pay prices for the company's products and services that create value for the owners. But the customer-employee-owner cycle is not linear; it does not stop with the owners. Value must be returned to employees in exchange for their contributions to the process. To sustain the success of the organization, value is created and shared throughout the customer-employee-owner cycle.

What Is Value for Employees?

Employees expect to receive rewards, or value, for their contributions to the firm. In general, employee value is derived from two sources. Depending upon the organization and the individuals involved, value for employees may be largely financial, or it might be dominated by psychological and social considerations. Examples of the former include money and benefits, and examples of the latter might be a sense of accomplishment, feelings of pride and commitment to the work being done, status, self-esteem, a meaningful existence, or contributions to a larger social cause.

Financial Value

Employees expect to receive financial rewards for their contribution to the organization. This includes a competitive salary and fringe benefits package, but it means more than that. Indeed, one component of a high performance management system is *contingent compensation,* that is, compensation that is tied to organizational performance.

Contingent compensation can take a number of different forms, including gain sharing, profit sharing, and stock options and ownership. Each of these compensation schemes shares a common thread: Employees receive financial rewards when

---

* These opposing views about employees are known as Theory X and Theory Y, developed by Douglas McGregor. Theory X assumes employees dislike work, have little ambition, and need to be directed and controlled. Theory Y assumes employees can be highly committed to the organization and can exercise a high degree of creativity and initiative. According to the theory, the proper management style is contingent upon the employees. In today's Information Age, where firms rely on employees to adapt, innovate, and grow, the Theory Y approach works well. This is implied in the discussion above.

the organization meets or exceeds performance standards. **Gain sharing** is a program whereby employees are rewarded for new programs or initiatives that result in measurable improvements in productivity. For example, produce department employees in a supermarket are rewarded for finding ways to cut the percentage of waste associated with fruits and vegetables that have to be tossed out because they exceed their shelf life. **Profit sharing** differs from gain sharing in that it focuses on bottom line profits. When the organization exceeds a predetermined profit goal, some portion of the excess profit is shared among employees.

Stock options and stock ownership plans (**stock-based compensation**) have become increasingly important ways to reward employees. A recent survey of 350 companies' proxy statements found 35 percent with stock options for most employees, more than double the total 5 years earlier.[30] Another survey found that 45 percent of companies with 5,000 or more employees now have options for all their employees. At smaller companies the usage is even higher. For companies with less than $50 million in sales, 74 percent offered stock option plans to all employees.[31]

Texas Instruments has quadrupled the number of option-eligible employees since 1993 and slashed its turnover rate among technical workers. Similarly, The Charles Schwab Corp., a discount broker, extended its stock options program to all 13,300 of its employees in 1998. These programs recognize that the interests of employees, owners, and customers are not incompatible or mutually exclusive; in fact, they are inextricably linked.

Some of the advantages of stock-based compensation are shown in Table 2-3. As the table describes, these advantages may include tax incentives, lower employee turnover, higher commitment, and higher rates of organizational growth.

Another way to provide financial value for employees is through the benefits package offered. Starbucks Coffee, for example, has taken the unusual step of providing both full-time and part-time employees with full benefits beginning 3 months after the date of hire. They believe the extra cost of providing full-time benefits to part-time employees is more than offset by their ability to hire and retain more and better people. Starbucks is also motivated by the desire to avoid the high cost of replacing employees who leave, estimated by the Food Marketing Institute to be over $1,500 per entry level employee.

Psychological and Social Value. Employees also seek social and psychological rewards from their work. For instance, there can be great psychological value in work that the employee finds meaningful or important to a larger cause. Employees also find value in a stimulating work environment that affords them opportunities for personal growth and development on the job. Perceptions of value may be influenced by the amount of training received by employees, feedback, and recognition for their performance, and in general, the respect they are accorded.

A great deal of research has been conducted over the years on employee motivation and on what employees value in an organization. One long-standing project attempts to identify the 100 best companies to work for in the United States, based on a variety of factors.[32] The research indicates that **value for employees** means much more than good pay. In fact, the social and psychological aspects of work are often more powerful motivators than money.

Table 2-3 Advantages of stock-based compensation

Companies install stock-based compensation plans to create value for employees and for the company:

- **Attraction and retention.** Stock-based compensation is a benefit that a company can provide to increase employees' pay. The company has the ability to design plans that can increase employee total compensation at a lower cost for the employer. The increase in compensation comes from improvements in the value of the company. The market rewards the employee through appreciation and the company reduces its total cash outlay. These programs may also reduce employee turnover, which cuts recruitment and training costs.

- **Company cash flow and tax incentives.** Using stock-based compensation plans allows the company to provide employee benefits with a lower cash outlay. When the company gives shares of stock or options to employees, the employees benefit from price appreciation without the company having to lay out cash individually.

  In addition, the use of qualified stock plans provides tax incentives for the company that further lowers cash outlays.

- **Awareness of success of the company.** Employees who have part of their compensation based on success of the company have more interest in following the value of the company. The employees' benefit statements and communications of stock or option awards are constant reminders to them that they have higher income potential.

- **More employee commitment to the company and greater satisfaction.** This awareness helps employees understand that they can enjoy even more benefits as the company succeeds. Commitment is further enhanced when stock based compensation is combined with a method for employee input. This combination leads to employees making more intelligent decisions.

- **Better organizational performance.** Companies with ESOPs have 8% to 11% faster growth than companies without them.

Source: "Employee Strategies for Stock-Based Compensation," *Compensation and Review Benefits* 31, no. 6 (November–December 1999): 41–54. Copyright © 1999 by Sage Publications. Reprinted by permission of Sage Publications, Inc.

Examples of nonfinancial programs and practices that create value for employees include the following:[33]

- **Team-building**—Organizations that help make people feel part of a team are valued. This includes open communication and the sharing of information on things such as financial results and strategy. Shared accountability for results and the reduction of status differences between managers and employees is also part of team-building.
- **Extensive training**—Training is an essential component of high performance work systems and an opportunity for employees to develop new skills and knowledge. It also should prepare employees to identify and resolve problems, to initiate changes in work methods, and to take responsibility for quality.
- **A pleasant work environment**—Attention and resources devoted to maintaining a clean, safe, positive work environment are valued by employees.

- **Employment security**—The idea of providing employment security in today's competitive world seems outdated and at odds with what most companies are doing, but employees are not likely to be innovative or embrace change if they fear that this will jeopardize their own job security. Try not to lay off people without first making an effort to place them in other jobs either within the company or elsewhere.
- **Recognition for a job well done**—Employees appreciate constructive feedback on their performance and acknowledgment for good work.

Genuardi's Family Markets is a chain of 35 supermarkets with about 6,000 employees in the mid-Atlantic region of the United States. Retail businesses in general, and the supermarket industry in particular, are notorious for high rates of employee turnover. A combined full-time and part-time turnover rate of 100 percent is about average among supermarkets. Genuardi's has been able to achieve turnover rates that are one-third of the industry average. Genuardi managers attribute their success not to higher wages or more benefits (although their pay and benefits are competitive) but to the culture of their organization, epitomized by their corporate slogan: "The Difference Is Our Family Pride." Posted in every store is their statement of "Core Values and Beliefs," which includes the following:

> Genuardi's Family Markets is an enduring family business. Our primary purpose is to serve our family of customers, employees, and industry associates. All that we believe in is a reflection of our "Family Pride" . . . Our customers and employees are a family in which every member is treated with respect, sincerity, and fairness.

Genuardi's looks for ways to make the work experience pleasant and rewarding. Examples of ways the family atmosphere is reinforced include matching each new employee with a mentor, promoting from within, investing in ongoing training and development programs, seeking opportunities to recognize and thank employees for their contributions, holding employee appreciation days, and honoring employees with small gifts and incentives.

These nonfinancial ways of creating value for employees are as important as, and often more important than, stock ownership programs and other financial approaches. According to the research by Pfeffer and Veiga, creating a corporate culture that values employees is a key to superior organizational performance: "When employees are owners, they act and think like owners. However, little evidence suggests that employee ownership, by itself, affects organizational performance. Rather, employee ownership works best as part of a broader philosophy or culture that incorporates other practices"[34] such as team-building, training, information sharing, and delegation of responsibility. Thus, providing opportunities for employees to develop skills and be a part of a team has its own rewards.

OWNERS AND VALUE CREATION

There has long been a vigorous debate on the importance of shareholder value relative to other significant measures of corporate performance such as employment, social responsibility, and the environment. Although we have argued against an exclusive, narrow focus on owners, the centrality of creating value for owners is not to be taken lightly. Managers of public corporations have a fiduciary responsibility, a legal obligation, to create value for stockholders. Failure to do so is a serious concern. The examples of CEO turnover and massive employee layoffs described at the beginning of the chapter are ample evidence.

The discipline imposed by shareholder capitalism and an attention to value creation have led the United States economy to a 20 to 30 percent edge in GDP per capita in comparison with other major developed countries. Productive and innovative companies also happen to be the ones creating value for their owners. These firms attract better workers, who further enhance value creation in a virtuous, repetitive cycle.

What Is Value for Owners?

When owners invest in a company, regardless of whether that company is private or public, they expect a financial return on their investment. In general we can say that **value for owners** is created when the worth of their investment increases beyond the cost of the capital invested.

In the case of public companies, shareholders expect the worth of their stock to appreciate, to receive a share of the profits of the firm (in the form of dividends), or both. Thus, from the shareholder's perspective, whether or not management is creating value is easy to determine—it is directly related to the movement of the company's stock price and its dividend payout. (Some companies, such as Microsoft, do not pay dividends but have been enormously successfully in creating value for owners because of the superior performance of their stock.) Shareholder value, then, is tied to stock price appreciation and dividend payouts. Stock price and dividends, in turn, are linked to the firm's ability to produce current profits and to expectations about future profits. So the bottom line on value for owners is the bottom line—value for owners depends on the organization's ability to produce a steady stream of profits over the long term. These relationships are shown in Figure 2-4.

For Chevron's common stockholders, value is not an abstraction. It means something concrete in terms of wealth enhancement. Having traded their money for an ownership interest in the enterprise, they expect the worth of that investment to increase. They also have certain expectations about current earnings emanating from the investment. In other words, Chevron's owners look to management's choice and implementation of strategic initiatives to create value for them. How? By earning a return on invested capital that is greater than the cost of that capital, and by enhancing market expectations regarding future company financial performance. This is a big job, but that is the focus of top management's attention. Economic or financial value creation is an imperative outcome.

Owners Are Last to Receive Value. Value for owners is received only after other stakeholders have gotten a share. Think of an income statement. The bottom line is profit, economic value for owners. Before getting to the bottom line, customers have gotten value from their purchases; employees have received wages, benefits, and other nonfinancial rewards; vendors have been paid for their supplies and materials; property, plant, and equipment have been purchased or financed; creditors have received payments on loans; distributors, if any, have been paid. Government has also received value in the form of tax payments. Only after all financial obligations

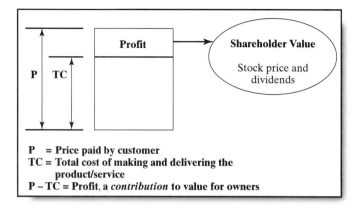

Figure 2-4
The concept of value for owners

P = Price paid by customer
TC = Total cost of making and delivering the product/service
P – TC = Profit, a *contribution* to value for owners

have been met does revenue from the top line of the income statement filter down to the bottom line, resulting in value for owners.

Strategy and Financial Performance

The process of value creation for owners has a great deal to do with the effective and efficient use of resources. Organizations are complex transformational entities: Input factors are combined in a way that the worth of the outputs exceeds the cost of the effort expended to create them. For the firm and its owners, profit (economic value) is created. Translating such value creation into wealth enhancement for owners is not always a "sure thing," but it is expected to occur.

When appropriate strategies are put in place and well executed, managers look to performance measures to help them make future value-creating decisions. Financial outcomes are one essential way to assess the appropriateness of the firm's strategy, the effectiveness of strategy implementation, and the efficiency with which execution of the strategy has occurred. Strategies drive performance outcomes, and to an extent, financial performance enables strategic initiatives.

There is no perfect measure of financial performance, nor is there a single metric that can capture all that is needed to assess every aspect of the strategic management process. Profitability measures, though, come closest to the ideal of an indicator that value creation has occurred for the firm and its owners.

Short-Term Value

The question of the *time horizon* for value creation been a contentious one. For example, much has been made of American companies' obsession with **short-term value**: quarterly financial performance, 10-day auto sales reports, weekly receipts by retail merchants, and the like, as against the supposed longer view taken by firms in Japan. What should be obvious is often overlooked in this debate: The long term is really just a connected chain of short terms. It's not as much the time dimension of the view taken as it is a stronger focus on value creation per se. A company that creates value in every short-run period has, by definition, created value in the longer-term analysis. By the same token, a company that focuses only on short-term profits can sacrifice its ability to create value in the long term.

The broader view of business as an ongoing enterprise allows little room for "get rich quick" or "fast in and out of the market" strategies on any large scale or for any extended length of time. Value creation for the impacted stakeholders, and shareholders in particular, demands that the business manager plan as if there will be no end to the growth and prosperity of the enterprise, while at the same time assuring that day-to-day operations provide appropriate value-creation rewards. These are not inconsistent goals! To survive, the firm must generate revenue, cover costs, produce a stream of available cash flows, and show a profit. In short it must create economic value.

Managing both short- and long-term value creation is a task that requires focusing on different metrics for the different tasks. Measuring value creation has a time dimension too. A significant difficulty for strategy development is that short-term financial measures (e.g., profit) often signal changes in the value creation process too late for corrective action to have an impact. Strategic management, with a view that transcends immediate and short-run aberrations, requires using measures of value that may differ from the popular short-term signaling ones that are so much a part of the daily stream of business news "sound bites." These measures are further discussed in Chapter 10.

Lasting Value

James Collins and Jerry Porras, authors of *Built to Last: Successful Habits of Visionary Companies*, liken the distinction between short-run profit making and long-term and persistent value creation to the difference between an ability to tell time and clock building itself. In the former case, the time teller, no matter how skilled and successful, eventually will disappear. In the other, the creation and building of a clock accounts for a long-lasting development that transcends the builder himself/herself. So it is with great business firms in their quest for value creation.

Lasting value for all stakeholders comes from building the enterprise itself, not a simple focus on profits this quarter, sales of a new product, or accomplishments of the latest cost-cutting program. Success at strategic management and creating value requires attention to a cluster of ideas and goals. Visionary enterprises, companies that bask in greatness for a long time, are guided by core values and ideologies that focus the business on purposes beyond short-term profit maximization.

Owner Value at the Expense of Customers and Employees. The risk of managing value creation for owners with a short-term perspective is the adverse impact this practice may have on the firm's long-term stakeholders (e.g., employees, customers, suppliers). The relentless pursuit of higher stock prices now can lead to reductions in investments in employees, research and development (R&D), and organizational processes and capabilities that are essential to long-term growth and value creation.[35] The result is that the firm mortgages its future for the sake of higher short-term stock prices.

The intrinsic value of a business undertaking must be seen as its ability to create good and lasting value for all stakeholders. For stockholders to benefit from the risk taken and the investment made, managers must avoid decisions that penalize the long-term cash-flow-generating ability of the company for the immediacy of short-term financial results. Lasting value is just that: sustained, market-besting total return to shareholders. This means meeting short-, medium-, and long-term objectives. It means managing strategy to provide significant wealth enhancement for stockholders without sacrificing value for other stakeholders. In short, it means understanding and managing the dynamics of the customer-employee-owner cycle.

EMERGING TECHNOLOGIES AND VALUE CREATION

Emerging technologies, including the Internet, have changed the way many firms attempt to create value, especially value for their customers. Some business analysts predict that technology will revolutionize the way business is transacted. They claim that we have only scratched the surface of the potential of technology. Others believe the impact of technology will be more limited but nevertheless agree that its role will be increasingly significant. Let's consider a few of the value-creating technologies now in use.

Laser scanners and *bar coding* are used to track product movement and sale through the channel of distribution and at the point of final sale. FedEx delivers packages overnight nationwide. Scanning technology is a necessary part of the FedEx system; without it, packages could not be routed correctly and within narrow windows of time required to reach both the hub and spokes of the FedEx system.

Electronic data interchange (EDI) between different firms in a channel of distribution permits automated flows of information regarding customer orders, transactions, inventory, and payment. Ford Motor Company has taken the lead in attempting to reinvent the supply chain in the auto industry by trying to become a model of efficiency in the Internet age. Aiming for a supply chain driven by Internet technology, the vision calls for factories that build cars to order, dealerships that report problems instantly to allow plants to make instantaneous adjustments, and suppliers that control inventories at Ford factories. Management at Ford feels that streamlining suppliers and distribution using the Internet could reap supply chain savings equal to 25 percent of the retail cost of the car. In addition, there is significant added value for customers who can get a custom-designed car delivered to their home in just a few days.[36]

Computer-aided design (CAD) and **computer-aided manufacturing (CAM)** enable mass customization or developing and manufacturing customized versions of products for individual customers. Dell Computer uses a direct-to-consumer sales model that is the envy of many industries, enabled by ordering and manufacturing processes that have been fine-tuned over the 16-year history of the company and updated using Web-based technology. Dell custom-assembled more than 25,000 different computer configurations for buyers in 1999 because the company works closely with all of its suppliers, especially the two dozen companies that make about 90 percent of its parts and components. The parts are designed for just-in-time delivery to Dell assembly plants and for snap-in assembly.[37]

Using digital technology, companies such as Adidas, Reebok, and Saucony have invested in high-tech devices to properly measure consumers' feet. A digital image of the foot can be used to produce a shoe that is partly standardized and partly customized to the individual shopper's foot. This represents a key for delivering customer value given that industry data suggest that over 60 percent of consumers have difficulty finding shoes that fit properly.[38]

Scanning purchases at the point of sale in food, drug, and mass merchandise retailers generates a wealth of transaction data. Advances in database technology permit rapid processing of large amounts of transaction data plus easy access to these data. Information suppliers such as ACNielsen and Information Resources, Inc. purchase and process these data. As a result, client organizations, mostly food and allied product manufacturers, have up-to-the minute reports on sales volume, volume changes, market share, share dynamics within categories, and information that allows volume and share to be correlated with price, display, use of promotional tactics, and other factors. These data are now available to subscribers on the Web so that local sales and marketing managers can base tactical decisions on the most recent market behavior.

E-Business and Value Creation

The explosive growth of business over the Internet is reflected in Table 2-4. From 1997 to 1999, electronic sales of the selected products quadrupled. The table shows that they are projected to almost quadruple again by 2002. These trends are driven by a host of factors, especially advances in technology associated with the new Information Age, but what is electronic business (e-business) and how can it be used to create value for organizations?

Table 2-4 Actual and projected online sales (U.S. sales only, in millions)

	1997	1999	2002
Travel	$911.30	$3,933.5	$11,699.4
PC Hardware	985.5	3,106.0	6,434.4
Books	151.9	1,138.8	3,661.0
Apparel and accessories	103.1	641.5	2,844.5
PC software	84.5	507.4	2,379.1
Grocery	63.3	350.3	3,529.2
Specialty gift	99.9	336.3	1,356.5
Music	36.6	280.6	1,590.6
Tickets	51.8	274.4	1,809.9
Videos	15.0	104.5	575.2
Consumer electronics	15.0	77.9	792.5
Health & beauty	2.0	65.5	1,182.9
Toys	2.0	52.6	555.3
Other	484.7	1,086.9	2,688.7
Total	$3,006.60	$11,956.30	$41,099.30

Note: U.S. sales only; consumers and small-office/home-office markets.
Source: Jupiter Communications, "The Online Revolution," The Wall Street Journal, July 12, 1999, R6.

E-business is a process that facilitates exchanges of information and transactions among organizations and individuals while employing state-of-the-art information technology. When e-business is successfully employed, it can contribute to value creation for organizations in several ways, including the following:

1. Improved communications and exchange of information between an organization and its customers, among its employees, and with its owners.
2. Increased operational efficiencies as it can help create less cumbersome workflow processes.
3. Quicker customer response time thus providing competitive advantage in today's fast-changing environment.
4. More and better customer relationships because it can be used to create a one-to-one relationship with every customer of the firm at an affordable cost.

Among other capabilities, Internet technology enables *direct-to-consumer marketing* plus the ability to track individual customer or household purchase patterns. Nike was slow to embrace the Internet but has invested heavily in Nike.com, which has been selling shoes since 1999. Recently, the site was upgraded to allow consumers to personalize athletic shoes by color and with names and jersey numbers.[39] Amazon.com homes in on individual customers by tracking purchases and attempted purchases, and communicating suggestions for products to established customers who jump on their Web site. An established customer orders a book on Amazon.com that happens to be out of print. That customer will be presented, the next time he or she logs on, with a number of other books on the same and related topics that are available for purchase with a single mouse click.

These examples demonstrate that emerging technologies and e-business have the potential to create value throughout the customer-employee-owner cycle. For customers, there is added convenience and more choices, employees can benefit from more and better customer relations, and owners have the potential of increased profits from more sales and lower costs. While this is the promise of emerging technologies, the ability to realize the promise continues to be a significant challenge for many organizations.

CONCLUSION

In order to create value for owners, profits must be earned. Earning profits depends on creating and delivering value to customers. Customer value is created and delivered by employees who possess the requisite knowledge, skills, direction, and commitment to perform value-creating tasks, in order to execute organizational strategies that take advantage of market opportunities. In return for their contributions to the value creation process, employees expect rewards. This dynamic cycle of value creation involving customers, employees, and owners is known as the customer-employee-owner cycle. It is the engine that powers the value creation process and serves as the focus of strategic management.

KEY TERMS AND CONCEPTS

After reading this chapter you should understand each of the following terms.

- Computer-aided design (CAD)
- Computer-aided manufacturing (CAM)
- Customer-employee-owner cycle
- Customer intimacy
- Customer value
- E-business
- Electronic data interchange (EDI)
- Gain sharing
- Lasting value

- Operational excellence
- Product leadership
- Profit sharing
- Short-term value
- Stock based compensation
- Value disciplines
- Value for employees (financial and nonfinancial)
- Value for owners

DISCUSSION QUESTIONS

1. What is the customer-employee-owner cycle and how is it related to the strategic management process?
2. Discuss why both Nordstrom's (high price, high service) and Wal-Mart (low price, low service) can provide value to their customers.
3. How have advances in information and communications technology enhanced the ability of organizations to create value for their customers?
4. What is the relationship between how firms manage their employees and value creation?
5. What is value for owners? How is it assessed?
6. Use the textbook's Web site to learn more about the current condition of Chevron. How well is Chevron currently creating value in the customer-employee-owner cycle?

EXPERIENTIAL EXERCISE

Value Creation: E-Commerce Versus Brick and Mortar. Evaluate an e-commerce Web site and a brick-and-mortar Web site for two companies in the same or a closely related industry. How do they compare on attention to value creation for customers, employees, and owners? What specific examples of value creation are evident?

ENDNOTES

1. Lublin, J. S., and M. Murray, "CEOs Depart Faster Than Ever as Boards, Investors Lose Patience," *The Wall Street Journal*, October 27, 2000, B1.
2. Bulkeley, W. M., "Polaroid to Slash Workforce by 2,000, to 5,500," *The Wall Street Journal*, June 14, 2001, A3.
3. Fernandez, B., "Chrysler to Cut 25,800 Jobs," *Philadelphia Inquirer*, January 30, 2001, A1.
4. Chevron, www.chevron.com., accessed January 20, 2000.
5. Chevron, www.chevron.com., accessed January 20, 2000.
6. J. P. Morgan Chase, www.chase.com, accessed March 7, 2000.
7. The Coca-Cola Company, www.cocacola.com, accessed February 11, 2000.
8. U.S. Airways, www.usairways.com, accessed July 22, 1999.
9. The Great Atlantic and Pacific Tea Company (A&P), "Becoming the Supermarket of Choice: Issue 3," February 1999.

10. Woodruff, R. B., and F. G. Sarah. *Know Your Customer.* Cambridge, MA: Blackwell Publishers, Inc., 1996.

11. Treacy, M., and F. Wiersema, "Customer Intimacy and Other Value Disciplines," *Harvard Business Review* (January–February 1993): 84–93.

12. Treacy, M., and F. Wiersema, "Customer Intimacy and Other Value Disciplines," *Harvard Business Review* (January–February 1993): 84.

13. Chevron, *Chevron Annual Report*, www.chevron.com, March 1999, accessed January 20, 2000.

14. Treacy, M., and F. Wiersema, "How Market Leaders Keep Their Edge," *Fortune* (February 6, 1995): 88–98.

15. Rocks, D., "Going Nowhere Fast in Cyberspace," *Business Week* (January 31, 2000): 58–59.

16. Treacy, M., and F. Wiersema, "Customer Intimacy and Other Value Disciplines," *Harvard Business Review* (January–February 1993): 84.

17. Simonds, W. C., and L. Lee, "They're Running as Fast as They Can," *Business Week* (July 12, 1999): 106–108.

18. Simonds, W. C., and L. Lee, "They're Running as Fast as They Can," *Business Week* (July 12, 1999): 106–108.

19. Reinhardt, A., "The New Intel," *Business Week* (March 13, 2000): 110–124.

20. Treacy, M., and F. Wiersema, "Customer Intimacy and Other Value Disciplines," *Harvard Business Review* (January–February 1993): 84.

21. Pfeffer, J., and J. F. Veiga, "Putting People First for Organizational Success," *Academy of Management Executive* 13, no. 2 (1999): 37.

22. Pfeffer, J., and J. F. Veiga, "Putting People First for Organizational Success," *Academy of Management Executive* 13, no. 2 (1999): 37.

23. Collins, J.C., and Porras, J. *Built to Last: Successful Habits of Visionary Companies.* New York: HarperCollins, 1994.

24. Senge, P. M., C. Roberts, R. Ross, B. Smith, and A. Kleiner. *The Fifth Discipline Fieldbook: Strategies and Tools for Building a Learning Organization.* New York: Doubleday/Currency, 1994, 299.

25. Taylor, F. *Principles of Scientific Management.* New York: Harper and Row, 1911.

26. Pfeffer, J., and J. F. Veiga, "Putting People First for Organizational Success," *Academy of Management Executive* 13, no. 2 (1999): 37.

27. Pfeffer, J., and J. F. Veiga, "Putting People First for Organizational Success," *Academy of Management Executive* 13, no. 2 (1999): 39.

28. Huselid, M. A., and B. E. Becker. "The Impact of High Performance Work Systems, Implementation Effectiveness, and Alignment with Strategy on Shareholder Wealth." Unpublished paper, Rutgers University, New Brunswick, NJ, 1997.

29. Chevron, www.chevron.com, accessed January 20, 2000.

30. "More Employers Motivate the Rank and File with Stock Options," *The Wall Street Journal*, May 18, 1999, A1.

31. "Employee Strategies for Stock Based Compensation," *Compensation and Review Benefits* 13, no. 6 (November–December 1999): 41–54.

32. Levering, R., M. Moskowitz, and M. Katz. *The 100 Best Companies to Work for in the United States*, New York: Addison-Wesley, 1984, ix.

33. This list of value-creating programs and practices comes primarily from two sources: Pfeffer, J., and J. F. Veiga, "Putting People First for Organizational Success," *Academy of Management Executive* 13, no. 2 (1999); and Levering, R. M., R. M. Moskowitz, and M. Katz. *The 100 Best Companies to Work for in the United States.* New York: Addison-Wesley, 1984.

34. Pfeffer, J., and J. F. Veiga, "Putting People First for Organizational Success," *Academy of Management Executive* 13, no. 2 (1999): 37.

35. Kennedy, A. A. *The End of Shareholder Value: Corporations at the Crossroads.* Cambridge, MA: Perseus Publishing, 2000.

36. Kerwin, K., M. Stepanek, and D. Welch, "At Ford, E-Commerce Is Job 1," *Business Week* (February 28, 2000): 74–78.

37. Kerwin, K., M. Stepanek, and D. Welch, "At Ford, E-Commerce Is Job 1," *Business Week* (February 28, 2000): 74–78.

38. Symonds, W. C., and L. Lee, " They're Running as Fast as They Can," *Business Week* (July 12, 1999): 106–108.

39. Lee, L., "Can Nike Still Do It?" *Business Week* (February 21, 2000): 120–128.

Chapter 3

Developing a Mission and Understanding Strategy

Chapter Outline
Core Values, Mission, and Vision
Types of Strategies
Porter's Generic Strategies
Types of E-Business Strategies
Conclusion
Key Terms and Concepts
Discussion Questions
Experiential Exercise
Endnotes

*C*onstancy and Change. Stability and transformation. These terms capture the essence of the paradox faced by strategic managers, the challenge of finding ways to manage the tension between constancy and change. Specifically, this challenge entails being able to stay true to an enduring organizational mission (stability) while operating in an evolving and dynamic world (change).

How can this paradox be reconciled? Can change and stability coexist within organizations? Merck & Co., a leader in pharmaceuticals, has found a way to do just that by remaining committed to an unchanging set of core values and its enduring organizational purpose while adapting to a constantly changing world. The mission and values of Merck carry on while new strategies are developed to adapt to an ever-changing competitive landscape.

Mission, vision, values, and strategy. These are the means to manage the dynamic tension between constancy and change, and are the focus of this chapter. The purpose of this chapter is to explain the concepts of mission, vision, and core values, and to discuss how they are developed. These concepts are the bedrock, enduring elements of strategic management. In addition, we provide an overview of the various types of strategies that organizations pursue that allow them to change and be transformed. An understanding of these strategy types is necessary before we can proceed to explore the remaining steps in the strategic management framework. After reading this chapter you should be able to answer each of the questions shown in Figure 3-1.

CORE VALUES, MISSION, AND VISION

Strategic management, as we have discussed, aims to create value for the organization, and by doing so over time, to achieve survival and well-being in the long term. Studies of *visionary companies,* that is, companies that have achieved enduring, long-term success, have found that they are characterized by a purpose and core values "that remain fixed while their business strategies and practices endlessly adapt to a changing world."[1] **Core values** are the fundamental beliefs and ideals of an organization.

In other words, visionary companies know how to manage constancy and change. Employees understand why the organization exists and where it is going. A sense of enduring and shared purpose pervades the organization, along with a vividly clear understanding of what the organization aspires to become. The ability to manage this constancy and change leads to superior organizational performance. According to the research, over a 64-year period, $1.00 invested in the visionary companies would have grown to $6,356 compared to $955 in non-visionary companies.

How is this commitment to an enduring and shared purpose fostered? Visionary companies attain their stature by finding ways to express their values, priorities, and sense of identity throughout the organization. Among the most prominent and important ways this is done is with their list of core values, and their mission and vision

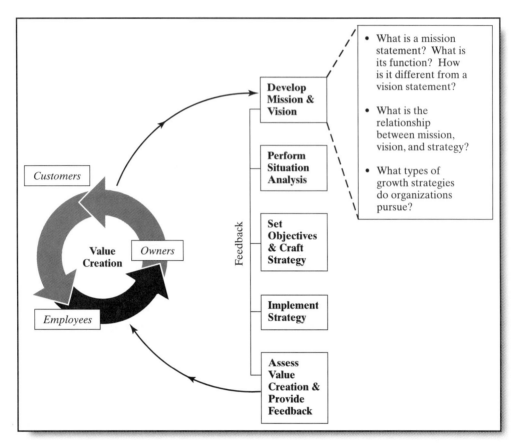

Figure 3-1
The strategic management framework

statements. As we can see in Figure 3-1, developing the mission statement (and vision and values) is the beginning step in the strategic management process.

Merck is considered one of the visionary companies that has achieved enduring success. Consistently ranked near the top of *Fortune's* "Most Admired Companies" list,[2] it is one of the world's most respected companies. Merck is admired not only for its financial success but also for its crystal clear and unwavering sense of mission and identity.

What is Merck's secret? The answer is simple: "people and the unifying values that bind them together." Decades ago, George W. Merck, the company's president and CEO from 1925 to 1950 articulated his philosophy: "We try to remember that medicine is for the patient. It is not for the profits. The profits follow, and if we have remembered that, they have never failed to appear . . . These words define who we are and why we do what we do."[3] Commitment to this philosophy cannot waiver.

George Merck's words have become a foundation for generations of employees, helping the company to understand and preserve its core values and corporate philosophy. The company's mission statement also reflects this commitment: Our mission is "to provide society with superior products and services—innovations and solutions that improve the quality of life and satisfy customer needs—to provide employees with meaningful work and advancement opportunities and investors with a superior rate of return."[4]

Merck's commitment to customers, employees, and owners is legendary, and is clearly evident in its mission statement. Merck also recognizes that its ability to meet these commitments depends on energized employees who embrace and embody those values. Merck's core values are shown in Table 3-1.

Being a truly visionary company requires more than writing a list of core values and a mission statement. After all, if these pronouncements are not understood by employees or infused into the culture of the organization, they can become nothing more than fluff—nifty public relations statements but irrelevant to the life of the firm. They are powerless to influence the behavior of employees and the direction of the organization. Developing and communicating a set of values, mission, and vision can be a helpful step in the process of building a visionary company. In fact, research shows that the visionary companies "wrote such statements more frequently than the comparison companies and decades before it became fashionable."[5]

Some organizations develop both mission and vision statements. From Chapter 1 we know that the mission statement answers the question "What is our business?" and the vision statement addresses the question "What do we want to become?" The goal of value creation for customers, employees, and owners begins to become more concrete with the development of mission and vision statements, helping to foster a unified focus or commonality of interests[6] among employees.

Table 3-1 Merck: Our values

1. **Our business is preserving and improving human life.** All of our actions must be measured by our success in achieving this goal. We value above all our ability to serve everyone who can benefit from the appropriate use of our products and services, thereby providing lasting consumer satisfaction.
2. **We are committed to the highest standards of ethics and integrity.** We are responsible to our customers, to Merck employees and their families, to the environments we inhabit, and to the societies we serve worldwide. In discharging our responsibilities, we do not take professional or ethical shortcuts. Our interactions with all segments of society must reflect the high standards we profess.
3. **We are dedicated to the highest level of** *scientific excellence* **and commit our** *research* **to improving** *human* **and animal health and the quality of life.** We strive to identify the most critical needs of consumers and customers, we devote our resources to meeting those needs.
4. **We expect** *profits*, **but only from work that satisfies customer needs and** *benefits humanity.* Our ability to meet our responsibilities depends on maintaining a financial position that invites investment in leading-edge research and that makes possible effective delivery of research results.
5. **We recognize that the ability to excel—to most competitively meet society's and customers' needs—depends on the integrity, knowledge, imagination, skill, diversity and teamwork of employees, and we value these qualities most highly.** To this end, we strive to create an environment of mutual respect, encouragement and teamwork—a working environment that rewards commitment and performance and is responsive to the needs of employees and their families.

Source: Merck & Co., Inc., "Mission Statement," www.merck.com/overview/philosophy.html, accessed March 9, 2000. Courtesy of Merck & Co., Inc.

The Mission Statement

The mission statement of Hershey Foods Corporation in the mid-1990s was:

> . . . to become a major diversified food company and a leading company in every aspect of our business as:
>
> The number-one confectionery company in North America, moving toward worldwide confectionery market share leadership.
>
> A respected and valued supplier of high quality, branded consumer food products in North America and selected international markets.[7]

This statement revealed Hershey's business, "a major diversified food company." It told what products Hershey sold, "confectionery and branded food products." The mission statement also indicated Hershey's geographic markets and its desired market share—"worldwide confectionery market share leadership." It provided the basis for allocating resources so Hershey could begin the journey to becoming a major diversified food company with worldwide leadership in the confectionery market. It was a signal, both to employees and to external stakeholders, that Hershey intended to become a global player in the consumer food products business, challenging Nestle and the Kraft Foods unit of Philip Morris. The mission indicated how Hershey was going to create value for customers, employees, and owners.

Throughout the 1980s and into the 1990s, Hershey pursued this mission through financing, investing, and operating decisions. Hershey acquired A.B. Marabou of Sweden, Franklin Restaurants, the Dietrich Corporation, maker of Luden's Throat Drops, the Canadian confectionery and snack nut operations of Nabisco Brands Ltd., and PeterPaul/Cadbury's U.S. candy operations. In the early 1990s Hershey acquired Ronzoni Foods Corporation from Kraft General Foods, which strengthened Hershey's position as a branded pasta supplier in the United States. Several acquisitions and investments were made to increase Hershey's international presence: Gubor Schokoladen, a German manufacturer and marketer of high-quality assorted pralines and seasonal chocolates; Sperlari, an Italian candy maker; and OZJ Jamin, a manufacturer of candy, cookies, biscuits, and ice cream for distribution in the Netherlands and Belgium. Hershey continued to build its position in the confectionery market in the United States through acquisitions, marketing, and the development of new products. Hershey's mission statement was being used as the focal point for decision making and communication.

By the mid 1990s, however, managers at Hershey began to realize that fulfilling this lofty mission was going to take a far greater commitment of resources and time than was anticipated or feasible. It was going to be almost impossible to challenge Nestle on a worldwide basis. Value creation in the customer-employee-owner cycle was beginning to weaken. Hershey's mission no longer seemed to match its current reality or its future possibilities. Actual or realized strategies were different from the original intended strategy, prompting Hershey to revisit the question of "What is our business?" By 1995, Hershey's mission statement was modified to read:

> Hershey Foods Corporation's mission is to be a focused food company in North America and selected international markets and a leader in every aspect of our business.[8]

This statement backs off from Hershey's aspiration to be a global leader in the confectionery market. Hershey's chosen path to value creation became more focused.

Table 3-2 Functions of a mission statement

- To establish a sense of direction within the firm and to guide the strategic management process by providing a basis for objectives and strategies
- To influence decisions about resource allocation
- To help build and communicate among employees a sense of shared purpose
- To communicate an attractive and compelling image to external stakeholders
- To support the core values of the organization

Hershey divested its European holdings, created more leasing agreements in the Far East, reorganized into four, then three divisions, and most recently sold all of its pasta businesses. At the beginning of the twenty-first century, Hershey is firmly committed to the North American confectionery market where it holds the number one position in the chocolate segment and is building share in the non-chocolate segment.[9]

The Role of a Mission Statement. The Hershey example reveals quite a bit about the nature of a mission statement. An effective mission statement may serve several purposes, both within the firm and for external stakeholders. Table 3-2 identifies some of the common functions of a mission statement. Among the most critical of these is to help build a sense of *shared purpose* in the organization, to establish direction, and to communicate that direction and purpose internally and to the public. A clear mission statement is needed to guide and set parameters for the strategic management process; it helps managers set objectives, make strategic choices, resolve their differences, and is a basis for allocating resources. A clear **mission** can set the tone within the organization and communicate a positive and compelling image to the outside world.

The Hershey example also shows that a mission, while enduring, is not stagnant. It may need to evolve over time. When Hershey's mission was to be a major player in the worldwide market, strategies were formulated and implemented to carry out that mission. The iterative nature of the process was revealed when Hershey evaluated its strategies in relation to its internal capabilities and external challenges and revised the mission statement. Then Hershey formulated and implemented new strategies to achieve the new mission.

The Components of a Mission Statement. Mission statements vary in length, content, format, and specificity (see Table 3-3 for several examples). If mission statements are too general they provide no direction and are worthless as decision making and communication tools. While some debate the usefulness of mission statements altogether,[10] ample evidence suggests that they are viable tools and are critical in a strategic management process that builds value. In a survey of executives, Bain and Company found that mission statements were ranked as the number one tool of strategic management every year since the study began in 1989.[11] While there is no single formula for the content of a mission statement, some common components are:[12]

- *Value creation.* How and for whom will the organization create value? Hershey will create value by being a leader in every aspect of its business. The current mission does not explicitly mention customers, employees, or owners.
- *Principal products and services.* What are the firm's major products and services? Hershey's current mission statement says that the principal product is food.

Chapter 3 Developing a Mission and Understanding Strategy   53

- *Geographical area.* Where does the firm compete? Hershey's geographic market is North America and selected international markets.
- *Philosophies.* What are the basic beliefs, values, and ethical priorities of the firm? Hershey's philosophy is to be a leader in every aspect of its business.
- *Self-image.* What are the firm's distinctive competencies or uniqueness? Hershey's current mission statement does not mention self-image.
- *Public image.* Is the firm responsive to social, community, and environmental concerns? Hershey's current mission statement does not mention public image.

Evaluating and Building a Mission Statement. An examination of the mission statement is part of the strategic management process. The components discussed above can be used to either break down the current mission statement for evaluation, or to build a new one. Because this statement helps all employees focus their efforts on the critical priorities, it is important to involve as many as possible in the process of evaluating or building the mission statement. To stimulate thinking and discussion, each person could be asked to consider the points listed in Table 3-4. This initiates discussion, but also gives some structure to the process.

Raising the question of "What is our business?" can trigger debate and reveal differences among those evaluating or building the mission statements. Negotiation,

Table 3-3 Examples of mission statements

FedEx Corporation

To produce superior financial returns for our shareowners as we serve our customers with the highest quality transportation, logistics and e-commerce solutions.

GUESS, Inc.

At GUESS, our mission is to be the leader in the jean market. We strive to make available the latest fashion trends and designs. By maintaining this mission, we will deliver profitability and growth that is necessary for the future success of our company.

Kellogg Company

Kellogg is a global company committed to building long-term growth in volume and profit and to enhancing its worldwide leadership position by providing nutritious food products of superior value.

Schering-Plough Corporation

Schering-Plough is a worldwide pharmaceutical company committed to discovering, developing and marketing new therapies and treatment programs that can improve people's health and save lives.

PepsiCo

PepsiCo's overall mission is to increase the value of our shareholder's investment. We do this through sales growth, cost controls and wise investment of resources. We believe our commercial success depends upon offering quality and value to our consumers and customers; providing products that are safe, wholesome, economically efficient and environmentally sound; and providing a fair return to our investors while adhering to the highest standards of integrity.

Sources: FedEx Corporation, "Mission Statement," www.fedex.com, accessed February 11, 2001; GUESS, Inc., "Mission Statement," www.guess.com/guessinc.asp, accessed March 7, 2001; Kellogg Company, "Our Mission," www.Kelloggs.com, accessed August 4, 2001; Schering-Plough Corporation, "Mission Statement," www.schering-plough.com, accessed August 31, 2000; PepsiCo, "Mission Statement," www.pepsico.com, accessed October 20, 2001.

Table 3-4 Evaluating and building the mission statement

COMPONENT	DESCRIPTIONS (KEY WORDS) OF OUR MISSION
Value creation	
Principal products and services	
Geographical area	
Philosophies	
Self-image	
Public image	

Source: Adapted from Ginter, P. M., L. M. Swayne, and W. J. Duncan. *Strategic Management of Health Care Organizations.* 3rd ed. Malden, MA: Blackwell Publishers, Inc., 1998, p. 148.

compromise, and eventual agreement on this important issue are critical to give focus to the rest of the strategic management process. This is especially important as more and more companies merge and develop alliances across national boundaries.

The Vision Statement

Vision statements are less common than mission statements. Neither Merck nor Hershey has one. Hershey's mission in the early 1990s, however, of becoming "a major diversified food company and a leading company in every aspect of our business" reads more like a vision because it speaks to what Hershey wanted to become rather than who they actually were. The vision statement of Marriott International, Inc. is "to strive to be the world's leading provider of hospitality services."[13]

A clearly articulated **vision** of the future is at once simple, easily understood, clearly desirable, and energizing.[14] A vision statement should address four key attributes: *idealism, uniqueness, future orientation,* and *imagery.*[15] As in the case of Marriott, vision statements tend to be very brief, forward-looking, inspirational, and attempt to evoke the emotions. A vision articulates a view of a credible but very attractive future for the organization. Like the mission statement, there is no single formula for crafting a vision statement. An effective vision statement, however, passes the *three C test*—it is *clear, concise,* and *compelling.*[16]

Evaluating and Building a Vision Statement. Table 3-5 may be used as a tool in the process of evaluating or building a vision statement. As with the mission statement process described above, each person involved could be asked to think about the points listed in Table 3-5. The table provides a list of vision statement components with space provided for participants to brainstorm and articulate key words to address each component. This initiates discussion and provides some structure for the process.

The Vision Framework

The superior financial performance of visionary companies has been partly attributed to a well-conceived vision framework. The concept of a **vision framework** includes the vision statement but goes further. It consists of two major components:

Table 3-5 Evaluating and building the vision statement

COMPONENT	DESCRIPTIONS (KEY WORDS) OF OUR VISION
Clear hope for future	
Challenging; inspires excellence	
Energizing to employees and customers/clients	
Memorable	

Source: Adapted from Ginter, P. M., L. M. Swayne, and W. J. Duncan. *Strategic Management of Health Care Organizations.* 3rd ed. Malden, MA: Blackwell Publishers, Inc., 1998, p. 157.

core ideology and envisioned future. The *core ideology* or *core purpose* defines the enduring character of the organization and is the glue that holds the organization together over time. Merck's core purpose for being, for example, is "to preserve and improve human life." Walt Disney wants "to make people happy," and Nike's core purpose is "to experience the emotion of competition, winning, and crushing opponents."[17] Core ideology is a constant over time.

For many companies, core ideology is expressed not in a vision statement but in a set of **core values** (see, for example, Merck's core values listed in Table 3-1). Johnson & Johnson's credo, found in Chapter 1, expresses its core ideology. Another leading competitor in the pharmaceutical industry is Pfizer, which strives to "abide by the enduring values that are the foundation of our business: Integrity, Innovation, Respect for People, Customer Focus, Teamwork, Leadership, Performance, and Community."[18]

The second component of the vision framework—*envisioned future*—includes two parts: a 10- to 30-year "audacious goal" plus vivid descriptions of what it will be like to achieve the goal. These vivid descriptions may be analogous to a vision statement as described above. The audacious goal is a very aggressive long-term goal that looks far into the future and requires thinking beyond the current capabilities of the organization. It "serves as a unifying focal point of effort, and acts as a catalyst for team spirit. It has a clear finish line, so the organization can know when it has achieved the goal . . . [the goal] engages people—it reaches out and grabs them."[19]

On May 25, 1961 U.S. President John F. Kennedy delivered a message before a joint session of Congress. In that message he established one of the great examples of an envisioned future:

> I believe that this nation should commit itself to achieving the goal, before this decade is out, of landing a man on the moon and returning him safely to the earth.

In 1961 the United States lagged behind the Soviet Union in space exploration and was far from capable of realizing the goal of landing on the moon. Kennedy's bold pronouncement, however, made in full view of the world, was a commitment and a powerful catalyst for focusing the nation's and NASA's resources and energy.

As a visionary company, Merck has set far-reaching, aggressive goals throughout its history. They include those found in Table 3-6.

Developing a Vision Framework. Synthesizing and crafting a vision framework is a challenging task. Intuition, perhaps even a spark of genius, are necessary "to

Table 3-6 Merck's goals over time

Early 1930s—to build a research capability so outstanding that it could "talk on equal terms with the universities and research institutes."
Early 1950s—to transform itself into a fully integrated pharmaceutical company in order to participate fully in the dramatic changes in medicine—backed by a "bet the company" acquisition of pharmaceutical giant Sharp & Dohme that gave Merck a well-established distribution and marketing network.
Late 1970s—"to establish Merck as the pre-eminent drug maker worldwide in the 1980s."
Late 1980s—to become the first drug maker with advanced research in every disease category.
Early 1990s—to "redefine the pharmaceutical paradigm" with a $6 billion acquisition of Medco to create more of a direct link with end customers.

Source: Collins, J. C., and J. L. Porras. *Built to Last: Successful Habits of Visionary Companies.* New York: HarperCollins, 1999, 205–206.

assemble—out of all the variety of images, signals, forecasts, and alternatives—a clearly articulated vision of the future that is at once simple, easily understood, clearly desirable, and energizing."[20] This synthesis requires:

- *Foresight*, to ensure that the vision will be appropriate for the future environment;
- *Hindsight*, so that organizational tradition and culture are not violated;
- *A worldview*, to capitalize on the impact of new developments and trends;
- *Depth perception*, to see the whole picture in perspective;
- *Peripheral vision*, to foresee possible responses from competitors;
- *A process of revision*, so that the vision is reviewed in light of changes in the environment.[21]

This discussion of core values, mission, and vision emphasizes that successful organizations have a clear sense of identity and purpose. Putting these pieces together and creating a vision framework allows the organization to send a strong and clear message to its employees and external stakeholders: "This is who we are and what we stand for. Anything less is not acceptable." Arthur Andersen, a worldwide leader in the management consulting field, provides a good example of how this is done. Andersen's vision framework is shown in Figure 3-2.

TYPES OF STRATEGIES

We began this chapter by discussing the paradox of constancy and change in strategic management. The company's core values and ideology anchor the company to an enduring purpose and provide a secure foundation for managing the turbulence of the business world. This is the constancy; but if organizations don't adapt with the times they go the way of the dinosaurs. How can firms remain true to their core ideology but also transform themselves to fit the changing world? That is where *strategy* comes into the picture. Strategy is the bridge that spans the gap from the organization's present to its future. While changing their strategies but remaining true to their mission and values, organizations are able to adapt and grow.

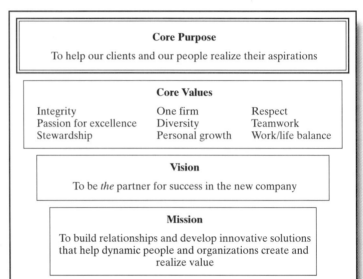

Figure 3-2
Arthur Andersen's
vision framework

Source: Arthur Andersen,
"Being" (An internal
company document),
2000, 2.

Before we move to Chapter 4 and the second step of the strategic management process—the situation analysis—we need to understand the concept of strategy. In this section we introduce and define the types of strategies that organizations can use to adapt and change with the times.

Classifying Strategies

With very rare exceptions, all organizations seek their own survival and most have a strong bias to continually improve performance to achieve greater productivity, more sales, lower expenses and higher profits, and for publicly-held companies to constantly strive to enhance shareholder value. Strategy is the means to achieve this goal. It is important to note that not all performance improvement strategies necessarily involve growth, but they all seek to enhance organizational performance in some way. Consider a basic model for measuring financial performance:

Performance = (Revenues less expenses)/invested assets

This formula suggests that strategies may be used to improve financial performance in one or more of three ways: (1) increasing revenues via one or more growth initiatives; (2) reducing expenses through greater efficiency; or (3) reducing the organization's asset base. In addition, organizations can pursue two modes of growth—internal or external. *External growth* is achieved through mergers, acquisitions, or strategic alliances involving more than one organization. By contrast, firms that grow on their own by introducing new products or expanding into new markets are pursuing *internal growth*. Internal growth occurs without partnering with another organization. Let's examine five types of strategies used by firms to improve or at least maintain their performance.

Expansion Strategies

Firms can pursue several avenues to achieve growth or expansion, each involving the basic strategic elements of products and markets. For example, new product development is a growth strategy aimed at achieving top-line sales increases, and is one of the strategic alternatives in the growth model shown in Figure 3-3. This model posits that the two major elements of strategy—products and markets—can be divided into two categories, that is, those that are current and those that are new.[22] Using a two by two matrix with four cells we can identify four different growth strategies:

1. *Market penetration*—achieving growth by selling more of our existing products in existing markets
2. *Market development* (or *market extension*)—achieving growth by taking existing products into new markets or market segments
3. *Product development*—the creation of new products for markets we currently serve
4. *Diversification*—branching out into new products for new markets; diversification suggests an expansion outside the firm's current core business(es)

These strategies may be achieved by either mode of growth, internal or external. However, diversification is typically an external growth strategy achieved via mergers and acquisitions, whereas the first three strategies listed above are often accomplished through internal expansion. Expansion strategies are not mutually exclusive. Several options may be pursued simultaneously. Let's look at each in more detail.

Market Penetration Strategies. Businesses can grow using current products in current markets through a strategy of **market penetration.** Penetration strategies typically include changing and/or increasing advertising and promotion, temporary price reductions, and promoting new uses. For example, Bayer A.G. has repositioned Bayer Aspirin, which was losing sales to alternative analgesic products such as ibuprofen (e.g., Motrin, Datril) and acetaminophen (e.g., Tylenol) as a remedy to aid in patient survival should a heart attack strike.

In November 1999, Campbell initiated a $95 million advertising campaign designed to increase sales and share of its flagship soup line. The campaign used the theme "We have a soup for that," attempting to position soup as a simple meal and lifestyle choice. Campbell can also increase the sales of certain soup flavors such as Cream of Mushroom or Cream of Shrimp by suggesting uses as sauces or ingredients in casseroles. These are all classified as market penetration strategies.

Market Extension Strategies. Alternatively, companies can grow by taking an existing product to new markets using a **market development** or **market extension**

		Markets	
		Present	New
Products	Present	Market Penetration	Market Extension
	New	Product Development	Diversification

Figure 3-3
The growth matrix

Source: Adapted from Aaker, D. A. *Strategic Market Management.* 5th ed. New York: John Wiley & Sons, Inc., 1998, 31.

strategy. Campbell's is a good example of a company that has been looking hard at expansion in overseas markets, while Tasty Baking, long a local and then regional company centered in Philadelphia, has now expanded distribution to 46 states plus Puerto Rico. After all, if you have close to an 80 percent share of the domestic prepared soup category (Campbell), or a close to 70 percent of snack cakes in the local market (Tasty Baking), how much can you grow via additional penetration of that market?

Comcast Corporation, whose major businesses are cable and cellular communications, grew domestically mostly through acquisition. The U.S. cable industry has consolidated dramatically, leaving few options for more acquisitions by Comcast. As the new century dawns, Comcast has turned its sights to Europe as one possible avenue for future growth. Through a company called Broadnet, a Brussels-based firm of which Comcast is a majority owner, Comcast has launched several bids to win national and regional wireless licenses throughout Western Europe, a market extension strategy.[23]

Product Development Strategies. Firms can grow by creating new products for existing or related markets. This strategy is called new **product development.** In the pharmaceutical industry, new product development is the lifeblood of the company. Merck, for example, pursues an ongoing strategy of discovering new medicines and uses for medicines through breakthrough research. Merck invests millions of dollars each year in research for new product development. Their track record for bringing new products through R&D and into the marketplace is exemplary. In 1999, 28 percent of Merck's global sales in the human health category were from new products. For example, Mevacor, Merck's cholesterol-lowering drug, has less than 1 year left on patent, but a similar and newer product, Zocor, has become Merck's best selling product.

Following its runaway success in traditional sports such as basketball and football, Nike tried to build credibility among fans of nontraditional and extreme sports, mostly teens. Many teenagers today identify with skateboarding and snowboarding instead of basketball and football, and do not see Nike the way that young adults did as teenagers who followed the NBA and NFL. To tap into the Generation Y cohort, Nike has created a division called ACG, which stands for "all conditions gear." This division is creating new products such as a $175 snowboarding jacket with a dozen pockets designed to hold items like goggles, headphones, a cellular telephone, gloves, and other essentials.[24]

Diversification Strategies

When organizations expand beyond the existing scope of their core business, they are pursuing a strategy of **diversification.** In other words, diversification entails entering a new industry. One justification for adopting a diversification strategy is to reduce risk, based on the logic that diversification allows the organization to spread its assets over a larger cross-section of industries. When one industry is down, another may compensate by being up. Ironically, many firms have found just the opposite to be true. Diversification may actually increase risk because the firm is expanding into a new and unfamiliar industry.

Diversification may either be related, in terms of the type of customer, technology employed, production process, distribution channels and so on, or unrelated or conglomerate, denoting expansion into a business that is entirely new and very different to the company. Diversification can be accomplished via internal development, but, as mentioned above, it is most often achieved through mergers, acquisitions, partnerships, or alliances.

Related Diversification

An example of **related diversification** is Nike's expansion from athletic shoes for track, then basketball and other sports, into athletic apparel and sports equipment, including its latest foray into golf. Pepsi's acquisition of Frito-Lay and Tropicana is another example of related diversification. Pepsi expanded outside its core industry of carbonated beverages but into related food and beverage categories.

Unrelated Diversification

An example of **unrelated diversification** is Kodak's acquisition of Sterling Drug Company. This move took Kodak into an entirely new business, quite different than its core business of film and imaging. Although Kodak later divested Sterling, the rationale for the acquisition was twofold: first, profit margins in pharmaceuticals were substantially higher than those in imaging products, and second, both industries were research-intensive and were built on research and development competencies. Unfortunately, the businesses were simply too different to provide the necessary synergy to manage them properly.

General Electric (GE) is a good example of a firm that has found a way to successfully manage unrelated diversification. GE competes in a wide spectrum of different industries from appliances to lighting, broadcasting (GE owns NBC), aircraft engines, and financial services. The Minnesota Mining and Manufacturing Company, more commonly known as 3M, which operates in office products, health care, industrial products, and other major markets, is another example of a successful firm with an unrelated diversification strategy.

Alliances and Integration Strategies

Like diversification strategies, alliances and integration strategies are typically achieved via external growth in partnership with other organizations. Let's take a closer look at each of these strategies.

Vertical Integration. Integration strategies may be either vertical or horizontal. Firms can integrate vertically by acquiring or developing their own sources of supply (known as **backward integration**) or by acquiring or developing their own distributors or retailers (known as **forward integration**). The two major motives driving vertical integration are the desire for (1) increased control over the channel of distribution, and (2) operational efficiencies.

Merck acquired Medco, a distribution company that delivers pharmaceuticals on a direct-to-consumer format. Merck distributes some of its own products through this operation, while Medco also distributes the products of other pharmaceutical manufacturers, putting Merck in the position of partnering with several of its key competitors. Medco now accounts for about half of Merck's total revenue.

Archer Daniels Midland is an integrated producer and processor of grain products, owning production at the farm level, intermediate processing into ingredients, and final processing into finished goods for sale at retail and through foodservice establishments. Another example of a vertically integrated firm is Chevron. We know from the last chapter that Chevron is involved in every aspect of the petroleum industry, from exploration and production to transportation, refining, and retailing to the final consumer.

Horizontal Integration.   When a firm acquires one of its competitors it is pursuing a *horizontal integration* strategy. This strategy has been very common in certain industries such as publishing, banking, accounting, and food. Industries that are experiencing a great deal of horizontal integration are going through what is known as *industry consolidation.* The aftermath of industry consolidation is fewer and much larger competitors. Because of their impact on competition and antitrust laws, horizontal mergers in the United States are subject to close scrutiny and must be approved by the FTC (Federal Trade Commission).

Examples of recent horizontal mergers and acquisitions are Ford Motor and Volvo (automobiles), PriceWaterhouse and Coopers & Lybrand (accounting/consulting), First Union and Core States (banking), PaineWebber and UBS Warburg (financial services), McGraw-Hill and Irwin (publishing), and Albertson's and Acme (food retailing).

An illustration of the integration strategies is shown in Figure 3-4.

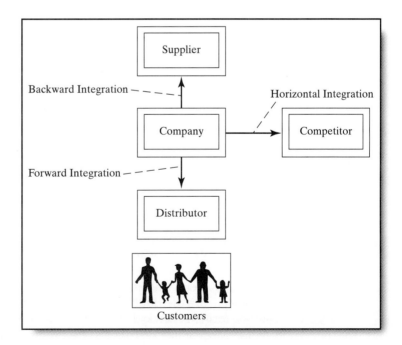

Figure 3-4
Integration
strategies

Strategic Alliances, Joint Ventures. A **strategic alliance** is a broad term encompassing many forms of cooperative agreement between two or more organizations. *Joint ventures* are a specific kind of strategic alliance with equity contributions (if appropriate) from partners to form a third, separate entity that stands alone for a specified time period. The two or more sponsoring firms establishing the joint venture share ownership rights in the new entity.

Strategic alliances and **joint ventures** are increasingly common and important ways to achieve growth. In 1991 Merck and E.I. Du Pont de Nemours formed a joint venture called The DuPont Merck Pharmaceutical Company (DMPC) to focus on cardiovascular, radiopharmaceutical, and central nervous system products. The venture achieved sales of $1.3 billion by 1997, but in 1998 Merck decided to sell its one-half interest in DMPC to Du Pont. Merck currently has joint ventures with Aventis—one called Merial to develop the field of animal health and poultry genetics, and another called Aventis Pasteur MSD, to act as the sole representative of Merck vaccines in Europe.

Strategic alliances are especially attractive in certain industries such as pharmaceuticals, automobiles, and computers. The alliances are driven by increasing cost pressures, shorter product life cycles, and the forces of global competition. The cost-sharing relationship of a partnership may improve the cost structures of the cooperating businesses and/or allow a business to gain access to new geographic markets or introduce new products. Another key advantage is speed. Alliances typically allow a company to achieve growth much faster than internal development.

Alliances tend to work well for firms whose products or geographic markets are complementary rather than overlapping. For example, Starbucks and Kraft formed an alliance to distribute Starbucks coffee in supermarkets. Kraft offered Starbucks a strong distribution system that it lacked while Kraft picked up a gourmet coffee, filling a gap in their product line. Both firms share the revenues from product sales. Similarly, Nestle, the giant Swiss food company with a powerful global distribution system, and General Mills, a company with strong domestic brands but a weak international presence, established a joint venture to sell Cheerios and other General Mills' cereals in the European market.

Retrenchment Strategies

The strategies discussed so far—expansion, diversification, integration, and alliances—are primarily thought of as alternative growth strategies. Firms attempt to improve performance not only through growth but also by controlling their expenses and asset base. Efforts to cut expenses and/or reduce assets are known as **retrenchment** or *consolidation* strategies. These strategies were a common way that firms tried to build shareholder value and please the investment community in the 1990s. There are risks associated with these strategies. Let's examine different types of retrenchment.

Cost-Cutting Strategies. ConAgra recently launched a major *restructuring* initiative designed to reduce expenses and boost earnings, typical goals of a restructuring effort. At the same time, virtually every major food company was forced to undertake cost-cutting strategies, including job reductions or *downsizing* and the improvement of operational efficiencies in order to boost profit margins in a slow-growth industry.

Cost-cutting strategies are often reactive, that is, in response to declining organizational performance. Bridgestone/Firestone, a maker of tires, found itself embroiled in a crisis after some of its tires were found to be defective and linked to deadly accidents on the highways. A safety recall of millions of tires ensued. Within weeks Firestone announced a downsizing, including a 10 percent workforce layoff. Similarly, Nike's layoff of 1,600 employees described in Chapter 1 occurred after a drop in company performance. While cost control is always a strategic imperative, these types of reactive cost-cutting strategies raise ethical concerns about employee rights and are not conducive to a healthy, productive corporate climate.

On the other hand, cost-cutting strategies need not be reactive nor involve employee layoffs. Merck, for example, continually seeks ways to reduce expenses through optimizing plant utilization, improving technology transfer between research and manufacturing, and redesigning or reengineering core and administrative processes.

The Risks of Downsizing. Researchers who have studied the relationship between layoffs and corporate performance have found mixed results. Downsizing may reduce costs and improve cash flow in the short term but may also damage customer relationships and the morale of surviving employees. One study found companies that announced mass layoffs or repeated layoffs underperformed the market over a 3-year period. A similar study found that 68 percent of firms using cost-cutting strategies did not achieve their profit goals for five years.[25] These studies suggest that layoffs cannot be a knee-jerk reaction during downturns. The firm's ability to create value depends not on short-term fixes but on serving customers, employees, and owners over the long term. Employee commitment to a shared purpose is not engendered when a company resorts to layoffs as their first line of defense.

Divestment and Liquidation. While cost-cutting focuses on the efficiency of operations, asset reduction strategies focus on eliminating assets. Two types of asset reduction are divestiture and liquidation. In a **divestiture** the firm reduces its asset base by selling off or divesting divisions and other parts of the organization. The divested division may continue as an ongoing concern but under different corporate ownership. **Liquidation** involves dissolving the business or a portion of it, and selling it for its tangible worth. It ceases to exist as an ongoing concern.

In an attempt to save $150 million per year and focus on core businesses, Campbell's divested seven non-core businesses in the late 1990s, including Swanson frozen foods, Vlasic Pickles, Swift Armour meats, and other international specialty foods business. A separate new publicly traded company, Vlasic Foods International, was created by the spin-off. Campbell's goal was to provide significant cost reductions for Campbell and the spin-off company (Vlasic Foods International) and allow Campbell to focus on its most profitable businesses with the highest growth potential. These include soup and sauces, biscuits and confectionery, and food service.

Subsequently, Campbell announced major cost-saving initiatives in its supply chain designed to deliver annualized savings of $100 million.

Dean Foods divested its vegetable company in 1998, generating cash to invest in its core dairy business while at the same time exiting from a category affected by the volatility of the vegetable commodities markets. Another example of a divestment strategy involves PepsiCo, which spun off its food service unit (KFC, Taco Bell, and Pizza Hut) in order to concentrate on the beverage and snack food industries with Pepsi and Frito Lay products. The food service businesses continue to operate under new ownership and a new name, Tricon Global Restaurants.

Bradlees, Inc. announced a liquidation strategy in December 2000 when it filed for protection pursuant to Chapter 11 of the U.S. bankruptcy code in order to conduct an orderly wind-down of its business and sale of its assets. Bradlees and its board of directors had explored a number of options, including consolidation, before determining that liquidating operations was the best alternative. Senior managers blamed a number of adverse factors that affected the company's ability to continue to operate. Bradlees was a general merchandise retailer of apparel and items for the home, and operated 105 stores and three distribution centers in seven Northeast states.[26]

In some industries, and specifically in the food processing industry, opportunities to improve performance through cutting expenses or reducing the firm's asset base are increasingly difficult to find. Many companies have already "cut to the bone" so that further reductions can only undermine the business's ability to create value for customers. Even in an economy characterized by slow population growth, mature markets, and cutthroat competition, the emphasis is ultimately on generating more revenue. This leads to the need to follow a growth strategy.

Stability Strategy

A final category of strategies seeks to neither grow nor cut but to stabilize operations. A successful company in a mature industry may seek to hold its competitive position but no more. The goal of a stability strategy is to maintain the status quo. A harvest strategy is a type of stability strategy used in portfolio planning, which is described in Chapter 6. A *harvest* strategy attempts to hold a competitive position with minimal reinvestment in the business.

Table 3-7 identifies the five categories of strategies and provides examples of each of the specific strategy types.

PORTER'S GENERIC STRATEGIES

Another useful and well-known model for understanding different types of strategies was developed by Michael Porter, professor and author of several important strategy books.[27] According to Porter, strategies allow organizations to achieve a competitive advantage in two ways: by establishing a position of either cost leadership or differentiation. *Competitive advantage* comes from creating customer value

Table 3-7 Types of strategies

Type	Strategy	Example
Expansion	Market Penetration	Campbell Soup's $95 million advertising campaign designed to increase sales and share of its flagship soup line.
	Market Development	The expansion of Comcast Corporation, a U.S. cable company, into European markets.
	Product Development	The ongoing commitment of Merck Pharmaceuticals in the research and discovery of new medicines and product development.
Diversification	Related Diversification	Nike's expansion from athletic shoes into sports apparel and equipment.
	Unrelated Diversification	The success of GE in different industries, including appliances, broadcasting, aircraft engines, and financial services.
Alliances and Integration	Vertical Integration	Chevron's involvement in every aspect of the petroleum industry, from exploration and production to transportation, refining, and retailing to the final consumer.
	Horizontal Integration	The consolidation of accounting firms Price Waterhouse and Coopers & Lybrand.
	Strategic Alliance	The alliance formed by Starbucks and Kraft allowing Starbucks to distribute coffee in supermarkets and Kraft to pick up a gourmet coffee line.
	Joint Venture	Coke and P&G formed a jointly owned company to develop and market juices and snacks.
Retrenchment	Cost Cutting	Firestone's 10% workforce layoff in the aftermath of its defective tire crisis.
	Divestment	Pepsi's spinning off of its food services businesses (KFC, Taco Bell, and Pizza Hut) in order to concentrate on the beverage and snack food industries with Pepsi and Frito Lay products.
	Liquidation	Bradlees ceased operations, closing all of its 105 stores and selling off its inventory.

and we know that customer value comes from offering a product with equivalent benefits at a lower price or unique benefits that more than offset a higher price.

The scope of competitive advantage may be realized either on a broad, mass-market basis or by focusing on a narrow market niche. These two dimensions—scope of advantage and type of advantage—may be used to identify generic strategies for competing in any business. Figure 3-5 shows the generic strategies.

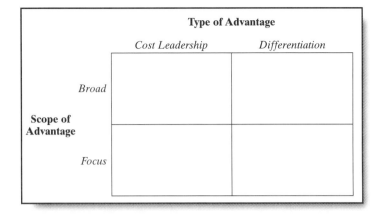

Figure 3-5
Porter's generic
strategies

Source: Adapted from
Porter, M. E. *Competitive
Advantage: Creating and
Sustaining Superior
Performance.* New York:
Free Press, 1985, p. 12.

Establishing a **cost leadership** strategy rests on the organization's ability to be more efficient than competitors and serve customers at a lower per-unit cost. Having this low-cost position allows the firm to charge a lower price (if it chooses to) and still generate a healthy profit margin. Southwest Airlines is a good example of a company that has established a very tight cost structure and passed that on to consumers in the form of lower airfares. Southwest has succeeded with a focused cost leadership strategy. As noted in the previous chapter, Wal-Mart is another company that has built a cost structure unrivaled by its competitors. These cost advantages allow Wal-Mart to charge lower prices that many other retailers have found it difficult if not impossible to match.

A **differentiation** strategy pursues competitive advantage in a different way, by producing products and services perceived to be unique in some way. Uniqueness is typically thought of in terms of product features but can actually be derived from any number of sources, including product or service benefits, quality, convenience, a special warranty, after-sale service, or a trendy image from successful marketing. When a product attains a position of uniqueness, customers are often willing to pay more for it. Customers perceive the extra value to be worth the extra price. For example, Nike athletic shoes are generally more expensive than alternative brands. But the perceived superior performance of Nike shoes makes the added price worthwhile to many customers. Ritz Carlton is a hotel chain that has successfully differentiated itself from other chains, and as a result is able to charge more for its rooms. Despite higher room rates, customer value remains high because of the perceived added benefits of staying at Ritz Carlton.

Stuck in the Middle

While advances in technology and changes in competition have created opportunities for firms to compete on both a low cost basis and on differentiation, one must still heed Porter's warnings about winding up "stuck in the middle." Failure to achieve one of the generic strategies leaves a company stuck in the middle with no competitive advantage and below-average performance. Sears held the position as the nation's number one retailer during the 1960s and 1970s, but lost its position as mass merchants such as Wal-Mart and Kmart (low price) and Nordstrom's (high service) eroded Sears' market share. Ultimately, Sears recast its strategy by focusing on brands such as Kenmore and Craftsman, plus opening up specialty hardware and furniture stores designed to provide deep assortments of a limited range of products in a convenient shopping format, thereby getting the company out of being stuck in the middle.

TYPES OF E-BUSINESS STRATEGIES

Another way of classifying strategy is from an e-business perspective. E-business strategies are a means to achieve growth, cut costs, or both. In this sense, e-business strategies are not new or different types of strategies than those just described; they are simply a different way to achieve the desired goal. Because of their increasing prominence in the global economy, however, they warrant special consideration.

Figure 3-6 identifies four types of e-business strategies based on the relationship between a business and its customers. Examples of each strategy are also shown in the figure.

The **business-to-consumer (B2C)** model allows firms to sell directly to consumers, bypassing intermediaries in the channel of distribution. Examples of this model include Amazon.com and E*Trade. The explosive growth of advertising for these dot.com businesses is evidence of their vitality.

The largest segment in terms of transaction volume is **business-to-business (B2B).** An example of this is VerticalNet Inc. (see www.verticalnet.com), which allows firms to find suppliers and industrial customers. Electronic Data Interchange (EDI) transactions have evolved over the years to support this model by allowing various information trading relationships, including one-to-one (direct linkage), one-to-many (e.g., Wal-Mart and their suppliers), and many-to-many (e.g., Visa Card's Private EDI Network, connecting merchants to banks).

A model that has increasingly captured the public's imagination is the **consumer-to-consumer (C2C)** segment. Through eBay Inc. (www.ebay.com) and other Internet auction firms, consumers can connect with other consumers all over the world.

Figure 3-6
Models of e-business strategy

Source: Adapted from M. P. Joshi, and I. Yermish, "The Digital Economy: A Golden Opportunity for Entrepreneurs?" *New England Journal of Entrepreneurship* 3, no. 1 (2000): 15–21.

	Consumer	Business
Business	**B2C** Amazon, E*Trade	**B2B** VerticalNet, SABRE system
Consumer	**C2C** eBay	**C2B** Priceline, Lendingtree

Finally, the **consumer-to-business (C2B)** model was imagined in theory only until the advent of the Internet. A well-known example is Priceline.com Inc. (www.priceline.com), a service that taps into the excess capacity of hotels and airlines, and allows consumers to bid for this excess capacity. Similarly, Lending Tree International (www.lendingtree.com) allows consumers to signal their interest in a mortgage and consider bids from competing mortgage companies. Classic economic theory suggests that the consumer should pay less for these services as more sellers compete.

CONCLUSION

Since 1995 Merck has launched more than 15 successful new medicines, accounting for almost 30 percent of their worldwide sales. In addition, Merck's revenue and profit growth remain healthy and strong despite some important medicines coming off patent. Through an unwavering commitment to research and introduction of new products and a steadfast focus on its core values, Merck is able to manage change from a base of stability. This is the paradox of change and constancy discussed throughout the chapter.

The organization's core values, mission, and vision help to establish an unambiguous and enduring focus. The process used to develop the mission, vision, and values is important as is the way they are communicated. When the process is open and includes employees, understanding and commitment are enhanced.

Organizations pursue various types of strategies as means to adapt to their changing circumstances. Most firms have a bias for growth, but other strategies are also important depending on the circumstances. Growth, retrenchment, integration, strategic alliances, and e-business strategies are just some of the important types of strategies that were explained in this chapter. Each strategy should contribute to achieving the organization's mission, vision, and core values.

KEY TERMS AND CONCEPTS

After reading this chapter you should understand each of the following terms.

- **Backward integration**
- **Business-to-business (B2B) strategy**
- **Business-to-consumer (B2C) strategy**
- **Consumer-to-business (C2B) stragegy**
- **Consumer-to-consumer (C2C) strategy**
- **Core values**
- **Cost leadership**
- **Differentiation**
- **Divestiture**
- **Focus**
- **Forward integration**
- **Horizontal integration**
- **Joint venture**
- **Liquidation**
- **Market development or extension**
- **Market penetration**
- **Mission**
- **Product development**
- **Related diversification**
- **Retrenchment strategy**
- **Strategic alliance**
- **Unrelated or conglomerate diversification**
- **Vision**
- **Vision framework**

DISCUSSION QUESTIONS

1. How are the concepts of vision, mission, core values, and strategy related? How are they different?
2. Critique the following mission statement of the Harley Davidson company.

   We fulfill dreams through the experience of motorcycling, by providing to motorcyclists and to the general public an expanding line of motorcycles and branded products and services in selected market segments.

3. Compare and contrast the core values of three leading pharmaceutical firms: Merck, Pfizer, and Johnson & Johnson. Use Johnson & Johnson's credo from Chapter 1, Merck's list of values in Table 3-1, and Pfizer's values listed under "The Vision Framework" in this chapter.
4. What are the advantages and disadvantages of strategic alliances compared to internal expansion strategies?
5. Discuss the four types of e-business strategies and how they may be used to create value for the firm.
6. Check the textbook's Web site to see if Merck's vision and mission statements have changed. If so, what might account for the changes?

EXPERIENTIAL EXERCISE

Building and Evaluating a Mission Statement. Select a company or organization that you know well (e.g., your university or your place of employment). Use the table below as a guide to write your own mission statement for the organization. Then obtain a copy of the organization's actual mission. How does your mission compare to the actual? Which do you think is better? Why?

COMPONENT	DESCRIPTIONS (KEY WORDS) OF MISSION
Value creation	
Principal products and services	
Geographical area	
Philosophies	
Self-image	
Public image	

ENDNOTES

1. Collins, J. C., and J. L. Porras, "Building Your Company's Vision," *Harvard Business Review* (September-October 1996): 65.
2. Brown, E., "America's Most Admired Companies," *Fortune* (March 1, 1999): 68–73.
3. Merck & Co., Inc., "Mission Statement," www.merck.com/overview/philosophy.html, accessed March 7, 2000.
4. Merck & Co., Inc., "Mission Statement," www.merck.com/overview/philosophy.html, accessed July 22, 1999.
5. Collins, J. C., and J. L. Porras, "Building Your Company's Vision," *Harvard Business Review* (September-October 1996): 65.
6. Quigley, J., "Vision: How Leaders Develop It, Share It and Sustain It," *Business Horizons* (September–October 1994): 39.

7. David, F. *Strategic Management Concepts.* 7th ed. Upper Saddle River, NJ: Prentice Hall, 1999, 30.
8. Ibid.
9. Ibid.
10. Ackoff, R. L., "Mission Statements," *Planning Review* 15, no. 4 (July–August 1987): 30–31.
11. Mosner, D., "Mission Improbable," *Across the Board* (January 1995): 1.
12. Pearce, J. A., III, and F. David, "Corporate Mission Statements and the Bottom Line," *Academy of Management Executive* 1, no. 2 (1987): 109–116.
13. Marriott International, "Vision Statement," www.Marriott.com, accessed March 7, 2000.
14. Bennis, W., and B. Nanus. *Leaders: The Strategies for Taking Charge.* New York: Harper & Row Publishers, 1985, 103.
15. Kouzes, J., and B. Z. Posner, "Envisioning Your Future: Imagining Ideal Scenarios," *The Futurist* 30, no. 3 (1996): 14–19.
16. Truskie, S. D. *Leadership in High-Performance Organizational Cultures.* Westport, CT: Quorum Books, 1999, 66.
17. Collins, J. C., and J. I. Porras, "Building Your Company's Vision," *Harvard Business Review* (September–October 1996): 69.
18. Pfizer, "Our Values," www.pfizer.com, accessed February 11, 2000.
19. Ibid, 73.
20. Bennis, W., and B. Nanus. *Leaders: The Strategies for Taking Charge.* New York: Harper & Row Publishers, 1985, 103.
21. Ibid, 102–103.
22. Aaker, D. *Strategic Market Management,* 5th ed. New York: John Wiley and Sons, 1998, 204.
23. Horn, P., "Comcast Seeking Growth in Europe," *Philadelphia Inquirer,* March 20, 2000, E-1.
24. Lee, L. "Can Nike Still Do It," *Business Week* (February 21, 2000): 120–128.
25. Ilsenrath, J. E., "Many Say Layoffs Hurt Companies More Than They Help," *The Wall Street Journal,* February 21, 2001, A2.
26. www.businesswire.com/webbox/bw.122600/203612129.htm, accessed February 21, 2001.
27. Michael Porter is the author of *Competitive Strategy* (New York: Free Press, 1980), *Competitive Advantage* (New York: Free Press, 1985), and *Competitive Advantage of Nations* (New York: Free Press, 1990) among other books.

Chapter 4

The Internal Audit

According to published reports in the business press, the heat was on Livio DeSimone, CEO of Minnesota Mining and Manufacturing Company (3M).[1] Would DeSimone be ousted from 3M, a company once lauded as one of America's best?[2] Some managers at 3M were extremely disgruntled, and had even gone so far as to take the drastic step of sending anonymous letters to the 3M board of directors complaining about DeSimone's leadership and the organization's performance. Would DeSimone survive the strife and retain his position as CEO? How did he find himself in this situation? What were the specific complaints against DeSimone, and why would 3M managers take the highly unusual, and some might argue inappropriate, step of sending those anonymous letters?

The answers to these questions are directly related to the topic of this chapter, the internal audit. As we know from Chapter 1, performing a situation analysis, that is, a thorough and ongoing assessment of the organization's external and internal circumstances, is the second step in the strategic management process. A situation analysis is conducted in two parts—by performing an internal audit and an external audit.

An **internal audit** is a systematic technique for evaluating and understanding the internal condition of the organization. The purpose of the internal audit is to identify the **competitively relevant strengths and weaknesses** of the organization. This information is a critical piece of the puzzle for making strategic decisions.

The strategic management framework, shown in Figure 4-1, reveals that the results of the situation analysis influence managers' choices about strategy, and through the feedback mechanism may also be used to alter or redefine the organization's mission, vision, and objectives. The external audit is discussed in Chapter 5. It focuses on monitoring and evaluating the forces and factors outside the organization, in the firm's external environment. The purpose of this chapter is to describe a four-step process for performing an internal audit. By applying this process to 3M and other companies we will demonstrate the internal audit process and answer each of the questions listed in Figure 4-1.

THE INTERNAL AUDIT PROCESS

As shown in Figure 4-1, an organization bases its strategic choices on a variety of considerations, one of the most important of which is its understanding of its own strengths and weaknesses. This understanding is a result of the organization's internal audit process. Using this information the organization can leverage its strengths to take advantage of emerging growth opportunities, to counteract the effects of external threats, or to attempt to overcome or improve its weaknesses.

Identifying a laundry list of strengths and weaknesses for a firm is relatively easy task but also a relatively useless one from a strategic management perspective. This

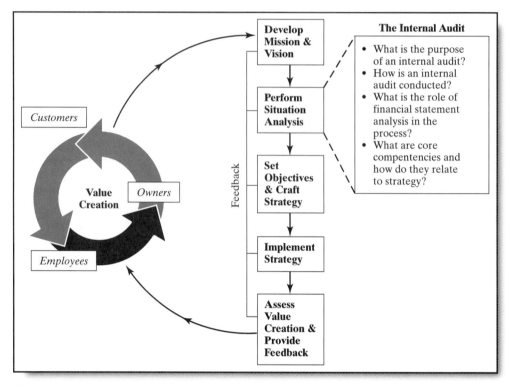

Figure 4-1
The strategic management framework

type of information tends to be too superficial and unfocused for decision-making purposes. The real challenge is to determine a *workable number* of competitively relevant strengths and weaknesses. This is not always an easy or obvious task. In fact, it is generally agreed in the strategic management field that the development of tools for analyzing the external environment has proceeded more rapidly than the development of tools for the internal audit.[3] By following a systematic process of internal assessment, however, these strengths and weaknesses can be determined.

Figure 4-2 provides an overview of a four-stage process for identifying an organization's competitively relevant strengths and weaknesses. The process requires that managers assess the organization's current and past performance at creating value, analyze the organization's value chain activities, understand its distinctive competencies, and, using this information, determine its strengths and weaknesses. Each step in the process is explained in the following sections. 3M is used as an example to illustrate applications of the process.

STAGE 1: ASSESSMENT OF PERFORMANCE

We know that a successful strategic management process is oriented to creating value for key stakeholders. The first stage of the internal audit process is an assess-

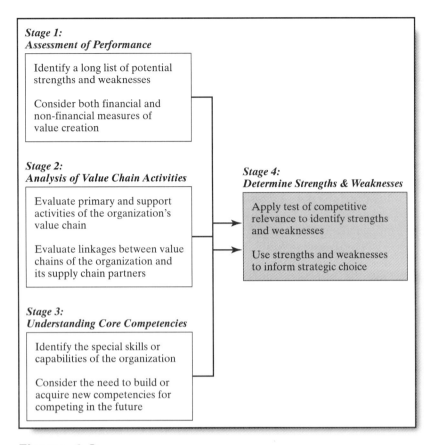

Figure 4-2
The internal audit process

ment of the organization's recent performance in value creation. This includes an evaluation of both financial and nonfinancial measures of organizational performance. The purpose of this stage is to get an accurate and current gauge of how well the organization's strategies are working. The outcome of this stage is a rather long list of *potential* strengths and weaknesses. Some of these potential strengths and weaknesses will filter through the screens employed in Stage 4 of the process. Those that do are considered *competitively relevant* and are included in a short list of strengths and weaknesses. The implication is that to be considered a strength or weakness, factors must be competitively relevant.

Assessment of value creation is an ongoing process in strategic management (this topic is covered in depth in Chapter 10). It allows managers to get a sense of the health of the organization. Depending on the nature of the firm, its mission, and objectives, firms will use different sources of information to assess their performance in Stage 1. Just about all organizations (and certainly all businesses) will analyze their financial reports for evidence of potential strengths and weaknesses. Other common sources of information for the Stage 1 assessment include customer and employee surveys and interviews, market share analyses, market research studies, internal staffing standards, and productivity reports.

Again, depending on the nature of the organization, different types of performance measures will be preferred by different organizations. The measures listed and defined in Table 4-1 are among the most common, however, and are recommended for this stage of the process. They can provide a good broad-brush assessment of the recent performance of the organization.

These tools by themselves provide useful information about the potential strengths and weaknesses of the company, but they are somewhat limited. To be more meaningful for strategic management purposes, other bases of comparison are needed. For example, suppose your company's sales increased by 4.5 percent from the previous year. Is this a strength, a weakness, or neither? While it appears to be a strength, without additional information, it is difficult if not impossible to answer the question.

Two bases of comparison will help to overcome this problem. First, you could perform a **trend analysis,** which calculates the rate of change over time. For example, suppose your firm averaged 10 percent sales growth per year over the past 5 years. Last year's rate of 4.5 percent is unimpressive in this light.

Another useful basis of comparison is to **benchmark** or compare the firm to *industry norms* and/or *key competitors.* In this example, industry norms would indicate the average rate of growth of companies in the industry. In some cases, norms for the industry are either not available or not relevant because the firm is diversified and competes in several industries. A direct comparison to a small number of close competitors is appropriate under these circumstances.

Table 4-1 Common assessment tools for Stage 1

NAME OF TOOL	DEFINITION/DESCRIPTION
Analysis of revenues	Growth rates of sales for the firm Sources of revenues (geographic markets, divisions, product lines)
Analysis of earnings	Growth rate of profits (could include gross, operating, net profit) for the firm Sources of earnings (geographic markets, divisions, product lines)
Analysis of return on equity (using DuPont formula)	After-tax profit for each dollar of investment by stockholders
Stock price performance	Change in the value of the firm's stock
Changes in market share	Changes in the firm's share of all purchases in the market
Employee turnover reports	Ability of the firm to retain its employees
Results of employee and customer surveys or interviews	May indicate degree of satisfaction, commitment, loyalty to firm

One tool in Table 4-1 that needs further explanation is the **DuPont Return on Equity (ROE)** formula. ROE is a measure of profitability and is expressed as a percentage. The formula for calculating this ratio in three parts is:

% ROE = net profit margin × asset turnover × equity multiplier

$$\frac{\text{Net Profits}}{\text{Sales}} \times \frac{\text{Sales}}{\text{Assets}} \times \frac{\text{Assets}}{\text{Equity}}$$

Efficiency	Effectiveness	Leverage
Operating	Investing	Financing

The advantage of computing ROE in three parts is the added information it provides. It allows the analyst to decompose ROE into measures of **efficiency** (how well the firm converted sales into profits), **effectiveness** (how many sales were generated by each dollar of assets), and **leverage** (what proportion of assets were paid for by owners' equity). Each component provides an indication of the results of management decisions in one of three areas—financing, investing, and operations (FIO). The ROE formula can also be modified to fit the unique circumstances of a company. For example, a retailer may want to use sales-to-inventory or sales-to-fixed assets as their measure of effectiveness.

Financial Ratio Analysis

After assessing the performance of the company using all or some combination of the tools listed in Table 4-1, the analyst has a general understanding of the current condition of the firm. This initial survey may indicate areas where further and more detailed analyses are needed. This is where **financial ratio analysis** may become important. If concerns are raised about the financial condition of the firm, for example, financial ratio analysis can help pinpoint the source of the problem. Four major categories of ratio analysis are: (1), liquidity, (2) leverage, (3) activity, and (4) profitability. Measures of **liquidity** provide information about the ability of the firm to pay its short-term obligations. **Leverage** ratios focus on the firm's capital structure, including its level of debt. **Activity** ratios indicate how well certain assets are being managed, and **profitability** focuses on the firm's ability to turn sales into various measures of profit. Table 4-2 lists selected examples of the four types of ratios and provides a definition and formula for each.

Limitations of Ratio Analysis. While ratio analysis is an important tool for decision making, it has limitations. The appearance of completeness and precision given by financial statements and ratio analysis can be misleading. Generally accepted accounting principles permit alternative treatments of many items such as depreciation, inventory valuation, taxes, and research and development expenses. The treatment management chooses will affect the numbers reported and thus any subsequent analyses (the books can be cooked!). Keep in mind that ratio analysis is just one indication, and sometimes a misleading one, of the health of a company. It is only one part of Stage 1 of the internal audit process. A thorough assessment of the health of any firm goes beyond ratio analysis to include both financial and nonfinancial measures of condition, such as those in Table 4-1 (and in the balanced scorecard discussed in Chapter 10). In addition, it includes the analyses discussed later as part of Stages 2 and 3 of the internal audit process.

Table 4-2 Selected financial ratios

RATIO	FORMULA	WHAT IT MEASURES
Liquidity Ratios		
Current Ratio	$\dfrac{\text{Current Assets}}{\text{Current Liabilities}}$	The extent to which a firm can meet its short-term obligations
Quick Ratio	$\dfrac{\text{Current Assets Minus Inventory}}{\text{Current Liabilities}}$	The extent to which a firm can meet its short-term obligations without relying on the sale of its inventories
Leverage Ratios		
Debt-to-Equity Ratio	$\dfrac{\text{Total Debt}}{\text{Total Stockholders' Equity}}$	The percentage of total funds provided by creditors versus by owners
Times-Interest-Earned Ratio	$\dfrac{\text{Profits Before Interest and Taxes}}{\text{Total Interest Charges}}$	The extent to which earnings can decline without the firm becoming unable to meet its annual interest costs
Activity Ratios		
Inventory Turnover	$\dfrac{\text{Sales}}{\text{Inventory of Finished Goods}}$	An indication of how efficiently a firm is managing its inventories
Total Assets Turnover	$\dfrac{\text{Sales}}{\text{Total Assets}}$	Whether a firm is generating a sufficient sales volume on its asset base
Accounts Receivable Turnover	$\dfrac{\text{Annual Credit Sales}}{\text{Accounts Receivable}}$	The average length of time it takes a firm to collect credit sales (in percentage terms)
Profitability Ratios		
Gross Profit Margin	$\dfrac{\text{Sales Minus Cost of Goods Sold}}{\text{Sales}}$	The total margin available to cover operating expenses and yield a profit
Operating Profit Margin	$\dfrac{\text{Earnings Before Interest \& Taxes (EBIT)}}{\text{Sales}}$	Profitability without concern for taxes and interest
Net Profit Margin	$\dfrac{\text{Net Income}}{\text{Sales}}$	After-tax profits per dollar of sales
Return on Total Assets (ROA)	$\dfrac{\text{Net Income}}{\text{Total Assets}}$	After-tax profits per dollar of assets; this ratio is also called return on investment (ROI)
Return on Equity (ROE)	$\dfrac{\text{Net Income}}{\text{Total Stockholders' Equity}}$	After-tax profits per dollar of stockholders' investment in the firm

3M Performance: Stage 1 Assessment

If we apply a few of the tools from Table 4-1 to 3M, problems are immediately apparent. We can begin to understand the reasons why some people were dissatisfied with the performance of 3M and its CEO. Trend analyses of 3M revenues and earnings are

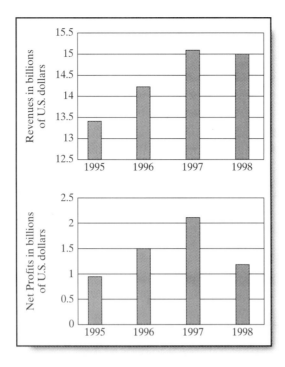

Figure 4-3
3M revenues and net profits (1995 through 1998, in billions of U.S. dollars)

Source: PriceWaterhouse Coopers, Edgar Scan, www.edgarscan.pwc-global.com, accessed June 2, 2000.

shown in Figure 4-3. From 1997 to 1998, revenue growth was flat and earnings dropped precipitously. Revenues by product segment for 1998 are shown in Table 4-3. 3M's stock price performance during the period was also discouraging—the stock lost a third of its value.

Table 4-3   Breakdown of revenue by product segment

3M PRODUCT SEGMENT	1998 REVENUES ($ IN BILLIONS)	PERCENT OF TOTAL REVENUE
Tapes	2.005	13.3
Abrasives	1.332	8.9
Automotive Products and Specialty Materials	1.687	11.2
Connecting and Insulating	1.733	11.5
Consumer and Office	2.611	17.4
Health Care	2.540	16.9
Safety and Personal Care	1.497	10.0
Other	1.616	10.8
Total	**15.021**	**100**

Source: Minnesota Mining and Manufacturing, 1998 Annual Report, www.3M.com, accessed August 4, 2000.

Table 4-4 3M's efficiency, effectiveness, and leverage

YEAR	EFFICIENCY	EFFECTIVENESS	LEVERAGE	=ROE (%)
1996	10.72	1.07	2.13	24.4
1997	14.07	1.06	2.39	35.6
1998	7.82	1.06	2.38	19.7

A further analysis of 3M revenues shows that international sales accounted for 52 percent of the total (no change from previous year). Almost half of all international sales were in Europe, 31 percent in Asia, and 20 percent in Latin America, Canada, and Africa.

These revenue figures for product segments and geographic markets could be compared to prior years (a trend analysis) to determine changes over time. We could conduct a similar analysis of operating income for 3M. These comparisons would help us to discover any potential strengths or weaknesses in our underlying business segments.

Using the three-part ROE analysis we can more precisely define some of 3M's problems.

ROE dropped below 20 percent in 1998. Looking at the measures of efficiency, effectiveness, and leverage (Table 4-4), it is clear that effectiveness and leverage were relatively stable during the 3-year period. 3M's efficiency measure, however, fell dramatically in 1998 and accounted for the significant decline in ROE. This indicates a problem with operations that needs to be carefully and thoroughly analyzed.

In addition to these financial concerns, at least some 3M employees were disgruntled, according to reports in the press: "dissatisfied researchers and scientists in divisions such as pharmaceuticals and telecommunications . . . were angered by what they saw as [the CEO's] lack of commitment to research. [The dissatisfaction] soon spread to other divisions such as industrial tape and abrasives, where compensation worries were high".[4]

Thus, a Stage 1 assessment of 3M reveals both financial and nonfinancial problems, including flat sales growth, a 44.6 percent drop in net profits, and festering employee morale issues. It is no coincidence that pressure from employees and stockholders surfaced at the same time 3M was failing to meet expectations of value creation.

STAGE 2: ANALYSIS OF VALUE CHAIN ACTIVITIES AND LINKAGES

The value chain, a concept developed by Michael Porter, is an important tool for strategic planning purposes. It identifies the activities performed internally by a firm and the relationships between those activities. Because no two firms are exactly alike (firms configure themselves differently), each firm's value chain is unique. In Stage 2 of the internal audit process a value chain analysis is performed in two parts: (1) an internal evaluation of the firm's value chain activities, costs, and profit margins, and

(2) an evaluation of the relationships between the value chains of the firm and its supply chain partners. Before we discuss this two-part analysis, let's further examine the concept of the value chain.

The Value Chain

The *value chain* is a tool to help managers visualize and analyze their organizations' value-creating activities. A general example is shown in Figure 4-4. The value chain emphasizes the fact that multiple and varied activities, performed in a coordinated and efficient manner, are necessary to create value for the firm's customers.[5] According to Porter, *competitive advantage* is a result of the value a firm is able to create for its customers that exceeds the firm's cost of creating it. Superior customer value stems from value chain activities that allow the firm to offer lower prices than competitors for equivalent benefits or provide unique or differentiated benefits that more than offset a higher price.[6] These generic strategies—low cost or differentiation (discussed in Chapter 3)—are a direct result of the activities performed by the firm in its value chain.

Primary Activities.   Value chain activities can be divided broadly into primary and support activities, as shown in Figure 4-4. The *primary activities* relate directly to the production, distribution, and sale of the product or service. Typical examples include inbound logistics, operations or manufacturing, outbound logistics, marketing, and sales. A strict time sequencing of these activities does not necessarily apply. For example, note in Figure 4-4 that marketing occurs after production. In reality, market-focused organizations base decisions about product design, production, and distribution on market information to achieve efficient and effective production of products that will satisfy customer needs.

Figure 4-4
The value chain

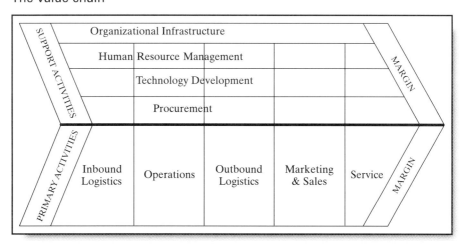

Source: Porter, M. E. *The Competitive Advantage of Nations*. New York: The Free Press, 1990, 41.

Support Activities.   *Support activities* are required to perform the primary activities. Examples of support activities include financing (raising the capital needed for operations), human resource management, technology development, and procurement of materials and supplies.

Let's consider an example of value chain activities, using the Campbell Soup Company. Campbell must procure a large number of items, including produce, ingredients and flavorings, packaging materials, labels, and other supplies and have these available at geographically dispersed production plants at specific times. If the items are received in improper quantity or in poor condition, or if they arrive late or early at the appointed destination, either unnecessary inventory will accumulate or production will be delayed. Most of the unprocessed produce used by Campbell as raw materials is produced seasonally and/or must be procured from foreign countries, complicating the process of having materials available when and where needed for production. Some of the items produced are intermediate goods, meaning that they require further processing before being packaged for distribution and sale, and some of these intermediate goods must be moved to alternative plants. Clearly, the processes of acquisition, inbound logistics, inventory control for ingredients and supplies, and production scheduling become quite complex.

Once final products have been produced, they must be moved to shipping points where orders for wholesale and retail customers are assembled. Campbell production plants produce only a portion of the total number of items in Campbell's full product line, but wholesale customers demand mixed loads of product to serve their retail customers. Thus this process includes shipping products from a variety of plants to a variety of shipping points, and assembling customized lots of goods for delivery to customers. These wholesale customers provide specific windows of time during which deliveries must be made in order to minimize their handling and inventory accumulation. Plus, wholesale customers demand orders that are correct, complete, and in proper condition so that retail customers may be served, and so on down the line to household consumers.

The emphasis on cost reduction in the channel has led to a demand that food processors, such as Campbell, play a significant role in helping to minimize food retail inventories while at the same time preserving high levels of both service and inventory availability. Ultimately, Campbell brands must be in the store and on the shelf at the precise moment the consumer wants to place the product in the shopping cart, with minimum total inventory commitment in the channel of distribution.

Cross-Functional Linkages

The Campbell example shows that value chain activities are intertwined and highly interdependent, characterized by a network of activities connected by linkages.[7] These cross-functional linkages occur when the performance of one activity affects the cost or effectiveness of the other activities.

Cross-functional linkages create trade-offs between activities, underscoring the need to focus on the efficiency and effectiveness of the whole set of activities, not just one activity, a concept long recognized in the field of logistics. For instance, higher design and materials costs may allow creation of a more reliable product that breaks down less frequently, lowering costs of after-the-sale service but also enhancing overall customer value by minimizing customer downtime. Campbell Soup has made an increased investment in aseptic packaging technology that has led to longer shelf life for prepared soups. This reduces the amount of product that deteriorates and the amount of product that "goes out of code" and is returned by the retailer, and protects inventory position at the wholesale and retail levels leading to fewer stock-outs and lost sales.

Linkages also mandate that activities be coordinated. In order to provide on-time delivery of products to customers, all aspects of the value chain must function together smoothly. A production slowdown at one plant, created by an inbound logistics or other supply problem, has a ripple effect on inventory and service levels throughout the system. Coordinated activities take trade-offs into account, improve overall quality, reduce cycle time, and create potential competitive advantage.

The value chain also recognizes the interdependence, not only of activities performed by one firm, but also of the value chains of multiple firms. An individual company's value chain for competing in a particular industry is embedded in a larger stream of activities that can be termed the value system. The *value system* includes suppliers to the firm's value chain (also known as *upstream* activities) and may also include distributors who handle the product on the way to the ultimate buyer (known as *downstream* activities). One firm's value chain often represents a supplier in another firm's value chain, who uses the products marketed by the first firm to perform value-creating activities of its own, as we have seen in the Campbell Soup example presented previously. Competitive advantage is therefore not only a function of how well a firm integrates and coordinates its own activities, but how well systems of firms integrate and coordinate activities. This philosophy is the foundation of what we now term *supply chain management.*

Internal Evaluation of the Value Chain

As stated previously, Stage 2 of the internal audit entails a two-part value chain analysis. In part one, the firm focuses internally on each discrete activity, function, or business process it performs and attempts to determine the costs of performing the activity or process versus the value it creates. The purpose of this step is for the firm to understand its *cost structure,* that is, the costs associated with each activity, and its profit engines, that is, where in the value chain profit margins are realized. A firm must especially understand its central costs, or *cost drivers,* as Porter calls them,[8] and monitor changes over time in these areas. A firm can lose its competitive advantage and ability to create value when even one key value chain activity is not functioning properly.

A case in point is Hershey Foods Company. For more than 1 year the company battled problems with on-time delivery of customer orders. The delays were due to a new $112 million automated distribution system, designed in part to avoid year 2000 computer glitches. Prior to its distribution problems, Hershey was able to ship 98 percent of its orders without a hitch. This rate dropped to about 60 percent and coincided with a 25 percent drop in the value of Hershey's stock.[9] Fortunately for chocolate lovers, the delays have been corrected and production, sales, and distribution functions are working in concert once again.

The internal value chain analysis includes not only a focus on discrete activities and processes but also on the cross-functional linkages between those activities and processes within the firm. Understanding these linkages is critical because the performance of one activity has spill-over effects for other activities, and may directly relate to the costs of later activities in the value chain. For instance, Skil Corporation, a maker of power tools, was able to cut its cost structure by streamlining the number of power drills in its product line, and redesigning the tools to reduce the number of parts in each drill and to maximize the interchangeability of parts. In this case, a change in one value chain activity (product design) directly affected the costs of later activities (manufacturing and service).

The Case of Southwest Airlines. Southwest Airlines is an example of a company that knows its cost drivers and effectively manages its value chain to create value and a competitive advantage. Table 4-5 shows that Southwest is a relatively small player in the airline industry. Its revenues are only about one-quarter of the bigger airlines. Despite its size, or perhaps in part because of it, Southwest achieves significantly higher profit margins than its competitors.

As we will see in Chapter 9, one of the most important factors accounting for the success of Southwest is their cost leadership strategy. Southwest has been able to control their cost structure by building a value chain expressly designed to eliminate what they consider to be unnecessary value chain activities and to minimize the costs associated with those activities considered essential. Their strategy is based on short haul, high frequency, point-to-point flights. To cut costs, they rely on a single type of aircraft (Boeing 737), serve no in-flight meals, use reusable plastic boarding passes, offer no baggage transfers, and turn their flights around faster than other competitors.[10] Southwest creates value by virtue of its ability to manage the cost drivers in its value chain.

Evaluation of Supply Chain Management

The second part of the value chain analysis conducted in Stage 2 is an evaluation of the relationships among firms in the supply chain. As we described above, a firm's value chain is embedded in a larger system of activities that includes the value chains of the firm's suppliers and downstream customers or partners.[11] The firm's cost competitiveness depends not only on the costs of internally performed activities (its own value chain) but also on the costs passed on to the firm by its suppliers, distributors, buyers, and other partners (the value chains of supply chain partners). These relationships are shown in Figure 4-5.

Table 4-5 A comparison of airlines

AIRLINE NAME	1999 TOTAL OPERATING REVENUES ($ IN BILLIONS)	1999 PRE-TAX PROFIT MARGIN (%)
United	18.0	10.5
American	16.3	6.5
Delta	14.7	12.4
Southwest	4.7	16.3

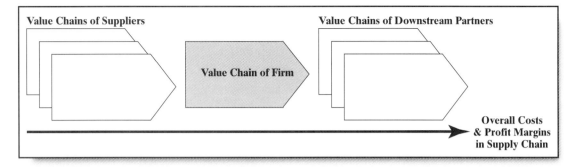

Figure 4-5
Relationships in the supply chain
Source: Reprinted with the permission of the Free Press, a Divion of Simon & Schuster, Inc.

Value creation and competitive advantage is enhanced or undermined, therefore, not only by how well a firm integrates and coordinates its own activities, but how well systems of firms integrate and coordinate activities. That is, value creation also depends on *supply chain management.* Wal-Mart is a good example of a firm that has exerted a considerable amount of control over its partners in the supply chain system to squeeze costs and sustain Wal-Mart's advantage as an everyday low-price retailer.

The outcome of Stage 2 of the internal audit process is a thorough understanding of the firm's internal cost structure and the cost structure of the entire supply chain. This information is critical for achieving the purpose of an internal audit—to determine the firm's competitively relevant strengths and weaknesses.

STAGE 3: UNDERSTANDING CORE COMPETENCIES

In Stage 1 on the internal audit process we evaluate the recent performance of the firm in both financial and nonfinancial terms to determine potential strengths and weaknesses. In Stage 2 we analyze value chain activities to determine and manage our cost structure and the cost drivers of the entire supply chain. These steps are necessary but not sufficient for a complete internal audit. In fact, if we were to stop here we may miss the real underlying strength of the firm.

To complete the audit we must understand the special skills, knowledge, and capabilities of the firm, in other words, its core competencies. A firm's core competencies cannot be understood by analyzing its financial statements and they may be missed in a value chain analysis. Core competencies are not assets on a balance sheet or activities in a value chain. Core competencies tend to reside in people and processes. In their seminal work on the topic, Hamel and Prahalad define **core competencies** as the collective learning, skills, and capabilities of the firm, especially relating to the coordination of diverse skills and the integration of multiple streams of technology.[12] Some authors distinguish between core competencies and *distinctive competencies.*[13] This distinction seems unnecessary and for our purposes the two terms are used interchangeably.* A competence must be something that the firm knows and does well relative to competitors. If it cannot be the basis of a competitive advantage in value creation, it is not considered a competence.

Consider a few examples. Toyota has a reputation for quality cars, such as the ever-popular Camry, but the Camry is an end product not a core competence. What underlies the success of the Camry, and the success of Toyota in general, is a knowledge of the complexities of the manufacturing process and an ability to produce consistently high-quality, dependable cars. This knowledge and ability reside not in some physical asset of Toyota, but in the accumulated knowledge of its people and engineering and production processes. Similarly, McDonald's invented the fast food industry. They were also the first to introduce innovations such as the drive-though window, a breakfast menu, and kids' meals. The core competence is not the kids' meal but the bundle of skills and knowledge that underlie McDonald's ability to develop successful new products and services over many years.

Companies exhibit many different types of core competencies and world class companies build and exploit several competencies. Examples include expertise in product design, an ability to identify and exploit opportunities for innovation, skills in developing and nurturing customer relationships, or the capability to provide superior after-sale service. In a particular industry different firms often build reputations for competencies in different areas. For example, in financial services, special knowledge and skill bases have been developed by different companies in investment management, foreign exchange, risk management, and consumer banking.

To be considered a core competence, a skill must pass three tests according to Hamel and Prahalad:[14]

- The first test is *customer value*. A core competence must make a significant contribution to perceived customer benefits of the end product. It is part of the reason the customer chooses the product or service. For example, Honda's competence in engines provides customers with benefits such as superior fuel economy, fast acceleration, and less noise and vibration.
- Second, to qualify as a core competence, a capacity must provide *competitor differentiation*. This means that the skills are not held equally by competitors in the industry. By extension, this also means that the core competence is not easily replicated by other firms.
- The third test is *extendibility*. This means that the competence provides potential access to a wide variety of markets. A competence may be used to leverage new opportunities in other markets. For example, Honda has used its competence in motors to enter the automobile, truck, and lawnmower markets.

The importance of core competencies for strategic management is a function of the potential competitive advantage they may provide for the firm. Core competencies are the roots of competitiveness, according to Hamel and Prahalad. Think of a

---

* The distinction made by some authors is that a core competence is something that a firm does well relative to other internal activities while a distinctive competence is something the firm does well relative to competitors. It is argued here that unless the competence is competitively relevant, it is not something on which to build strategy. A competence must have at least the potential for a competitive advantage to be considered important for strategic management purposes.

tree as an analogy for a firm. "The trunk and major limbs are core products, the smaller branches are business units; the leaves, flowers, and fruit are the end products. The root system that provides nourishment, sustenance, and stability is the core competence. You can miss the strength of the firm by looking only at its end products, in the same way you miss the strength of the tree if you look only at its leaves."[15] Thus, core competencies are important because they are key strengths that allow the firm to grow new products and expand into new markets. In turn, strategies may be used to build or acquire new core competencies.

There are two ways to think of any business according to Hamel and Prahalad—the core competence perspective and the strategic business unit (SBU) perspective. Most companies adopt the SBU perspective, though not necessarily by conscious choice. These firms build their corporate identity around market-focused entities, often called strategic business units, rather than around core competencies. Hamel and Prahalad argue that it is "entirely appropriate to have a strong end-product focus in an organization, [but] this needs to be supplemented by an equally explicit core competence focus. A company must be viewed not only as a portfolio of products or services, but a portfolio of competencies as well."[16]

Firms are vulnerable to at least three risks when they ignore core competencies and focus exclusively on end products.[17] First is the danger of underinvestment in developing core competencies. A company focused only on end products tends to focus on competing today and may fail to invest in developing new core competencies, the root system for competing in the future.

A second danger is imprisoned resources. A common problem with the SBU mentality of management is that SBU managers, accustomed to working independently of other SBUs, develop a proprietary attitude toward their resources and competencies. "The people who embody these competencies are seen as the sole property of the SBU in which they grew up. . . . SBU managers are not only unwilling to lend their competence carriers but they may actually hide talent to prevent its redeployment in the pursuit of new opportunities."[18] In contrast, the core competence perspective is built on resource sharing and cross-functional teamwork.

A third risk of ignoring core competencies is bounded innovation. SBUs tend to pursue innovation opportunities within their predefined industry domains. This scope often limits innovation to marginal product line extensions, "new and improved" products, or geographic expansions. In contrast, the core competence approach seeks unbounded innovation that allows the firm to create entirely new industries or to rewrite the rules of industry success. Firms are encouraged to find ways to redeploy existing competencies and develop new ones in order to "create products customers need but have not yet even imagined."[19] Examples include fax machines, laptop computers, and the Post-It Note. This type of innovation emerges only when managers "take off their SBU blinders" and think beyond the confines of their immediate business.

Figure 4-6 is a framework for establishing a core competence agenda. The framework distinguishes between existing and new core competencies, and between existing and new product markets. Each cell in the matrix raises questions about growth opportunities relying on core competencies. The message inherent in the framework is to find new ways to exploit current competencies and to seek new competencies for competing in the future. New competencies may be developed internally over

Figure 4-6
The core compe-
tence agenda

Source: Hamel, G., and
C. K. Prahalad.
Competing for the Future.
Boston, MA: Harvard
Business School Press,
1994, 227.

		Existing	New
Core Competence	New	What new competencies will we need to protect and extend our position in current markets?	What new competencies would we need to participate in the most promising markets of the future?
	Existing	How can we improve our current position by better leveraging our existing competencies?	What new products or services could we develop by creatively redeploying our current competencies?

Product Markets

time, acquired via an acquisition or alliance with another company, or outsourced to suppliers or other strategic partners.

In Chapter 3 we mentioned a strategic alliance between Kraft Foods and Starbucks that combines their respective competencies.[20] The partnership brings the premium coffee to supermarket shelves throughout the United States. Starbucks will combine its strength in coffee procurement and roasting with Kraft's strength in supermarket sales and distribution, relying on its army of 3,500 salespeople.

Core Competencies and 3M

3M is a world class company and as such it has several core competencies. One of its competencies is its special ability to innovate based on its history of turning apparent failures into success and its corporate culture that nurtures entrepreneurial behavior. 3M has succeeded in part because of its ability to "turn lemons into lemonade." One of the company's first true successes came from a mistake. The company was founded in 1902 when five businessmen agreed to mine a mineral deposit for abrasives.[21] The deposits turned out to be hopelessly low-grade. Instead of panicking, 3M developed a new and improved sandpaper for automobile manufacturers in Detroit. Sandpaper, in its many varieties, has turned out to be a core product for 3M.

A similar example is the story of 3M's Post-it Note.[22] Scientists at 3M were working on a new adhesive compound, which at first glance seemed to be a total failure. The adhesive failed to pass any of the conventional 3M tests for tackiness and aggressive adhesion. Instead of dismissing the new compound as a mistake, the scientists began to consider its properties and potential market uses. One of its most interesting properties was that the adhesive was strong enough to hold papers together, but weak enough to not tear paper fibers when it was removed. One day while singing in his church choir, the answer came to 3M scientist Art Fry. The new compound could be used as a bookmark for his hymnal. The advantage was that the bookmark was "permanently temporary." It would never fall out on the floor and lose its place yet it could be easily removed and reused when necessary. From this initial insight the Post-it Note was born. Over the last two decades, the Post-it product line has grown to include Post-it Flags, Post-it Memoboard, Post-it Notes and Cubes, Post-it Fax Notes, Post-it Easel Pads and Rolls, Post-it Notes in Business Card Size, Post-it Correction and Cover-up Tape, Post-it Dispensers and Organizers and more.[23]

Reflecting its emphasis on innovation, one of 3M's strategic goals is to generate 30 percent of total revenues each year from products that have been on the market for less than 4 years. This ability to innovate has differentiated 3M from its competitors and been used to launch the company into a wide variety of new markets. It is also at the root of one of the complaints against the CEO. Critics have faulted DeSimone for his hesitancy in making decisions and "his failure to fund important products for future growth."[24]

3M's ability to innovate operates on a simple principle that no market or product is too small to be ignored. Using the analogy of the tree discussed earlier, "3M has adopted a policy of allowing people to sprout tiny twigs in response to problems and ideas. Most twigs won't grow into anything. But anytime a twig showed promise, 3M would allow it to grow into a full branch—or perhaps into a full-fledged tree. This branching approach became so conscious at 3M that it sometimes explicitly depicted its product families in branching tree form"[25] (see Figure 4-7 as an example).

The ability to innovate is not 3M's only core competence. Consider the following list of 3M products and the 3M advertisement shown in Figure 4-8. Among other products, 3M produces sandpaper, Scotch Tape and Magic Tape, Post-it Notes, laser disks, audio and videotapes, and microflex circuits (see Figure 4-8). What do these seemingly diverse products have in common? The first four share an adhesive base as a key product element, and indeed 3M has a knowledge of adhesives that is perhaps unsurpassed by any company. What the entire list of products has in common though is a shared core competence of coating and bonding. 3M likes to think of itself as a company that specializes in two-dimensional (flat) products. This is because of their special knowledge and ability to attach things to flat surfaces. Many of their core products are a direct result of this core competence. While these 3M products may appear diverse and unrelated, that appearance belies a fundamental commonality—their core competence in coating and bonding.

STAGE 4: IDENTIFYING STRENGTHS AND WEAKNESSES

The final stage of the internal audit process is to take the information generated by the first three stages and identify the firm's internal strengths and weaknesses. These strengths and weaknesses are critical factors in making strategic choices. The final list of strengths and weaknesses should be manageable in size. Eight to 12 factors are typical but it is important to emphasize that there is no rigid formula to follow. The appropriate number will depend on the unique situation that is faced.

The list will include both financial and nonfinancial strengths and weaknesses from Stage 1, key success factors from the value chain analysis of Stage 2, and a set of core competencies from Stage 3. Each factor should address issues that affect the firm's ability to create value for customers, employees, and owners.

Another important characteristic of the final list of strengths and weaknesses, as we have emphasized, is that they must be competitively relevant. A weakness is

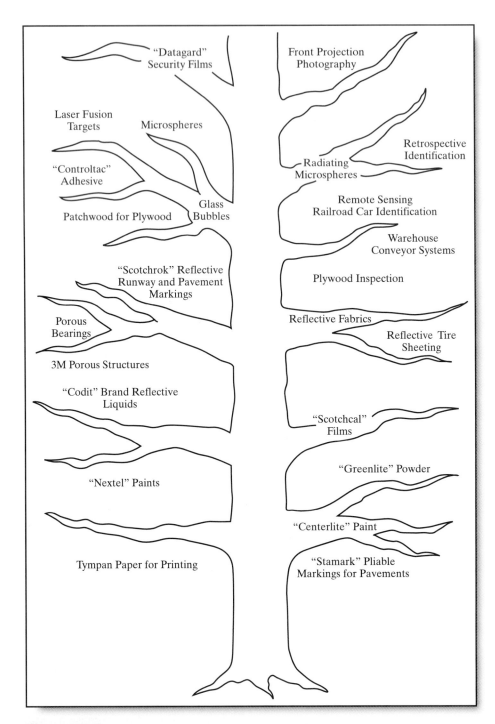

Figure 4-7
A branching tree at 3M

Source: Collins, J. C., and J. I. Porras, "Built To Last: Successful Habits of Visionary Companies," *Harper Business* (1994): 154. Reprinted with permission of Harvard Business School Press.

Figure 4-8
A 3M ad for microflex circuits

Source: Courtesy of 3M.

competitively relevant if it places the organization in a competitive disadvantage (or makes it vulnerable to a potential disadvantage) and/or undermines the organization's ability to create value for customers, employees, and owners. To determine whether a potential strength is real and competitively relevant, Jay Barney states that managers must address four important questions: (1) the question of *value,* (2) the question of *rareness,* (3), the question of *imitability,* and (4) the question of *organization.*[26]

The question of value focuses on whether the firm's "resources and capabilities add value by enabling it to exploit opportunities and/or neutralize threats. . . . 3M has used its skills and experience in substrates, coatings and adhesives, along with an organizational culture that rewards risk taking and creativity, to exploit numerous market opportunities in office products, including invisible tape and Post-it Notes."[27] A real strength offers something of worth to customers.

The question of rareness asks how many competitors already possess the resources and capabilities in question. If a particular resource or capability is widespread in the industry, it may be a minimum threshold for competing but it does not offer the potential for a competitive advantage. Similarly, the potential strength must pass the third test of competitive relevance by being difficult to imitate. A firm may develop a rare capability, but if it is easily learned and copied by competitors, it may be important in the short term but it does not offer the prospect of sustainable competitive advantage.

The final test of relevance focuses on whether the firm is organized to exploit the competitive potential of the resource or capability in question. "Numerous components of a firm's organization are relevant when answering the question of organization, including its formal reporting structure, its explicit management control systems, and its compensation policies."[28] Unless these aspects of the organization are aligned to support the potential strength, its potential cannot be realized. 3M's competence in innovation is fostered by a corporate culture that expects scientists to "bootleg" a portion of their time, or work independently on their own pet projects, and by a reward system that encourages and supports new product champions.

These four questions may be used to screen the long list of potential strengths and weaknesses generated in Stages 1 through 3, and to identify those that are important for value creation and competitive advantage. Those that pass the test of competitive relevance are used in later steps of the strategic management process.

What Happened to the CEO of 3M?

There is a happy ending to the story about 3M and its CEO. 3M bounced back from its weak performance in 1998 to record strong growth and profitability in the following years. 3M sales in 1999 grew 4.3 percent and net income was up 12.2 percent versus 1998. This was followed by another strong year in 2000, with sales and net income up 6.2 percent and 9.4 percent, respectively. Mr. DeSimone weathered the storm to keep his position as CEO. In April 2001, DeSimone left 3M just before the age of 65. He was replaced by W. James McNerney, an 18-year veteran from General Electric. It appears that the board's patience with DeSimone and its commitment to stay the course were rewarded.

CONCLUSION

Assessing the organization's internal environment for strengths and weaknesses is part of the second step in the strategic management process. This is accomplished by an internal audit based on a four-stage process. The audit requires an evaluation of the current performance of the firm, a value chain analysis, an understanding of the firm's core competencies, and a determination of which strengths and weaknesses are competitively relevant. Essentially, the audit attempts to find internal factors that either enhance or undermine the firm's ability to create value for employees, customers, and owners. Some of the critical questions to be answered in the internal audit include:

- What are the firm's financial strengths and weaknesses?
- How well does the firm manage customer relationships? What does the firm do or not do that creates or loses value for customers?
- What are the cost and profit drivers in the firm's value chain and in the supply chain?

- What are the firm's core competencies? What core competencies will be needed in the future to compete successfully?
- Are employees competent, committed to the organization's mission, and satisfied with their association with the firm?

Accomplishing the internal audit is a matter of extensive research and analysis, and includes examining financial statements, staffing and productivity standards, information resources, organization charts, customer and employee surveys, and interviewing both internal stakeholders (e.g., managers and staff) and external stakeholders (suppliers, distributors, customers).[29]

The information generated by the internal audit is combined with the opportunities and threats identified during the external audit to complete the situation analysis. The external audit is the focus of the next chapter.

KEY TERMS AND CONCEPTS

After reading this chapter you should understand each of the following terms.

- Activity ratio
- Benchmark
- Competitively relevant strengths and weaknesses
- Core competencies
- DuPont return on equity (ROE)
- Effectiveness
- Efficiency

- Financial ratio analysis
- Industry norms
- Internal audit
- Leverage
- Leverage ratio
- Liquidity ratio
- Profitability ratio
- Trend analysis

DISCUSSION QUESTIONS

1. What is the purpose of an internal audit?
2. Describe how to perform an internal audit. What are the four stages for conducting the audit?
3. Discuss the benefits and limitations of financial ratio analysis and explain the following statement: "For ratio analysis to be meaningful, there must be a basis of comparison."
4. Choose a company and identify its supply chain partners. Which company or companies in your example seem to capture the most value? How do you know?
5. Select two different companies from the same industry (e.g., Ford versus Honda, Wal-Mart versus Kmart). What core competencies do the two companies have? Does one set of competencies provide more of an advantage than the other? Explain.
6. Check the textbook's Web site to determine 3M's current financial performance. Has it changed? If so, what might account for the changes?

EXPERIENTIAL EXERCISE

Analysis of Financial Strengths and Weaknesses. Either in teams or on your own, select a company and conduct a complete analysis of the company's current financial condition. Identify financial strengths and weaknesses.

In addition to absolute indicators of the firm's financial performance, consider trend analyses, industry norms, competitive benchmarks, and the firm's mission and stated goals. For guidance on the types of indicators that may be examined, see Table 4-1 (Common Assessment Tools for Stage 1) and Table 4-2 (Selected Financial Ratios). You may also wish to consult financial reporting services (e.g., Standard and Poor's, Value Line, Bloomberg, Moody's, Compustat, Dun & Bradstreet) for data on financial operations, results, trends, and future prospects.

ENDNOTES

1. Weimer, D., "3M: The Heat Is on the Boss," *Business Week* (March 15, 1999): 82–84.
2. Peters, T. J., and R. H. Waterman, Jr. *In Search of Excellence.* New York: Harper and Row, Publishers, 1982.
3. Duncan, W. J., P. M. Ginter, and L. E. Swayne, "Competitive Advantage and Internal Organizational Assessment," *Academy of Management Executive,* August 1998, 12, 3, 6–16.
4. Weimer, D., "3M: The Heat Is on the Boss," *Business Week* (March 15, 1999): 82.
5. Porter, M. E. *The Competitive Advantage of Nations.* New York: The Free Press, 1990, 40.
6. Ibid, 41.
7. Ibid, 42.
8. Porter, M. *Competitive Advantage.* New York: The Free Press, 1985, 37–43.
9. Egan, C., "Hershey Says Its Troubles Are Over," *The Philadelphia Inquirer,* February 26, 2000, C-1.
10. Hartley, R. F. *Management Mistakes and Successes.* 5th ed. New York: John Wiley & Sons, Inc., 1997, 127–141.
11. Porter, M. *Competitive Advantage.* New York: The Free Press, 1985, 34.
12. Prahalad, C. K., and G. Hamel, "The Core Competence of the Corporation," *Harvard Business Review* (May–June 1990): 82.
13. See for example, A. A. Thompson and A. J. Strickland. *Strategic Management.* 10th ed. Boston, MA: Irwin/McGraw Hill, 1998, 108.
14. Hamel, G., and C. K. Prahalad. *Competing for the Future.* Boston, MA: Harvard Business School Press, 1994, 204–206.
15. Hamel, G., and C. K. Prahalad. *Competing for the Future.* Boston, MA: Harvard Business School Press, 1994, 82.
16. Hamel, G., and C. K. Prahalad. *Competing for the Future.* Boston, MA: Harvard Business School Press, 1994, 221.
17. Ibid, 86–88.
18. Ibid, 87.
19. Ibid, 80.
20. "Fresh growth," *Progressive Grocer* (November 1998): 12.
21. Minnesota Mining and Manufacturing Co. (3M), "3M History: A Quick Glance," www.3m.com/profile/looking/history.html, accessed August 12, 2000.
22. Minnesota Mining and Manufacturing Co. (3M), "Art Fry and the Invention of Post-it Notes," www.3m.com/about3m/pioneers/fry.jhtm, accessed November 20, 2001.
23. Minnesota Mining and Manufacturing Co. (3M), "3M History: A Quick Glance," www.3m.com/profile/looking/history.html, accessed August 12, 2000.

24. Weimer, D., "3M: The Heat Is on the Boss," *Business Week,* (March 15, 1999): 83.
25. Collins, J. C., and J. I. Porras, "Built to Last: Successful Habits of Visionary Companies," New York: Harper Collins, 1994.
26. Barney, J., "Looking Inside for Competitive Advantage," *Academy of Management Executive* 9, no. 4 (1995): 50.

27. Ibid, 50.
28. Ibid, 56.
29. Ibid, 7.

Chapter 5

The External Audit

To the Stockholders and Employees of the Wm. Wrigley Jr. Company:

In many ways, 1999 was a transitional year for us, as we came to grips with a number of changes both within and outside the Company. We also faced a wide range of market conditions that affected our business performance.

The U.S. chewing gum market had lost momentum over the past few years. Wrigley shipment trends reached a low point in mid-1999, as our second quarter U.S. volume experienced a sharp drop from the prior year, reflecting competitive activity and retail inventory consolidations. Our management and marketing teams took a fresh look at the situation and revised our business plans for the second half of 1999. With some new trade initiatives, additional advertising investments, and a recharged sales team, we were able to inject new vitality into our U.S. business. . . .

Wm. Wrigley Jr. Company

Founded in 1886, Wm. Wrigley Jr. Company is the world's largest manufacturer and seller of chewing gums. Wrigley has 14 factories around the world and sales in over 140 countries exceed $2 billion. Principal brands are Wrigley's Spearmint, Doublemint, Juicy Fruit, Big Red, Freedent, Hubba Bubba, Orbit, Airwaves, Ice White, Eclipse, Bubble Tape, and Extra. Wrigley commands a 50 percent share of the U.S. gum market and almost 60 percent of Wrigley's sales are from outside the United States. To learn more about Wrigley visit www.wrigley.com.

Turning to our overseas business, we weathered some economic upheavals in Russia without slowing down our plant construction in St. Petersburg or reducing the size of our hard-working local team. . . . While Russia remains unsettled because its economy and government are still in transition, we continue to be positive about the long-term market prospects.

Our business in the Philippines, also complicated by difficult economic conditions, improved during the second half of 1999, though it was below 1998 levels for the full year. At our new and expanded factory, located in Antipolo City, our Philippine associates continue to gear up production capacity to serve recovering export markets across Southeast Asia.[1]

It may seem amazing that Wrigley has survived and grown while producing a simple leisure product, gum. However, we can tell from his comments above that William Wrigley Jr., the firm's 36-year-old president and chief executive officer, recognizes the importance of aligning Wrigley's strategies with the external environment. This is part of the reason why Wrigley has continued to create value for customers, employees, and owners for over a century.

Two key external trends threatened the Wrigley Company. The first trend was the loss of momentum in the United States gum market, reflected by a 3-year decline in traditional gum sales and a corresponding increase in candy mint sales.[2] This decline was due largely to the youth market, the heaviest consumers of gum and candy in the United States, increasingly preferring non-gum products, especially mints. The second trend was the political and economic upheavals in Russia and the Philippines. These trends, along with others such as the weaknesses in foreign currencies and the activity of competitors, influenced Wrigley's decisions about new products, levels of advertising expenditures, top management team composition, international market expansion, and cost control initiatives. In turn, Wrigley's actions influence competitors, customers, and suppliers. In forming its strategies for the future, the Wrigley Company must continue to be aware of this give-and-take relationship with its external environment.

In the previous chapter we discussed the internal audit, one component of a situation analysis. The purpose of this chapter is to describe the second component of a situation analysis—the external audit. The strategic management framework shown in Figure 5-1 indicates the position of the external audit in the strategic management process and identifies questions addressed in this chapter.

An **external audit,** also known as *environmental scanning,* is a systematic, ongoing process of analyzing the external environment to identify **opportunities** and **threats** facing an organization. A firm uses its strengths and avoids or overcomes its weaknesses by formulating strategies that take advantage of opportunities and/or mitigate threats. It is a basic premise of strategic management that organizations shape or fit their strategies in the context of their external environment.[3] For example, the Wrigley Company could neither stabilize the Russian economic and political climate, nor improve the difficult economic conditions in the Philippines, but when these

Figure 5-1
The strategic management framework

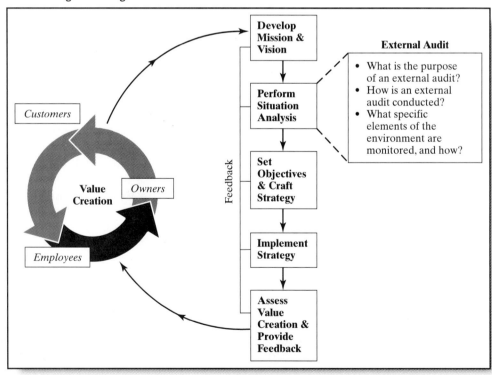

trends were identified as threats, Wrigley revised its international market growth strategy to counter their negative effects.

Research has found that when firms achieve an environment-strategy fit, financial performance levels are consistently better.[4] Thus, the external audit coupled with the internal audit informs decisions about mission, vision, objectives, strategy, and implementation. In the next section we explore why an external audit is crucial to value creation.

ENVIRONMENT-ORGANIZATION RELATIONSHIP

Organizations are *open systems,* meaning that they interact with and respond to their external environments, taking in inputs (human, informational, physical, and financial resources) and producing outputs (goods and services). Resources that are indispensable to a firm's current and future operations come from the external environment. Additionally, the environmental context is a source of change and uncertainty, impacting organizational decisions. In the open systems perspective, organizations are not just passive entities that react to the environment; they also try to shape and influence the environment through their strategies.[5]

The external audit becomes important in understanding how to secure resources, in reducing uncertainty, avoiding surprises, and in creating the future. There is ample evidence that inattention to external forces can be risky, if not fatal to an organization. Barnes and Noble did not take advantage of the emerging Internet technology to sell books online until after Amazon.com did so. Amazon.com identified the Internet as an opportunity and reinvented the retail book industry. Ultimately, Barnes and Noble had to respond to the threat posed by Amazon.com by developing a fully operational online bookstore to complement its physical stores.

Goals of an External Audit

Because organizations are open systems, it is not difficult to see that an external audit is critical to a firm's future, limiting as well as creating strategic options. The goals of an external audit are to: (1) identify and analyze important current issues and trends; (2) articulate or forecast likely emerging issues and trends; (3) foster strategic thinking and action throughout the organization; and ultimately to (4) identify opportunities and threats for planning purposes.

Through the external audit process, current data and information is gathered, aggregated, and classified. Ways to evaluate issues as opportunities or threats must also be set up. In addition to the identification of current issues, the external audit process attempts to detect signals that may identify emerging issues. Strategic managers must go beyond the known and speculate on the future nature of the external environment. This process often stimulates creative thinking concerning the organization's present and future products and services. When all levels throughout the organization are cognizant of the relationship of the organization to its environment, a higher level of responsiveness and proactiveness is likely. Strategic thinking fosters adaptability and openness to change.[6]

Challenges of an External Audit

There are several important challenges of the external audit process. First, environmental change is accelerating and the significance of changes may be difficult to determine. Second, an external audit is time consuming. Third, an external audit cannot foretell the future. Fourth, pertinent or timely information may be difficult or impossible to obtain. Fifth, managers' strongly held beliefs inhibit detection and rational interpretation of issues and organizational limitations.

The external environment is a source of uncertainty, so even the most comprehensive and well-organized external audit process will not detect all of the changes in the external environment. Perhaps the most limiting factor though is the preconceived beliefs of management. Often, what managers already believe about the external environment inhibits their ability to perceive or accept signals for change. There is often a need to unlearn or forget the past.[7] For example, decision makers at IBM in the 1960s did not see personal computers as a threat to their successful mainframe computer business. Bill Gates, CEO of Microsoft, thought the World Wide Web was a passing phenomenon that few would use. A rigorous external audit process that questions current worldviews is essential to creating a vision of the future. Despite the challenges of doing an external audit, this process is critical to the value creation cycle.

Before we look at the steps for conducting the external audit, it is important to define the factors that make up the external environment. What specific external elements do we examine in an external audit?

THE SEGMENTS OF THE EXTERNAL ENVIRONMENT

There are two main segments of the external environment: the **macro environment** (also known as the *general environment*) and the **task environment** (also known as the *industry environment*). The macro environment includes four clusters of general forces outside the control of the organization: economic, demographic/sociocultural, political/legal, and technological. The task environment includes those groups of variables that directly affect and are affected by an organization's operations, such as competitors, suppliers, customers, substitute products, new entrants, and other stakeholders (e.g., communities, creditors, labor unions, special interest groups, and trade/professional associations).

Figure 5-2 graphically depicts the external environment and its relationship to the organization. What we can't depict in a diagram, but which is critical to understand, is that this is a dynamic, interactive landscape. Trends in the external environment have significant and unequal effects on firms in different industries and in different locations. After we look at each of the external environment segments in detail, we'll discuss a process for dealing with this dynamic environment.

Defining the Macro Environment

The macro environment includes four variables and forces that are largely uncontrollable by the organization but may directly impact it. These forces are assessed as having either a positive impact (opportunity) or negative impact (threat) on the

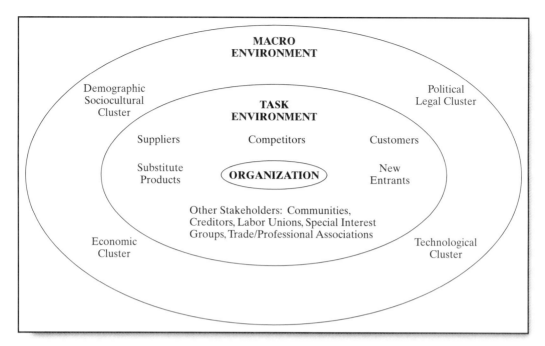

Figure 5-2
The external landscape

potential attractiveness of strategic decisions, on organizational operations, and on organizational performance. Let's look at each of the four forces in detail.

Economic Forces. **Economic forces** consist of a set of variables that measure the levels and patterns of economic activity in areas such as industrial output, consumption, income and savings, investment, and productivity.[8] For example, Gross Domestic Product (GDP) is a measure of all production located in a specific country and is calculated by adding up the contributions to final output of every firm in the economy. Often GDP is reported as percentage increases from year to year, as well as on a per capita basis (derived by dividing the total value of GDP by the population). GDP is often used to indicate the size of national markets, while per capita GDP is a measure of living standards. Another important economic variable is *purchasing power*, measured as disposable income per capita. Disposable income is the amount of current personal income minus personal income taxes that households have to spend or to save divided by a nation's population. Table 5-1 identifies economic variables that are often assessed for evidence of opportunities or threats.

Some industries are particularly vulnerable to interest rate fluctuations. The interest rate is the price paid to borrow capital, and there are many different kinds of interest rates, such as long-term Treasury bill rates, and corporate bonds. Although it may be difficult to predict the direction of future interest rates, we know some of the relationships of interest rates with other factors. For instance, interest rate fluctuations affect strategic decisions about expansion because as long-term interest rates rise, funds for capital expansion become more costly and may result in projects

Table 5-1 Key economic variables

Availability of credit	Disposable personal income
Consumer debt levels	Money market rates
Consumer Price Index	Monetary policies
Currency values/exchange rates	Per capita income
Government budget deficit	Price fluctuations
Gross Domestic Product (GDP)	Savings rates
Gross National Product (GNP)	Stock market trends
Housing starts	Trade balances
Industrial investments	Tax rates
Inflation rates	Unemployment rates
Interest rates	Workforce productivity

rejected or put on hold. Interest rates also affect sales. Rising mortgage rates decrease sales of new homes (a threat to a real estate company), but increase sales in the home repair market (an opportunity for Home Depot) because people fix up or expand their current homes rather than move to new ones.

Demographic/Sociocultural Forces. **Demographic forces** pertain to the study of the characteristics of the human population, including size, growth, racial and ethnic composition, and education levels. Examples of important demographic variables are shown in Table 5-2.

Table 5-2 Key demographic variables

VARIABLE	TYPICAL CATEGORIES
Age distributions	Under 6, 6–11, 12–19, 20–34, 35–49, 50–64, 65–75, 76+
Gender	Female, Male
Family size	1–2, 3–4, 5+
Family life cycle	Young, single; young, married, no children; young married, youngest child under 6; young, married, youngest child over 6; older, married, with children; older, married, with no children under 18; older, single; other
Income ($)	Under 10,000; 10,001–15,000; 15,001–20,000; 20,001–30,000; 30,001–50,000; 50,001–70,000; 70,001–100,000; over 100,000
Occupation	Professional and technical; managers, officials, proprietors; clerical, sales; craftsmen, foremen; operatives; farmers; retired; students; unemployed; other
Education	Grade school or less; some high school; high school graduate; some college; college graduate; post-college education
Religion	Catholic; Protestant; Jewish; Muslim; Hindu; None; other
Race	White; Asian; Hispanic; African American; Native American; other

Sociocultural forces pertain to societal traditions, values, attitudes, beliefs, tastes and patterns of behavior in a nation or region. Examples are provided in Table 5-3. Changes in demography or social values can create either opportunities for new products/services and markets or threats to product/service offerings or to the very existence of the firm. For example, a large and growing youth market in the United States (demographic factor) should have represented an opportunity for Wrigley. Unfortunately, this generation prefers mints to gums (social factor), so instead a threat emerged. What did Wrigley do? First, they modified their market penetration strategies by crafting different advertising and promotional spending strategies. For example, Wrigley began to sponsor the extreme sports X-Games and award trips to MTV tapings from its Juicy Fruit Web site. Second, Wrigley introduced new products, mint-like gum pellets, Eclipse and Everest, packaged in Altoids-like tins.[9]

Monitoring shifts in demographic and sociocultural forces is part of the external audit process. Let's take the case of the United States. The Census Bureau estimates a dramatic shift in the racial composition of the United States, with Hispanics surpassing African Americans as the largest U.S. minority group. These projections are shown in Table 5-4.

To take advantage of this demographic trend, food companies in the United States have introduced an increasing variety of ethnic products based on the belief that demographic groups exhibit consistent buying habits (sociocultural trend). Tasty Baking Company, a snack cake company, introduced four varieties of a snack cake, Tropical Delights, targeted for the Hispanic population.[10] Restaurants have also increasingly diversified menu offerings and advertising campaigns. McDonald's has a yearlong program for Hispanic consumers, including national advertising on Spanish-language outlets, a new bilingual Internet site, several promotional events, and Hispanic celebrity endorsements.[11]

When Toshifumi Suzuki, the 67-year-old CEO of 7-Eleven Japan Co., made plans to turn 7-Eleven into an online shopping giant, he studied the buying habits of Japan's small but growing Internet population of 20 million users. He had the Web site designed for ordering online, but payments and pick-ups were to be handled at the 7-Eleven convenience store. Why? Because "polls indicate that as many as 70 percent

Table 5-3 Key sociocultural variables

Attitudes toward saving and investing	Importance of social responsibility
Attitudes toward material goods	Importance of technology
Attitudes toward business	Lifestyles
Attitudes toward women and minorities	Quality-of-life issues
Attitudes toward work and careers	Regional tastes and preferences
Attitudes toward product/service quality	Value placed on short term versus long term
Attitudes toward leisure time	Value of education
Gender roles	Value of individual freedom
Importance of environmental issues	Willingness to accept change
Importance of family and religion	

Table 5-4   Projections of racial composition in the United States (%)

GROUP	1999	2005	2015
White	71.7	68.7	64.7
Black	12.7	13.2	13.7
American Indian	0.9	0.9	0.9
Asian	3.8	4.6	5.6
Hispanic	10.9	12.6	15.1

Source: Standard & Poor's, *Standard & Poor's Industry Surveys: Food & Nonalcoholic Beverages*, vol. 167, no. 48, section 2, New York: Standard & Poor's, December 2, 1999, 8. Used with permission of Standard & Poor's.

of Japanese dislike using credit cards for online purchases." Mr. Suzuki will continue to monitor Japanese attitudes for changes.[12]

Political/Legal Forces.   **Political/legal forces** represent power relationships, national stability, constraining and protecting laws, and administrative, regulatory, and judicial institutions at the federal, state, and local levels.[13] It is important to keep track of current and potential legal, regulatory, and political changes in any country in which an organization does business or is considering doing business. In looking at the example of Wrigley in the opening case, we know that political instabilities in both Russia and the Philippines were threats to Wrigley's strategic plans. A summary of key political and legal variables that can be evaluated as opportunities or threats is shown in Table 5-5.

An important regulatory consideration for any organization is human resource (HR) legislation. Table 5-6 gives some examples of U.S. labor laws. Let's look at the most recent work of the Occupational Safety and Health Administration (OSHA)

Table 5-5   Key political/legal variables

Government regulations or deregulations	Tariff regulations
Consumer laws	Trade treaties/alliances
Local, state, and national elections	Location and severity of terrorist activities
Judicial system	Number, severity, and location of government protests
Level of defense spending	Patent and copyright laws
Level of government subsidies	Tax laws
Political systems	Environmental protection laws
Political stability	Human resources laws
Government agencies	Quality-of-life laws
Voter participation rates	Local, state, or regional laws
Attitudes toward the legal system	Antitrust legislation and merger approval process
Size of government budgets	Attitudes toward intellectual property
Government fiscal and monetary policy	

Table 5-6 Examples of significant U.S. human resource legislation

---

Occupational Safety and Health Act of 1970
Requires employers to provide a working environment free from hazards to health.

Equal Employment Opportunity Act of 1972
Forbids discrimination in all areas of employer-employee relations.

Worker Adjustment and Retraining Notification Act of 1988
Requires employers with 100 or more employees to provide 60 days' notice before a facility closing or mass layoff.

Americans with Disabilities Act of 1990
Prohibits employers from discriminating against individuals with physical or mental disabilities or the chronically ill; also requires organizations to reasonably accommodate these individuals.

Civil Rights Act of 1991
Reaffirms and tightens prohibition of discriminations; permits individuals to sue for punitive damages in cases of intentional discrimination.

Family Medical Leave Act of 1993
Grants 12 weeks of unpaid leave each year to employees for the birth or adoption of a child or the care of a spouse, child, or parent with a serious health condition; covers organizations with 50 or more employees.

---

established by the Occupational Safety and Health Act of 1970. OSHA has been developing ergonomic (science of equipment design to reduce operator fatigue and discomfort) guidelines for workplace musculoskeletal disorders (MSDs) caused by repetitive-motion activities. Business and government disagree on the extent of the problem, the correct solution, and the annual cost of compliance. After a decade-long debate, it is still not clear what is going to happen.[14] This uncertainty and the expense of compliance are considered a threat by some organizations.

Technological Forces. The concept of technology relates to the development and application of knowledge. Technology can have an enormous impact on products, such as it has in healthcare, pharmaceuticals, and consumer electronics, and in how products or services are marketed and sold, such as it has in retailing. Examples of **technological forces** are listed in Table 5-7.

A common mistake in analyzing technological forces is to focus only on end-product changes. In addition, we need to be alert to inventions, innovations, and

Table 5-7 Key technological variables

Biotechnology	Superconductivity
Consumer electronics	High-definition graphics
Robotics and artificial intelligence	Number of patents
Handling industrial/chemical waste	Lasers
Food additives	Biogenetics
Satellites and satellite imaging	Wireless technology
Total federal spending for R&D	Changes in telecommunications
Changes in information technology	

Chapter 5   The External Audit

diffusions. *Inventions* are basic research into principles and relationships in nature resulting in increased knowledge of how the world works. *Innovation* occurs when basic knowledge is transformed into trial products. *Diffusion* occurs when many people adopt the innovation. Inventions, innovations, and diffusions can radically alter the entire external environment and make a company's products and services obsolete. For example, companies, like Blockbuster, that rent videos are faced with the threat of obsolescence due to changing technology. Table 5-8 provides examples of the technology development and application process.

Let's look at an example of how an organization reacted to technological forces. Sweden Post realized early in the 1990s that the traditional world of letter and parcel delivery was being slowly replaced by fax, telephone, and e-mail (see Table 5-9). Where others sensed peril, Sweden Post saw an opportunity and began fighting back by reinventing the postal industry. Sweden Post diversified into e-commerce and created one of Europe's most popular online shopping malls, providing deliveries for purchases made online. Sweden Post is also involved in business-to-business (B2B) commerce, with online handling of all aspects of product supply, delivery, and invoicing for its business customers.

Technological changes are also radically altering the health care field. Magnetic resonance imaging (MRI), electronic patient records, DNA mapping, protein-based and biotech drugs, video camera pills for exploring the intestines, and the use of the Internet to deliver and monitor patient care are just a few examples.

Figure 5-3 shows the multiple linkages among the variables in the macro environment and reveals the interdependent nature of the clusters. The importance of the

Table 5-8 Technology development and application process

TYPE OF ADVANCEMENT	DESCRIPTION	SPECIFIC EXAMPLE
Inventions	Basic research into principles and relationships	Studying a sugar molecule in an interstellar cloud in the middle of the Milky Way galaxy to increase understanding about how life began on earth.[1]
Innovations	Transforming knowledge into a prototype from	Memory designer, Rambus, Inc. unveiled a new memory bus—the expressway leading from a computer processor to the memory chips—for speeds more than 30 times faster than today's typical PC. Likely use: video games and digital televisions.[2]
Diffusions	Putting knowledge into a form that can be adopted by others	Optical networks convert information into bits of light (photons) that are sent over fiber-optic cables made of glass. These networks are starting to take hold in local phone markets because costs are dropping and demand for capacity is rising.[3]

[1] Arnst, C. "Life is Sweet, Scientifically Speaking," *Business Week* (July 10, 2000): 101.
[2] Arnst, C. "Burning Rubber down Memory Lane," *Business Week* (July 10, 2000): 101.
[3] Rosenbush, S. "Charge of the Light Brigade," *Business Week* (January 31, 2000): 62–66.

Table 5-9 World communications market

TYPE OF COMMUNICATION	1995 VOLUME (%)	2005 VOLUME (%)
Physical mail	20	15
Fax and telephone	75	75
Electronic mail	5	10

Source: Strassel, K. A., "As Mail Volume Slips, Sweden Post Takes Lead on the Internet," *The Wall Street Journal,* June 23, 1999, A1, A15.

clusters and the nature of their effects are unique to each organization. These assessments are part of the audit process and are based on the judgments of the managers and analysts. We will more closely examine the interpretation of the macro environment after defining the task environment.

Defining the Task Environment

The task environment of a firm includes the set of forces, organizations, and stakeholders that directly interact with the firm. Common elements of the task environment are competitors, suppliers, customers, substitute products, new entrants, and other stakeholders like communities, creditors, labor unions, special interest groups, and trade or professional associations. These forces, like those in the macro environment, are assessed as either an opportunity (positive impact) or a threat (negative impact).

The organization's task environment is often related closely to its industry. An **industry** is a collection of firms offering similar products and services, thereby sharing customers. Industry size, growth rates and concentration, identification and analyses of competitors, and market share analyses are important variables in the task environment. Although the boundaries of an industry may seem intuitively apparent, defining the relevant competition is increasingly difficult and complex.[15] For example, should a definition of the soft drink industry be confined to carbonated beverages, or should it also include bottled water, ice tea, and juice, which are increasingly seen as substitutes? The answer may have important implications for a firm's strategy.

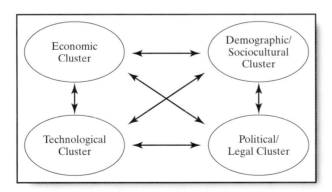

Figure 5-3
Cluster interactions in the macro environment

Source: Narayanan, V. K., and L. Fahey, "Macroenvironmental Analysis: Understanding the Environment Outside the Industry." *The Portable MBA in Strategy,* eds., L. Fahey and R. M. Randall. New York: John Wiley & Sons, Inc., 1997, 195–223. Used with permission of John Wiley & Sons, Inc.

One source of information for defining industries is the government. For example, the United States Census Bureau, through the **Standard Industrial Classification (SIC)** system, has grouped businesses by product/service type and has a large database of statistics by each level of code (e.g., volume amount of shipments, dollar amount of shipments, number of establishments, number of employees, etc.).[16] These statistics are aggregate numbers without reference to specific firms and are used to determine industry growth rates. The coding system works in such a way that the definitions progressively become narrower with each successive addition of numerical digits. Table 5-10 provides an example using Wrigley.

The SIC is gradually being replaced by the **North American Industry Classification System (NAICS).** The United States, Canada, and Mexico developed NAICS jointly to provide new comparability in statistics on business activity across all of North America. Wrigley is included in the NAICS code sequence shown in Table 5-11.

These examples suggest that we can define Wrigley's industry in many ways, from "food manufacturing," a broad definition, to "chewing gum, bubblegum," a narrow definition. We can also see that the NAICS codes provide a greater level of detail than the SIC and ultimately will also include data from Mexico and Canada. A firm's SIC code can be obtained from sources such as Dun & Bradstreet's *America's Corporate Families* or *America's Corporate Families and International Affiliates*[17] and Hoover's online.[18]

Industries are also defined in desktop reference books and increasingly in online sources. Some of these include *Value Line Investment Surveys, Standard & Poor's Industry Surveys, Research Insight (Compustat),* and *Dun & Bradstreet's D&B Industry Norms and Key Business Ratios.* Dun & Bradstreet compares the financial performance of a single company against the average financial performance of its entire industry by asset size, geography, and SIC Code. Looking at Wrigley, *Value Line Investment Surveys* includes Wrigley within the "food processing industry" with 47 other firms such as Campbell Soup, Hershey Foods, Interstate Bakeries Corporation, Nabisco Holdings, Co., Quaker Oats, Tootsie Roll Industries, and Unilever P.L.C. Composite industry statistics and forecasts are given, as well as a discussion of the important industry trends.[19] Another example is the Wall Street Research Network (www.wsrn.com),

Table 5-10 SIC code sequence for chewing gum, bubble gum manufacturers

SIC CODE	TYPE OF CODE	DESCRIPTION
	Group	Manufacturing
20	Sector	Food and kindred products
206	3 digit sub-sector	Sugar and confectionery product manufacturing
2067	4 digit sub-sector	Chewing gum, bubblegum, and chewing gum base

Source: U.S. Census Bureau, "1997 NAICS and 1987 SIC Correspondence Tables," www.census.gov/epcd/www/naicstab.htm, "1997 NAICS and 1987 SIC Correspondence Tables."

Table 5-11 NAICS code sequence for chewing gum, bubble gum manufacturers

NAICS CODE	TYPE OF CODE	DESCRIPTION	1997 VALUE OF PRODUCT SHIPMENTS ($1,000)
311	3 digit subsector	Food Manufacturing	423,262,220
3113	4 digit subsector	Sugar and confectionery Product manufacturing	24,301,957
31134	Industry code	Non-chocolate Confectionery Manufacturing	
311340	U.S. industry code	Non-chocolate Confectionery Manufacturing	5,080,263
3113404	Product class	Chewing gum, bubblegum, and chewing gum base	1,310,938

Source: U.S. Census Bureau, "3113 Confectionery Manufacturing from Purchased Chocolate," 1997, www.census.gov/epcd/naics/NDEF311.HTM#N31133, accessed August 4, 2000. U.S. Census Bureau, "1997 Economic Census: Manufacturing United States," 1997, www.census.gov/epcd/ec97/US_31.HTM#N311, accessed August 31, 2000.

which provides detailed information on companies as well as industries. Table 5-12 is a sample informational table comparing Wrigley and its competitors.

Organizations are another good source for understanding relevant competition. Wrigley, for example, states: "The Company's principal competitors in the United States are the Warner-Lambert Company and RJR Nabisco Holdings Corp."[20] Warner Lambert is not listed in any of the published sources as a competitor of Wrigley, but looking more closely, we find that Warner-Lambert manufactures and markets a broad line of chewing gums, bubble gums, breath mints, and cough/throat tablets (e.g., Chiclets, Cinn-A-Burst, Dentyne, Trident, Bubblicious, Certs, and Halls). In 1999, $2 billion of Warner Lambert's $12.9 billion in revenue was from their confectionery segment. In 2000 Warner-Lambert merged with Pfizer and confectionery revenues were about 6 percent of the $31 billion in total corporate revenues.[21]

Wrigley's other self-identified competitor, RJR Nabisco, is in the food processing industry. If we look at RJR Nabisco product lines we find gum, mints, and non-chocolate confectionery items such as Beech Nut, Carefree, Bubble Yum, Breath Savers, Now & Later, and Life Savers. Nabisco combines these product revenues with other foods and reports them by geographic areas (U.S. Foods Group or the International Foods Groups). In 2000 Nabisco also ceased independent operations when the food segment, Nabisco Holdings, was sold to Philip Morris Companies, uniting the Kraft and Nabisco families of food brands.[22]

Thus, industry definitions are inexact: part art and part science. Nevertheless, the process is important for identifying the relevant competitors. In the process of an external audit we can dispel some of the ambiguities of industry definition by using multiple definitions based on four dimensions of scope.[23]

Table 5-12 Industry comparison of Wrigley and its competitors

Company Name	Last Close Price ($)	Return On Equity (%)	Debt-to-Equity Ratio	% Change EPS Last Quarter	Earnings Growth Rate (%)	Market Value ($M)
Hershey Foods Corp	45.38	41.9	0.80	−67.5	17.4	6224
Rocky Mtn Chocolate	4.97	13.1	0.45	150.0	NA*	10
Tootsie Roll Industries	35.88	16.6	0.02	4.0	14.4	1777
Wm. Wrigley Jr. Co	79.13	27.1	0.00	8.3	8.2	7251

Source: Adapted from The Wall Street Research Network, www.wsrn.com, accessed August 31, 2000.
*NA-not available.

Four Dimensions of Industry Scope. Industries may be defined along four dimensions of scope—horizontal, vertical, geographical, and competitive. The issue of **horizontal scope** has been highlighted in the Wrigley example. When it is unclear whether a narrow horizontal definition (chewing gum) offers complete information, it may make sense to analyze the industry based on both narrow, midsize (non-chocolate confectionery), and broad (food processing) definitions. The narrow definition focuses the analysis on the current direct competitors, and the midsize and broad definitions prevent Wrigley from being blindsided by unexpected new competitors and permit the discovery of opportunities in related segments.

In regard to **vertical scope,** the key issue is how much of the total processing involved in providing a particular good/service is typically performed within a single company. Tight coupling is seen in the oil and gas industry because most firms marketing gasoline and petroleum products are vertically integrated back to oil exploration. In this case it makes sense to look at all of these activities as part of the same industry. However, the coupling between agriculture and retail grocery stores is very loose. The majority of the grocery stores are not vertically integrated back to the farm, so it makes sense to study the agriculture industry separate from the retail grocery industry.

Geographical scope pertains to whether physically separate markets should be treated as being served by the same industry or distinct industries. For example, does it make more sense to talk of the U.S. pharmaceutical industry or the global pharmaceutical industry? Interdependence across markets is higher for pharmaceutical companies than in the chewing gum industry, suggesting that the pharmaceutical industry should generally be defined at a global level. As the connectivity around the world increases through advances in telecommunications and transnational mergers (for example, Daimler/Chrysler), more and more industries are being defined globally.

Competitor scope looks at the additional complexities arising if competitors differ significantly in terms of their revenues, breadth of products or services, or some other identifiable dimension. We may want to use *strategic group maps,* which are conceptual clusters formed to facilitate understanding and analysis of the industry.

Strategic groups within an industry are sets of firms competing in similar ways for similar customers and interacting more directly within each group than with competitors drawn from other strategic groups in the industry.[24] It is possible to define strategic groups along any dimensions that seem relevant (age of capital equipment and level of diversification; price and image; price and product breadth, etc.).

Figure 5-4 illustrates a strategic group map for chain restaurants in the United States based on price and product-line breadth dimensions. We can see which competitors cluster together because they are similar in price and product-line breadth. For example, both Pizza Hut and Chi-Chi's are moderately priced with limited menus. We can also see that there are some areas, such as low price and limited menus, where there are no major chain restaurants in the United States; this might be viewed as a *strategic window* of opportunity. These simple charts convey a great deal of information, such as the selection and partial understanding of an industry's critical structural characteristics, competitive dynamics, evolution, and areas of "white space."[25]

Five Forces Model of Competition

Another tool for identifying and assessing the industry environment is Michael Porter's **Five Forces Model**.[26] The Five Forces Model expanded the definition of task environment to include not only rivalry among direct competitors, but also the power of suppliers, power of customers, threat of substitute products or services, and threat of entry of new competitors (these terms are defined later). Together these five forces determine the nature and extent of competition in an industry and shape the strategies of firms by limiting options (such as pricing) and affecting performance. The underlying premise is that the weaker the five forces, the more attractive the profit potential of the industry. Thus, when the forces are judged to be weak, there is an opportunity allowing for greater profit potential, either through lower

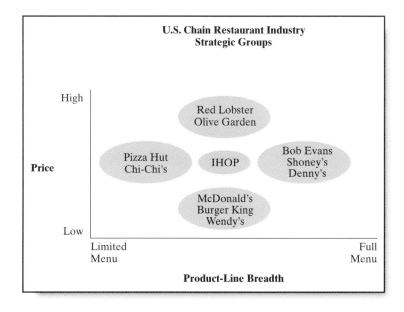

Figure 5-4
Strategic group map of U.S. chain restaurant industry

Source: Adapted from Hunger, J. D. and T. L. Wheelen. *Essentials of Strategic Management,* 2nd ed. Upper Saddle River, NJ: Prentice Hall, 2001, 44.

costs, increased prices, or a combination of both. On the other hand, when the forces are strong, it is a threat, because firms may encounter higher costs, lower prices, or both.

Stakeholder Model of Competitive Forces.   The Stakeholder Model may also be used to understand and evaluate the task environment. The Stakeholder Model complements the Five Forces Model by recognizing the impact on industries of stakeholders not specifically considered in the Five Forces Model, such communities, creditors, labor unions, special interest groups, and trade and professional associations.[27] In certain industries these stakeholders are especially important. Labor unions play a critical role in the airlines industry. Special interest groups keep a close watch on energy companies. Figure 5-5 graphically combines the Five Forces and Stakeholder models.

Strategic leaders focus on identifying the most appropriate and defensible strategic positions and selecting strategies that maintain or improve positions in each industry in which a firm competes. Different forces take on prominence in shaping competition in each industry. Analyzing these forces is also helpful when considering a diversification strategy into new industries or industry segments. Let's examine each force more closely.

Rivalry among Firms.   Head-to-head competition between direct competitors is perhaps the most obvious of the competitive forces. Examples include Coke versus Pepsi, Ford versus Toyota, and Nike versus Adidas. **Rivalry among firms** helps determine the extent to which the value created by the industry will be dissipated in the competitive effort. Price competition, product/service differentiation, product/service innovation, and/or advertising battles are the common forms of com-

Figure 5-5
Forces driving industry competitiveness

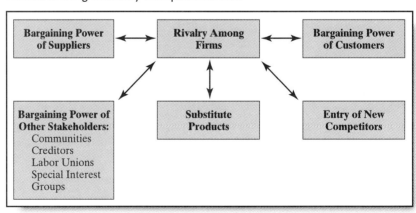

Source: Adapted from M. E. Porter. *Competitive Advantage: Creating and Sustaining Superior Performance,* New York: The Free Press, 1985, 5.

petitive moves. According to Porter, the intensity of the rivalry among the firms is related to the presence of a number of factors such as those listed in Table 5-13.

Bargaining Power of Suppliers. The **power of suppliers** can be seen when organizations supplying raw materials or services to an industry affect the profitability of the buying industry by either raising prices or reducing the quality or quantity of goods or services. Powerful suppliers are obviously a threat to the buying industry. A supplier or supplier group may gain power when:

- There are few suppliers.
- Satisfactory substitute products/services are not available.
- Industry firms are not a significant customer for the supplier group.
- Suppliers' goods are critical to the customer's marketplace success.
- The effectiveness of suppliers' products create high switching costs.
- Suppliers are a credible threat to integrate forward into the customer's industry.

The Organization of Petroleum Exporting Countries (OPEC) illustrates how a supplier can use its power to affect the profitability of numerous buying industries. When OPEC increases crude oil production, costs are lower for industries such as trucking, airline, electrical power generation, and oil refining. When OPEC decreases crude oil production, fuel costs increase. There is little that petroleum buyers can do in the short run to negotiate lower prices for oil. They are forced to pay more.

Bargaining Power of Customers. The **power of customers** influences the terms and conditions of a sale. When the balance of power favors buyers, they can capture more of the value created in an industry by bargaining for lower prices, better quality at the same prices, and/or additional services. Thus, powerful customers are a

Table 5-13 Factors involved in firm rivalry

RIVALRY FACTORS	RIVALRY INTENSIFIERS
Concentration and balance of competitors	Competitors are numerous or roughly equal in size.
Industry growth	Slow growth; market share battles.
Product or service characteristics	Product or service is very similar no matter which firm sells. Customers can switch easily.
Fixed or storage costs	High fixed costs and perishable products encourage price-cutting to either cover the fixed costs or salvage sales before spoilage.
Capacity	New plants often lead to overcapacity that leads to price-cutting.
Exit barriers	High costs to leave the industry, for example, specialized assets and management loyalty.

threat to the supplying industry. A customer or customer group may gain power when:

- A customer purchases a large proportion of the seller's product or service.
- Alternative suppliers are plentiful because the product is undifferentiated.
- Changing suppliers is not costly (i.e., low switching costs).
- A customer has the potential to integrate backward by producing the item itself.
- The customer industry has large firms.

Retail discount stores, such as Wal-Mart and Toys R Us, are able to negotiate favorable contracts with manufacturers such as Procter and Gamble and Mattel because these retail discount stores are large and account for a significant percentage of the manufacturers' sales. In this case the retailers have bargaining power over the manufacturers.

Entry of New Competitors.   **Entry of new competitors** can bring new capacity, new rivalry for market share, substantial resources, and increased diversity, thus disrupting the established patterns of competition. The threat of new entrants depends on the *entry barriers* that existing firms have erected to protect their positions in the industry and the attractiveness of the industry. The lower the barriers, the greater the threat of new entrants, assuming, of course, the industry is attractive. Starting your own house painting business is easy and, therefore, more competitive and less profitable than starting your own environmental law firm. Entry barriers for the latter are much higher than the former. Examples of entry barriers are listed and explained in Table 5-14.

Sometimes, despite high barriers to entry, new firms enter an industry with lower prices and or better ways to distribute the product. Dell and Gateway are two firms that were able to enter the PC industry despite the strength of IBM and Apple.

Substitute Products.   **Substitute products** put an upper price limit on an industry's products or services because consumers will switch to other less expensive substitute

Table 5-14   Entry barriers

BARRIERS TO ENTRY	EXPLANATION
Economies of scale	Cost advantage due to large size of production, research, marketing
Product differentiation	Customer loyalty to the brand
Capital requirements	Requirements to do business in the industry, not only for fixed facilities but also for R&D or marketing
Disadvantages other than size	Familiarity with the industry (learning and experience curve); relationships with suppliers, favorable locations
Distribution channels	Access to wholesale or retail channels
Regulation and/or licensing requirements	Special approvals needed before being permitted to compete in an industry

products/services if these satisfy the same need. For example, glass containers for beverages are much less common today than years ago, having been replaced by less expensive plastics. Similarly, steel fenders on cars have been replaced by less expensive molded plastics.

Competitive pressures arising from substitute products/services also come from technological advancements or deregulation. Examples are the online discount brokerage firms competing with financial services companies and CD-ROM versions of reference works competing with conventionally published reference works. Deregulation of the telephone industry in the United States served as an impetus for the development of substitutes to the traditional telephone, such as e-mail, cellular phones, and the Internet.

Bargaining Power of Other Stakeholders.   Other stakeholders may also impact the nature of competition in an industry by limiting strategic options or increasing compliance costs, for example. The intensity of the effects varies widely across industries. Let's take a look at some examples of the **power of stakeholders.**

The influence of local communities is differentially exerted on industries depending on the nature of the products/services. For example, in industries such as chemicals, paper and forest products, metals and mining, and utilities and power, communities may exert pressure on organizations to respect the environment and comply with federal and local environmental laws. In other industries, such as food, banking, and discount and fashion retailing, communities are less powerful forces. Even here, though, community zoning laws often restrict organizations.

The power of creditors to influence profitability in an industry is contingent upon the need for debt financing. Debt financing is most often significant in capital intensive industries, such as power generation and airlines, or if equity financing is not an option (nonprofits and privately held firms).

Labor Unions may limit management options and increase the cost structure of companies. The power of labor unions to influence the competitive environment within industries depends on the number and variety of unionized firms in an industry and the size of the unions. US Airways, for example, must negotiate with several strong unions including the Airline Pilots Association (ALPA), the Association of Machinists, and the Association of Flight Attendants (AFA).

Special Interest Groups lack the official power of government agencies and exert clout by using the media to call attention to their positions. Prominent interest groups include Mothers Against Drunk Drivers (MADD), the National Rifle Association (NRA), and the League of Women Voters. For several years, Nike, Gap, and most other leading U.S. garment manufacturers have tried to placate anti-sweatshop activists who want full disclosure of working conditions in garment and shoe factories around the world.[28]

Trade and Professional Associations are voluntary organizations. They often have power over how business is transacted in an industry by setting performance, output, and quality standards. OPEC is an example of a powerful trade association. The International Electronic and Electrical Engineers (IEEE) association has considerable power in the electrical and electronics industry.

Now that we have defined the macro and task environments, let's look at the external audit process.

During the external audit, the organization monitors or **SEES** the external environment. SEES represents the four steps of the external audit process as shown in Figure 5-6:

- Scanning to collect information about the environment
- Estimating the future direction of the external forces
- Evaluating the information to identify the opportunity or threat potential of each issue
- Sharing the information

Scanning the External Environment

Scanning is the process of continuously searching for current and emerging information and organizing that information into useable formats or categories. Imagine a radar screen or instrument panel where the external environment is constantly being monitored over time.[29] It is a dynamic, ongoing process that is ever alert and vigilant for patterns and changes in both the macro and task environments.

Increasingly, computers are used to tap into an extensive array of electronic databases. You can sign up with newsgroup services that will deliver news items to your desktop on pre-selected topics. Some organizations hire vendors, such as Dun and Bradstreet and a number of consulting firms, to scan for them. Panels of in-house experts and outside consultants may be established to receive inputs about changes in the external environment. The amount of information available may depend on

Figure 5-6
The external audit process: SEES

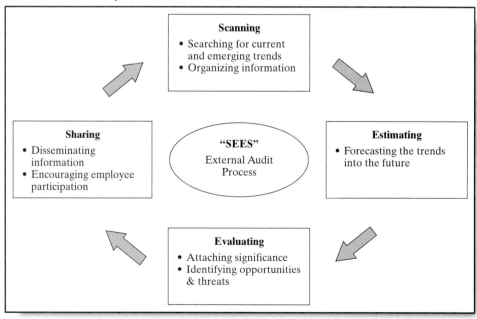

the industry. In industries dominated by large, public firms (e.g., automotive), detailed and complete industry figures abound. In smaller and less mature industries or product lines (e.g., picture framing), statistics may be very difficult to obtain.

Asking questions in critical areas can guide the scanning process. Table 5-15 offers some frequently asked questions to frame the search for current and emerging trends in the macro and task environments.

Estimating the Future Impact

Estimating is a process of forecasting the future impact of the trends, developments, dilemmas, and events that the organization is monitoring. Both quantitative and qualitative techniques are available for this task. Estimates can be generated by the organizations as well as by outside experts or from published reports. For example, *The Futurist,* a journal of the World Future Society, has been publishing forecasts, trends, and ideas about the future since 1962.

Quantitative forecasting techniques are most appropriate when historical data is available and relationships among the key variables are expected to remain stable. As the historical relationships become less stable, quantitative forecasts become less accurate. Commonly used quantitative forecasting techniques are econometric models such as regression analysis and trend extrapolation. Advancements in both hardware and software have made quantitative forecasting techniques faster, more reliable, and less expensive.

We can again look to Wrigley for an example. The total value of shipments in the United States for chewing gum was $1.10 billion in 1992 and $1.31 billion in 1997. In 5 years the total growth was about 19 percent, or approximately 3.5 percent average annual growth.[30] We can use the 3.5 percent growth rate to estimate the future industry revenue growth and calculate yearly forecasts for 3 years. If we also assume that Wrigley wants to maintain a 50 percent share of the U.S. market, we can calculate an estimate of Wrigley's future U.S. revenues as shown in Table 5-16.

Qualitative forecasting approaches may also be important. These approaches typically involve collecting and analyzing the opinions and judgments of customers, experts, or other key groups of people. Some qualitative approaches include:

- Focus groups—bringing together 10 to 15 key individuals to discuss, develop, evaluate, and reach conclusions regarding future trends or issues.
- Opinion surveys of either customers (current or potential) or experts.
- Scenario analysis—a story about the future based on a number of plausible alternative futures.[31]
- Delphi technique—anonymous collection of individual opinions on a selected topic going through several rounds until consensus is reached.[32]
- Brainstorming—group members are encouraged to present any ideas that occur to them. Ideas are recorded but not criticized.

Evaluating the Information

The third step of the external audit is evaluating, the process of making sense and attaching significance to the information gathered in the scanning and estimating processes. The critical or strategic issues are identified and the labels of opportunity

Table 5-15 Scanning process questions

Macro Environment:

1. What are the relevant segments of the macro environment?
   a. Which clusters are most important?
   b. Which variables within each cluster are most important?
   c. Which geographic areas are important?
2. What are the current and emerging trends and patterns?
   a. What are the emerging trends or patterns?
   b. What are the indicators (measures) of these trends or patterns?
3. What is the historical trend or pattern to these indicators?
4. What is the degree of change?
   a. Is the degree of change minor or major?
   b. Does the change need monitoring or require immediate action?

Task Environment

1. How is the industry defined?
   a. What is the horizontal, vertical, geographic, and/or competitive scope?
2. What is the financial performance of the industry?
   a. What is the approximate size of the market in dollars and/or volume? Growth rate?
   b. What is the average level of profitability?
   c. How much does it vary from year to year?
   d. What are the important industry-specific indicators of performance?
3. Who are our competitors? In which markets?
   a. What share of the defined market does each have? How is it changing and at what rate?
   b. Who is the market leader (largest share)?
   c. Who is the most profitable competitor?
   d. Who is the competitor most like us?
   e. Who is the fastest-growing competitor?
   f. Who do outside sources consider our competitors to be?
4. What do we analyze about our competitors?
   a. Sales
   b. Profits
   c. Objectives
   d. Strategies
   e. Competencies
5. What is the relative importance and strength of the forces of competition?
   a. Current rivalry?
   b. Entry of new competitors?
   c. Substitute products?
   d. Bargaining power of suppliers?
   e. Bargaining power of customers?
   f. Bargaining power of other stakeholders?
6. Who are our customers?
   a. How are they changing?
   b. What needs do our products/services serve?
   c. How are these needs changing?

Table 5-16 Estimate of Wrigley's future revenues

	ACTUAL 1997 (000)	ANNUAL GROWTH RATE (%)	1998 (000)	ESTIMATES 1999 (000)	2000 (000)
Overall industry revenue	$1,310,938	3.5	$1,356,821	$1,404,309	$1,453,460
U.S. Wrigley revenue (assuming 50% share)	655,469	3.5	678,410	702,155	726,730

or threat are often given to these issues. As we have stated, an opportunity is a positive trend or force that the organization can take advantage of and a threat is a negative trend or force that the organization needs to defend against.

In the evaluation process, the information is interpreted and assessed most often in a group. Information that is collected or generated is already complex and fraught with uncertainty and the group decision-making process complicates the situation. Different decision makers, even when evaluating identical issues, may assess meaning quite differently. The perceptions, values, and past experiences of decision makers influence the evaluating process.

A common form of group decision making takes place face-to-face. However, face-to-face groups often censor and pressure individual members toward conformity. The *nominal group technique* and *group decision support systems (GDSS)* are two ways to reduce many of the problems inherent in face-to-face decision making. When using the nominal group technique, participants identify and evaluate, in writing, their view of the important external trends and issues. Then all ideas are presented without discussion. There is time for questions and then the evaluations are ranked. The final evaluation is determined by the highest aggregate ranking.[33] GDSS are configurations of computer hardware and software that generate messages displayed on a central public projection screen. Ideas are presented anonymously and a skilled facilitator guides the session.[34]

Worksheets and decision matrices, such as the one shown for Wrigley in Table 5-17, may also be useful for organizing and evaluating environmental data. As illustrated in Table 5-17, the evaluation of external forces includes the identification of forces by cluster, entry of current and future trends, and the designation of the trend as an opportunity or threat. Not all forces present opportunities or threats. For example, the economic and political stability forecasted in Table 5-17 are neither an opportunity nor threat for Wrigley.

Sharing Information

The final step of the process is sharing, or disseminating the audit results throughout the company, especially to key decision makers. Sharing also involves encouraging employee involvement in scanning, estimating, and evaluating the environment.

Table 5-17 Sample macro forces—external audit worksheet for Wrigley[a]

FORCES	CURRENT (C) YEAR	FORECAST C+1	C+2	C+3	OPPORTUNITY	THREAT
Economic Force: Gross Domestic Product (% Change)	2.2%	2.3%	2.3%	2.2%		
Demographic Force: Generation Y—born between 1979 and 1994 is large	60 billion (21% of total U.S. population)	Purchasing power will grow			√	
Sociocultural Force: Generation Ys likes and dislikes are different from parents	Mints are preferred over gum	Trend expected to continue				√
Political/Legal Force: Political stability	Very stable	Will continue				
Technological Force: Internet B2B commerce	$43 billion	$1.3 trillion			√	

[a]Region or country: United States

The size of the organization influences the sharing process. In a small or medium-sized organization, employees may be in closer contact with both the external environment and senior managers, making information sharing easier to achieve. In larger organizations, the sharing process will be more complicated and may involve many people. Encouraging employees in closest contact with the environment to share information, particularly customer representatives who often have the most up-to-date information on customer needs, is an important component of this step.

CONCLUSION

Organizations need a continuous, systematic external audit process. This process includes an understanding of the macro and task environments. The macro environment includes four clusters of forces (economic, demographic/sociocultural, political/legal, and technological). The task environment encompasses industries defined along horizontal, vertical, geographical, and/or competitor scopes and in which dynamic forces of competitors, suppliers, customers, new entrants, substitute products/services, and other stakeholders interact.

The external audit process is conducted in four steps (SEES). Scanning is a process of continuously searching for current and emerging information and organizing that information into useable formats or categories. Estimating is a process of extending the trends, developments, dilemmas, and events into the future. Evaluating is a process of making sense and attaching significance to the information gathered. Sharing is a process of circulating the information and encouraging all employees to participate in the external audit process.

KEY TERMS AND CONCEPTS

After reading this chapter, you should understand each of the following key terms:

- Competitive scope
- Demographic/sociocultural forces
- Economic forces
- Entry of new competitors
- External audit
- Five Forces Model
- Geographical scope
- Horizontal scope
- Industry
- Macro environment
- North American Industry Classification System (NAICS) codes
- Open system
- Opportunity
- Political/legal forces
- Power of customers
- Power of stakeholders
- Power of suppliers
- Qualitative Forecasting
- Quantitative Forecasting
- Rivalry among firms
- SEES
- Standard Industrial Classification (SIC) codes
- Strategic groups
- Substitute products
- Task environment
- Technological forces
- Threat
- Vertical scope

DISCUSSION QUESTIONS

1. What are the two segments of the external environment and how do they relate to each other?
2. What kind of variables are included in the economic, demographic/sociocultural, political/legal, and technological clusters?
3. How has the definition of "industry" changed? How do you think the definition of industry might change in the next 5 years?
4. Choose an industry in which you would like to compete. Use the expanded Five Forces Model to explain why you find the industry attractive.
5. Discuss the following statement: Major opportunities and threats usually result from an interaction among key external trends rather than from a single external event.
6. What are the steps of the external audit process of SEES? How would you rate the importance of each component?
7. Check the textbook's Web site to determine if the external trends Wrigley identifies as opportunities and/or threats have changed. If so, what might account for the changes?

EXPERIENTIAL EXERCISE

Perform an External Audit of an International Business. Either in teams or on your own, select an organization that competes in international markets and conduct a complete analysis of its macro environment in the United States, using the format suggested in Table 5-18. Identify the most important opportunities and threats faced by the organization. Cite your sources of information.

Next, repeat the process for one of the organization's most important international markets. Compare the results of the U.S. and international audits. What are the implications for the firm's strategy?

Table 5-18 External audit of an international business

Region or Country:						
FORCES	CURRENT (C) YEAR	C+1	FORECAST C+2	C+3	OPPORTUNITY	THREAT
Economic:						
Demographic:						
Sociocultural:						
Political/Legal:						
Technological:						

ENDNOTES

1. Wm.Wrigley Jr. Company, *Annual Report,* March 2000, www.wrigley.com, accessed August 12, 2000.
2. Ginsburg, J., "Not the Flavor of the Month," *Business Week* (March 20, 2000): 128.
3. Powell, T. C., "Organizational Alignment as Competitive Advantage," *Strategic Management Journal* 13 (1992): 119–134.
4. Jan, J. J., and R. J. Litschert, "Environment-Strategy Relationship and Its Performance Implications: An Empirical Study of the Chinese Electronics Industry," *Strategic Management Journal,* 15 (1994): 1–20; Tsai, W. M., I. C. MacMillan, and M. B. Low, "Effects of Strategy and Environment on Corporate Venture Success in Industrial Markets," *Journal of Business Venturing* 6 (January 1991): 9–28; Venkatraman, N., and J. E. Prescott, "Environment-Strategy Coalignment: An Empirical Test of Its Performance Implications," *Strategic Management Journal* 11 (January 1990): 1–23.
5. Barnard, C. *The Functions of the Executive.* Cambridge, MA: Harvard University Press, 1938; Duncan, R. B., "Characteristics of Organizational Environments and Perceived Uncertainty," *Administrative Science Quarterly* 17 (1972): 313–327; Kast, F. E., and J. E. Rosenzweig, "General Systems Theory: Applications for Organizations and Management," *Academy of Management Journal* (December 1972): 447–465; Lawrence, P. R., and J. W. Lorsch. *Organization and Environment: Managing Differentiation and Integration.* Boston, MA: Division of Research, Harvard Business School, 1967; Pfeffer, J., and G. R. Salancik. *The External Control of Organizations: A Resource Dependence Perspective.* New York: Harper & Row, 1978; Varadarajan, P. R., T. Clark, and W. M. Pride, "Controlling the Uncontrollable: Managing Your Market Environment," *Sloan Management Review* (winter 1992): 39.

6. Hamel, G., and C. K. Prahalad. *Competing for the Future.* Boston, MA: Harvard Business School Press, 1994.

7. Hamel, G., and C. K. Prahalad. *Competing for the Future.* Boston, MA: Harvard Business School Press, 1994.

8. Narayanan, V. K., and L. Fahey, "Macroenvironmental Analysis: Understanding the Environment Outside the Industry." In *The Portable MBA in Strategy,* eds., L. Fahey and R. M. Randall. New York: John Wiley & Sons, Inc., 1997, 195–223.

9. Ginsburg, J. "Not the Flavor of the Month," *Business Week* (March 20, 2000): 128.

10. *Annual Report,* Tasty Baking Company, 1998, 3.

11. Kramer, L. "McD's Set to Launch Hispanic Ad Effort" *Crain's Chicago Business* 22, no. 51 (December 20, 1999): 26.

12. Kunii, I. M. "From Convenience Store to Online Behemoth?" *Business Week* (April 20, 2000): 64.

13. Narayanan, V. K., and L. Fahey, "Macroenvironmental Analysis: Understanding the Environment Outside the Industry." In *The Portable MBA in Strategy,* eds., L. Fahey and R. M. Randall. New York: John Wiley & Sons, Inc., 1997, 195–223.

14. Verespej, M. A. "Can OSHA Make Its Proposal Stick?" *Industry Week,* 249, no. 8 (April 17, 2000): 51, 3p, 1c.

15. Collis, D., and P. Ghemawat. "Industry Analysis: Understanding Industry Structure and Dynamics." In *The Portable MBA in Strategy,* eds. L. Fahey and R. M. Randall, New York: John Wiley & Sons, Inc., 1997, 171–194.

16. United States Census Bureau, 2000, www.census.gov.

17. Dun & Bradstreet, "Products and Services for All Your Business Information Needs," 2000, www.dnb.com/english/products/default.asp. Also available in most libraries.

18. Hoover's Inc., "Hoover's Online, the Business Network," 2001, www.hoovers.com.

19. *Value Line Investment Surveys,* May 12, 2000, 1461–1510.

20. Wm. Wrigley Jr., Inc. 10K Report, 1999. p. 4

21. Pfizer, Inc., "Merger News," June 19, 2000, www.pfizer.com/pfizerinc/investing/mergerclearance.html.

22. www.nabisco.com/frames.asp?pg=investorrelations/nabsale.html, accessed October 20, 2000.

23. Collis, D., and P. Ghemawat. "Industry Analysis: Understanding Industry Structure and Dynamics." In *The Portable MBA in Strategy,* eds. L. Fahey and R. M. Randall, New York: John Wiley & Sons, Inc., 1997, 175.

24. Hunt, M. S. "Competition in the Major Home Appliance Industry, 1960–1970." Ph.D. diss., Harvard University, 1972; Porter, M. *Competitive Strategy.* New York: Free Press, 1980, 129; Reger, R. K., and A. S. Huff, " Strategic Groups: A Cognitive Perspective," *Strategic Management Journal* 14 (1993): 103–123.

25. Nath, D., and T. Gruca, "Covergence Across Alternatives for Forming Strategic Groups," *Strategic Management Journal* 18 (1997): 745–760; Smith, K. G., C. M. Crimm, and S. Wally, "Strategic Groups and Rivalrous Firm Behavior: Towards a Reconciliation," *Strategic Management Journal* 18, (1997): 149–157.

26. Porter, M. *Competitive Advantage.* New York: Free Press, 1985, 5.

27. Donaldson, T., and L. E. Preston, "The Stakeholder Theory of the Corporation: Concepts, Evidence, and Implications," *Academy of Management Review* 20 (1995), 65–91; Freeman, R. E. *Strategic Management: A Stakeholder Approach.* Boston: Pitman, 1984.

28. Lee, L., and A. Bernstein, "Who Says Student Protests Don't Matter?" *Business Week* (June 12, 2000): 94–96.

29. Slywotzky, A. J. *Value Migration.* Boston: Harvard Business School Press, 1996.

30. U.S. Census Bureau, "Nonchocolate Confectionery Manufacturing, 1997," December 1999, www.census.gov/prod/ec97/97m3113f.pdf.

31. Schoemaker, P. J. H., "Multiple Scenario Development: Its Conceptual and Behavioral Foundation," *Strategic Management Journal* (March, 1993): 195; Schriefer, A., "Getting the Most Out of Scenarios: Advice from the Experts," *Planning Review* 23, no. 5 (1995): 33–35.

32. Lutz, S., "Hospitals Reassess Home-Care Ventures," *Modern Healthcare* 20, no. 37 (September 17, 1990): 22–30.

33. Robbins, S. P. *Essentials of Organizational Behavior.* 5th ed. Upper Saddle River, NJ: Prentice Hall, 1997, 105.

34. Jessup, L. M., and J. S. Valacich. *Group Support Systems.* New York: Macmillan Publishing Company, 1993.

Chapter

6

Setting Objectives and Making Strategic Choices

*D*ue to both a pending antitrust case by the U.S. Justice Department and a collapsing technology sector, the dawn of the new millennium saw Microsoft facing some significant challenges. On the legal front, Microsoft had to defend itself against a Justice Department antitrust action and a judicial order to break up the company. On the strategic front, the shakeout of many Internet-based startup companies in the wake of the NASDAQ crash of 2000 has led to a leaner technology sector with the most significant growth opportunities in areas other than desktop computing, which has been Microsoft's core business and greatest stronghold.

Industry observers generally agree that the major growth markets in computing and communications will be in wireless communications, devices, and back-end servers. Wireless communications are growing as the Internet is merging with the growth of cellular telephones. On the other hand, growth in personal computers and desktop computing has slowed. Faced with a transition from PC-based to Internet-based computing, and the move to greater dependence on handheld, portable, wireless devices, Microsoft has had to create a new technical platform for its products. Microsoft faces significant strategic choices about investing in new technologies while continuing to support and expand its Windows 2000 and other core businesses.

The third step in the strategic management framework, shown in Figure 6-1, is setting objectives and choosing a strategy. Microsoft is an example of a company that is reconsidering its objectives and strategies in light of challenges from the external environment. As a firm's internal or external situation changes, its objectives and strategies may also have to change.

In this chapter, we will discuss the key concepts of setting strategic objectives and generating, evaluating, and choosing strategies. Tools for strategic choice at both the corporate and business levels of strategy are introduced and discussed. In addition, strategic choice in a global business setting is examined. The influence of behavioral dimensions of strategic choice is also considered. After reading this chapter, you should be able to answer each of the questions posed in Figure 6-1.

Many companies operate beyond the borders of the United States for a variety of reasons. We truly live in a global world in the twenty-first century, with a global economy and a global business system. Thus, our discussion of strategic choice will cover issues and principles involved in crafting a global strategy. Finally, organizations of all types consist of people who make and implement decisions. We will discuss the behavioral dimensions of strategic choice, specifically the influence of corporate culture, the charac-

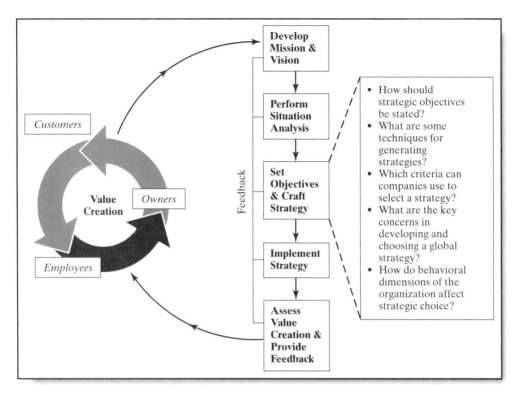

Figure 6-1
The strategic management framework

teristics of senior managers, company politics, and both ethical and social responsibility considerations on an organization's choice of strategies.

SETTING OBJECTIVES

Objectives define what the organization wants to achieve while strategies represent the pathways by which the organization will achieve the objectives. **Strategic objectives** are targets set to both motivate and direct organizational activity. They represent levels of performance we wish to achieve within a defined time frame, as well as standards of performance against which we can evaluate our progress in achieving the organizational mission and vision. Objectives reflect the priorities of the company, and if set properly, should help to create coordination of activities across functions and activity centers, thereby fostering synergies. An organization without objectives is an organization without a specific direction, one that will drift aimlessly toward an end that is uncertain.

Objectives also help stakeholders understand their role in an organization's future and provide a basis for consistent decision-making by managers whose values and backgrounds differ. In addition, objectives provide the bases for company organization and job design. Finally, objectives serve as standards by which divisions, departments, work groups, and individuals can be evaluated.

Sometimes a distinction is made between the terms "goal" and "objective." For example, some view goals as specific performance targets at intermediate levels of the firm while objectives are seen as more overriding, corporate targets.[1] We will use these terms interchangeably.

Long-Term and Short-Term Objectives

Long-term objectives broadly specify the major direction of the organization and link the mission of the organization to organizational actions. The specific numbers are derived from past performance or based on the external and internal audits. Strategies are then developed to achieve the long-term objectives. The long-term objectives also form the basis for strategy implementation, especially when used to set short-term objectives.

Long-term objectives are stated for a planning period of more than 1 year, such as 3 years or 5 years. In industries where the pace of change tends to be much faster than for the economy as a whole, such as information technology, long-term objectives must necessarily be set for a shorter time horizon, such as 3 years or less. Objectives set for periods longer than this are rendered fundamentally meaningless by the pace of change in such industries.

Sales of Microsoft's core Windows and Office product lines have slowed as worldwide demand for personal computers has dipped, and Microsoft finds it more difficult to upgrade to new versions of its products. In response, Microsoft has set long-term goals to develop new products for Internet applications such as online shopping and e-mail, as well as new Internet programs for businesses.[2]

Short-term (or annual) **objectives** establish specific performance targets for a period of 1 year or less. They may focus on the rate of sales growth, market share targets, profitability measures, or other targets. For example, an automobile company may set a specific 1-year goal in terms of the number of vehicles that it intends to sell in that year. A university identifies a specific number of incoming freshmen to be recruited for a given class. Short-term objectives must contribute specifically to the achievement of long-term objectives.

Short-term objectives can also be set for periods shorter than one year, such as a specific promotional period. A retailer with a backlog of accumulated inventory might offer an inventory reduction sale and set specific targets for the amount of merchandise, in terms of both units and dollars, that it wants to move during the sale period.

Writing Strategic Objectives

Objectives can be effective in their various roles only if stated properly. The **SMART format** is one way to state objectives in a clear, action-oriented way. Objectives must be:

- **S**pecific
- **M**easurable
- **A**ggressive
- **R**ealistic
- **T**ime-bound

The SMART format reflects the fact that objectives must be stated for specific dimensions of performance (e.g., ROI, sales, market share), in quantitative terms if possible (e.g., 10 percent, plus 15 percent, increase by 2 share points), and for a defined time period (e.g., over the next 3 years, by the end of the fiscal year). Stating objectives such as "our company will increase our share in the children's outerwear category by 3 percentage points by the end of 2003" allows a firm to determine if objectives have been achieved or not, and to use objectives as standards by which to evaluate performance. In addition, objectives should be realistic or attainable given our asset and resource base and with a reasonable level of effort, yet challenging and motivating. We can only "get to the next level" if we reach beyond what we have accomplished up to the present time.

Motorola saw its market share in the mobile phone market dwindle from 26 percent to 14 percent from 1996 to 2001 while Nokia increased its share from 20 percent to 36 percent during the same period. To counteract the decline, Motorola's CEO, Christopher Galvin, laid out a turnaround plan that included the following objectives:

1. increase gross margins from 20 percent to 27 percent by 2002;
2. reduce the number of phone types by 84 percent to 20 and the number of silicon components by 82 percent to 100 by 2003;
3. cut sales, marketing, and administrative expenses from $2.4 billion to $1.6 billion in 2000.

Motorola's objectives meet the SMART format test.[3]

Performance Areas. Managers set long-term objectives in several key performance areas, including profitability, productivity, growth, market position, shareholder wealth, technological position, employees, organizational reputation, and social responsibility. These are graphically depicted in Figure 6-2. The specific metrics within each performance area will vary depending upon the size and type of organization (profit, nonprofit, government) and its values.

Examples of common objectives include the following. Notice that many, but not all, of the objectives are evaluated based on financial metrics.

1. Growth:
   • Achieve earnings growth of 15 percent annually.
   • Double enrollments by the end of the 2003 to 2004 academic year.

2. Productivity:
   • Lower cost of goods sold from 57 percent to 52 percent by 2004.

3. Employees:
   • Increase annual employee retention rates to 80 percent within 3 years.

4. Market position:
   • Increase market share of the family-sized pie and cake category to 20 percent within 3 years.

5. Profitability:
   • Increase net profit margin from 7.5 percent in 2000 to 10 percent in 2005.
   • Increase return on stockholder's equity (ROE) from 13.8 percent in 2002 to 15.2 percent in 2004.

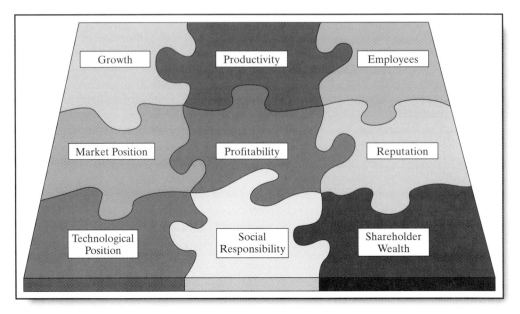

Figure 6-2
Long-term objectives—common performance areas

6. Reputation:
   - Move from number 53 to the top 25 on the *Fortune* magazine list of "Most Admired Companies."
   - Become the number one rated school in our region in the 2003 *Business Week* ranking of best regional universities.

7. Technological position:
   - Increase number of patents applied for and granted by 10 percent by 2003.
   - Increase the percentage of revenue generated by products introduced within the past 2 years to 30 percent by 2003.

8. Social responsibility
   - Donate 7.5 percent of after-tax profits to charities each year (e.g., Ben & Jerry's).[4]

9. Shareholder wealth
   - Earnings per share (net income divided by the number of outstanding shares): increase earnings per share from $1.20 to $1.30 by 2003.
   - Increase dividends by 15 percent in the next year.

STRATEGIC CHOICE

Once strategic objectives are set, the firm can begin to consider alternative strategies to achieve the objectives. *Strategic choice* involves identifying alternative courses of action designed to move the firm toward its strategic objectives, and assist in selecting the course(s) of action deemed most appropriate. These courses of action are known as *strategic alternatives.* These alternatives do not just materialize; the company's existing strategies, mission and vision, objectives, and understanding of both the internal and external environments guide the creation of strategies.

Strategic choice requires a consideration of six elements or dimensions of strategy.[5] The first four of these apply to any business while the remaining two apply to organizations with more than one business unit. In order to craft a strategy, we must make choices regarding:

1. The product market in which the business will compete, which defines not only the markets it wishes to serve but the competitors with whom it will compete.
2. The level of investment made in a business, which can vary from the significant investment required to enter or grow a market, to investment to maintain current position in a market, to investment designed to maximize short-term profit while preparing to exit the business.
3. The functional area strategies needed to compete in a market, such as product positioning, pricing, sourcing, manufacturing, distribution, and information technology.
4. The strategic assets or competencies that underlie a strategy and provide sustainable competitive advantage.

For organizations with multiple businesses, two other decision areas remain:

5. The allocation of financial and nonfinancial resources over the business units.
6. The development of *synergistic effects* across businesses, that is, the creation of value by having business units that support and complement one another.

Choosing or crafting a strategy involves generating feasible strategic alternatives, evaluating these alternatives, and selecting a strategy that will create value. While strategic choice should be based on specific criteria, it is not strictly the result of analytical thinking. Strategies are also influenced by factors such as the firm's culture, the characteristics of the strategic management team, politics in the company, ethical considerations, and social responsibility. In addition, boards of directors are exercising more control over strategic choice in today's organizations. These behavioral dimensions of strategic choice will be discussed in more depth later in this chapter.

TOOLS FOR CORPORATE LEVEL STRATEGIC CHOICE

In Chapter 1 we stated that corporate or organizational level strategy focuses on two major issues: determining the organization's business scope (i.e., the choice of business(es) in which to compete), and how organizational resources are allocated to these businesses. In virtually every organization, an underlying bias toward growth exists and drives strategic choice, at least in the long run. Most organizations, particularly those in rapidly changing markets, follow the philosophy "grow or die!" However, external conditions and internal realities sometimes create a scenario in which the firm may be more interested in attaining or maintaining stability. In other cases, conditions may become so negative that the best approach may be to consolidate or retrench. Once the orientation toward growth is established, managers select strategies consistent with that approach.

Fundamental relationships exist between business units in a diversified organization; these units rarely stand completely alone. Top management must promote cooperation among business units in order to achieve synergy and improve the overall position of the organization. Resources and costs must be shared among businesses. Some businesses are in the early stage of the life cycle and must be infused with cash while others are more mature and generate cash. Some businesses are positioned in markets with great growth potential while others have limited potential for further growth. Some businesses are in low-risk positions while other businesses reflect a great deal of risk. Portfolio theory is applicable as an analytical tool in addressing corporate level strategic decisions involving multiple, interrelated business units.

Portfolio Models

Portfolio models of strategic management rely on certain principles from the finance discipline as tools of strategic choice. For example, portfolio models treat business units as investments and, therefore, can be used to guide decisions related to allocation of investment capital and other organizational resources, and the overall achievement of a balanced portfolio.

The business literature includes several portfolio models, the two most popular of which are the **Boston Consulting Group (BCG) Matrix** and the **GE-McKinsey Business Screen.** Portfolio models use a two-dimensional grid, with dimensions representing internal and external factors, to define and position business units so that relationships between and among different units can be easily noted. These dimensions are either single criterion dimensions, as in the case of the BCG Matrix, or composite dimensions, as in the case of the GE-McKinsey model. The positioning of the organizational units in the matrices has specific strategic implications, as we will explain below.

The Boston Consulting Group (BCG) Matrix. The BCG Growth-Share Matrix uses single-criterion dimensions of market growth rate and relative market share. *Market growth rate* is defined as the growth rate of the industry (not the company). Market growth rate is a surrogate indicator of the attractiveness of an industry. Analysts use different approaches. In some versions, the midpoint of the market growth rate axis is zero; in others, market growth rates that exceed the growth rate of the economy as a whole are considered high growth. The second dimension of the matrix, *relative market share,* defined as the ratio of the firm's share of market to that of its largest competitor in the industry, is an internal variable and is a surrogate indicator of the strength of the business. If the relative market share of a business exceeds 1.0, that business is considered to be a high-growth business. The model uses relative instead of absolute share because a given share of market, say 20 percent, has much different implications for business strength if the leading competitor has a 50 percent share as opposed to a 10 percent share.

Businesses are measured on both the relative market share and market growth dimensions, and then are positioned in a two-by-two matrix as shown in Figure 6-3.[6] The model portrays each business unit or SBU as a circle, with the size of the circle

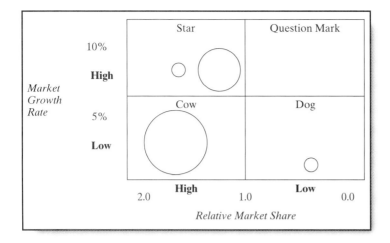

Figure 6-3
Boston consulting group matrix

Source: Adapted from Boston Consulting Group, *Perspectives on Experience,* Boston, MA: The Boston Consulting Group, 1974.

corresponding to the proportion of total revenue generated by the business unit. Some versions of the model also show the percentage of corporate profits generated by the business as a pie-shaped wedge in the circle. Based on its position on the two dimensions, a business is placed into one of four categories with the colorful labels of stars (high growth, high share), cash cows (low growth, high share), question marks (high growth, low share), and dogs (low growth, low share).

Figure 6-3 shows the outcome of a BCG analysis for a corporation with four business units. Its largest business unit is a cash cow, followed by a star. It also has two smaller units—one star and one dog. This mix of businesses represents a fairly balanced portfolio and would be considered attractive (all other things being equal).

Businesses with high relative share typically achieve high margins and high profits. Empirical data from the PIMS project (Profit Impact of Marketing Strategies, an initiative of the Marketing Science Institute in Cambridge, MA) has shown that there is a significant positive correlation between relative market share and return on investment. Conversely, businesses with low relative share tend to generate lower profits. High growth rate businesses require cash to fuel additional growth that may, in turn, lead to cost advantages relating to scale economies of manufacturing and distribution experience. Low growth rate businesses, which may be in the mature stage of the life cycle, require only maintenance levels of investment.

Implications. Businesses labeled as *stars* are in high relative share positions in high-growth markets, implying that while such businesses are profitable, they need heavy infusions of investment capital to continue strengthening their competitive position and take advantage of possible cost economies due to both scale and experience. As the industry matures, the star will move down and become a *cash cow,* provided that the business maintains its relative market share. The cash cow moniker represents a business with high relative share in a low-growth industry, leading to high profits and low demand for cash. As the term suggests, such a business generates cash that can be used to fuel businesses in high-growth arenas (i.e., stars and question marks).

Question marks are businesses that have a relatively weak position in high-growth industries, suggesting three alternative strategies. Firms can invest in these businesses to move them into more dominant, and therefore more potentially profitable, competitive positions. Alternatively, firms can redefine the market and use a niche strategy to gain a strong position in a smaller business. Finally, firms can prepare to exit the business, sometimes using a harvesting strategy to reap available profits before liquidating or selling the business. A *harvesting strategy* suggests minimal investment in a business to reap maximum short-term returns. It is important to remember that too many question marks will consume a lot of cash, so firms may wish to divest any question mark without significant long-term growth potential. *Dogs* (low-share, low-growth businesses) represent potential cash traps due to the fact that they typically absorb cash with little return. Dogs can sometimes bounce back from poor performance with a turnaround or retrenchment strategy. In addition, a business labeled as a dog may actually generate stable and respectable profit margins for a company.

Prudent judgment must be exercised when choosing a strategy for a business regardless of where it is positioned in the BCG model. Keep in mind that many business units may be in slow-growth categories, and thereby be considered either cash cows or dogs. Choosing cookie-cutter strategies based solely on the positioning of a business in the BCG Matrix is unwise and potentially lethal; it is also an abdication of corporate management's responsibility.

The GE-McKinsey Business Screen.   The GE-McKinsey model, shown in Figure 6-4,[7] is also known as the market attractiveness-business strength matrix. This model is similar to the BCG Matrix in theory but uses composite dimensions and a three-by-three matrix for a more comprehensive analysis of both internal and external factors.

The *market attractiveness* dimension of the model is a function of market size and growth, customer satisfaction levels, the quantity and nature of competition, price and margin levels, technology, regulation, and sensitivity of the category to economic trends. The second dimension of the matrix, *business strength,* evaluates the ability to compete in a market and is a function of the size and growth rate of the firm, market share by segment, customer loyalty, margins, distribution channels, technology skills, patent positions, and marketing and organizational skills. The dimensions may be modified depending on what internal and external factors are considered most relevant to the business.

The two dimensions are used to plot each business unit in the matrix. Similar to the BCG model, the size of each circle can represent the proportion of total revenues generated by the unit, while a shaded wedge of the circle represents the unit's proportion of corporate profits. The cells of the matrix can be colored-coded as in Figure 6-5 to signify go (growth strategies), caution (stability or maintenance strategies), and stop (retrenchment, turnaround or exit strategies) as a way of making the model more illustrative of appropriate strategies.

As with the BCG Matrix, each cell of the GE-McKinsey model suggests a different investment strategy for the business. Suggested strategies are shown in Figure 6-5.[8]

Summary and Evaluation.   The BCG model highlights the cash flow, investment needs, and performance of various business units. Strategists can use the model to identify how corporate resources can best be deployed to maximize future growth and profitability.[9] The approach is relatively simple to both understand and to use, which is both an advantage and a disadvantage. The notion of a balanced portfolio,

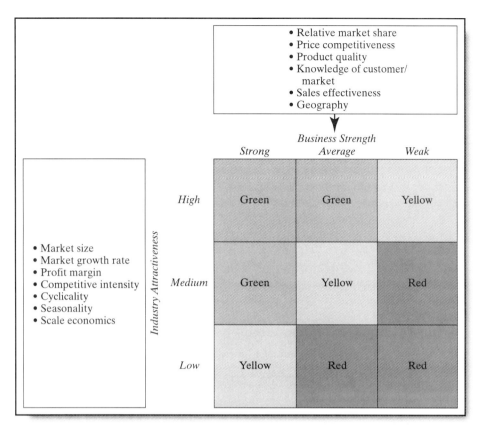

Figure 6-4
The GE-McKinsey business screen

Source: Paley, N. *The Manager's Guide to Competitive Marketing Strategies.* 2nd ed. Boca Raton, FL: CRC Press, 1999, 154.

defined in terms of the use of cash from businesses in slow-growth markets to fuel businesses in high-growth markets, is both useful and intuitively logical. However, the BCG model tends to be overly simplistic, relying on single-criterion dimensions to guide significant investment decisions. Many businesses tend to fall in the middle of the matrix and this leads to ambiguous implications for strategy. Also, if the market is defined too broadly, businesses with strengths in small segments may be misidentified as dogs.

The relationships posited by the BCG between relative share and cash generation are predicated on the assumption that firms could achieve significant cost advantages through both experience and scale effects. The experience curve posits a relationship between cumulative output and unit cost. Experience effects suggest that firms invest heavily in building market share and expanding output in order to achieve a cost advantage that will grow with accumulated experience. However, production technologies, such as the availability of computer-aided design and computer-aided production, have rendered experience effects inoperable in many situations, thereby invalidating the relationship between relative share and profitability.

	Business Strength		
	Strong	*Average*	*Weak*
High	Premium—Invest for Growth: • Provide maximum investment • Diversity worldwide • Consolidate position • Accept moderate near-term profits • Seek to dominate	Selective—Invest for Growth: • Invest heavily in selected segments • Share ceiling • Seek attractive new segments to apply strengths	Protect/Refocus—Selectively Invest for Earnings: • Defend strengths • Refocus to attractive segments • Evaluate industry revitalization • Monitor for harvest or divestment timing • Consider acquisitions
Medium	Challenge—Invest for Growth: • Build selectively on strengths • Define implications of leadership challenge • Avoid vulnerability— fill weaknesses	Prime—Selectively Invest for Earnings: • Segment market • Make contingency plans for vulnerability	Restructure—Harvest or Divest: • Provide no unessential commitment • Position for divestment or • Shift to more attractive segment
Low	Opportunistic—Selectively Invest for Earnings: • Ride market and maintain overall position • Seek niches, specialization • Seek opportunity to increase strength (for example through acquisition) • Invest at maintenance levels	Opportunistic—Preserve for Harvest: • Act to preserve or boost cash flow • Seek opportunistic sale or • Seek opportunistic rationalization to increase strengths • Prune product lines • Minimize investment	Harvest or Divest: • Exit from market or prune product line • Determine timing so as to maximize present value • Concentrate on competitor's cash generators

(Vertical axis label: Industry Attractiveness)

Figure 6-5
Strategy options using GE-McKinsey model

Source: Paley, N. *The Manager's Guide to Competitive Marketing Strategies.* 2nd ed. Boca Raton, FL: CRC Press, 1999, 155.

Finally, the model potentially leads to self-fulfilling prophecies with damaging results. For example, a BCG analysis may show declining sales in a category leading to the conclusion that a business has entered the mature stage of its life cycle and cash should be pulled back and redeployed in other businesses with higher growth rates. The model may be reacting to a false signal created by some extraneous or short-term event, but the mere fact of pulling back on the cash to support a business will lead to declining sales and profits.

The GE-McKinsey model is more comprehensive than the BCG model, but is more subjective and qualitative. Both models suffer from the same drawback in that the performance analysis is static—a view of internal and external factors at one point in time. Portfolio models treat businesses as relatively independent units. In reality, firms with multiple business units typically require some type of organized process to facilitate exchanges of technologies, skills, assets, and people across both functions and divisions.

Portfolio models first came into vogue as strategic planning tools in the 1970s, an era of much unrelated or conglomerate diversification. As a result of companies becoming increasingly diversified in unrelated businesses, it became important to manage the firm as a set of investments, similar to the way one would manage a financial portfolio. Over time, corporate strategy has evolved and the name of the game currently is for companies to focus their activities in related businesses that build upon and extend core competencies and assets. This trend has resulted in substantially less unrelated diversification. Nevertheless, portfolio models continue to be utilized to help guide strategic choice.

Overall, these models are useful as analytical tools to help guide corporate and business unit strategy. The visual representation of business units reveals some useful insight, but the weaknesses of portfolio analyses mean they should be used along with other considerations and tools, and should not be relied upon in isolation. Advantages and limitations of portfolio models are summarized in Table 6-1.

TOOLS FOR BUSINESS LEVEL STRATEGIC CHOICE

Business level strategy focuses on how to compete within an industry. The goal is to gain a competitive advantage that allows a firm to outperform its competitors and achieve above-average returns.[10] As we know from Chapter 3, achieving a **competitive advantage** depends, in part, on the firm's ability to realize a position of either cost leadership or differentiation. Failure to achieve one of these positions leaves a company stuck in the middle, with no real advantage over competitors.

Once a firm decides on its generic business strategy (i.e., cost leadership or differentiation) and once business level objectives are set, managers are faced with the

Table 6-1 Advantages and limitations of portfolio models

• *Advantages*
Encourages top management to evaluate each business individually and to set objectives and consider resources
Helps managers to recognize the inherent financial relationship between different business units
Requires the use of external data to supplement managerial judgment
Graphic representation makes interpretation and communication straightforward
• *Limitations*
The analysis is static in that it is based on a view of internal and external factors at a point in time
Market definitions can be somewhat arbitrary and therefore misleading
Understanding the success requirements for an industry is not always easy
Using standardized strategies or a cookie-cutter approach to strategic choice is overly rigid and may lead to both missed opportunities and impractical or even dangerous strategies
Portfolio analysis may give strategists an illusion of scientific rigor and objective analysis, when in fact much intuition and qualitative assessment is necessary to use portfolio models
Some of the posited relationships that drive portfolio models have questionable validity given changes in production technology

challenge of generating specific strategic alternatives to achieve those objectives. As we have emphasized, business strategies must build on internal strengths, minimize or help to overcome internal weaknesses, take advantage of opportunities presented by the environment, and avoid environmental threats. In other words, the SWOT analysis conducted during the internal and external audits will influence the strategies we consider. Let's examine two techniques for generating strategies: (1) the SWOT matrix and (2) scenario planning.

The SWOT Matrix

The **SWOT Matrix** is a simple tool that may be used to generate alternative business level strategies. Constructing the matrix is a straightforward process of listing the organization's key strengths, weaknesses, opportunities, and threats, as shown in Figure 6-6. These factors were identified during the situation analysis. Four different sets of strategic alternatives may be generated by matching strengths and weaknesses with opportunities and threats. We formulate SO strategies by considering ways in which our relative competitive strengths can be used to exploit opportunities. By contrast, ST strategies incorporate ways by which we can use our strengths to avoid threats. We generate WO strategies to take advantage of opportunities by addressing weaknesses. In an attempt to minimize our weaknesses and avoid threats, we generate WT strategies.[11]

It is important to emphasize that the purpose of the SWOT Matrix is to generate strategic alternatives, not to make strategic choices. The tool is best used to brainstorm possible strategies. The goal is to generate an extensive list of possibilities and then later to go back to screen and evaluate the ideas. Thus, not all strategies identified in the SWOT Matrix will be selected for implementation.

Aprilia SpA has grown to be Europe's second largest motorcycle manufacturer, following fellow Italian company Piaggio SpA. Aprilia was founded as a bicycle

Figure 6-6
The SWOT matrix

Source: Adapted from David, F. R. *Strategic Management Concepts,* 7th ed. Upper Saddle River, NJ: Prentice Hall, 1999, 182.

	STRENGTHS - S List strengths	**WEAKNESSES - W** List weaknesses
OPPORTUNITIES - O List opportunities	**SO STRATEGIES** Use strengths to take advantage of opportunities	**WO STRATEGIES** Overcome weaknesses by taking advantage of opportunities
THREATS - T List threats	**ST STRATEGIES** Use strengths to avoid threats	**WT STRATEGIES** Minimize weaknesses and avoid threats

company in the 1960s and expanded into motorbikes in the 1970s. After unsuccessful attempts at expanding into other product categories such as office furniture, Aprilia has regained profitability through a combination of focus on its core business—motorcycles—and growth by acquisition. Now Aprilia is faced with challenges to future growth in its core markets.[12] A situation analysis yields the information in Table 6-2.

Using the matching approach suggested by the SWOT Matrix, one clear strategic alternative (SO strategy) is to expand geographically into foreign markets, particularly those in the United States and Japan. This alternative is based on matching S2 (strong cash position) and S1 (worldwide exposure and strong brand name in racing) with O2 (expanding overseas markets). Another possible strategy (ST strategy) is to attempt to preempt Harley-Davidson's entry into Italy (T2) through the development and launch of bigger, more powerful motorcycles (S3).

Microsoft has strengths in their financial resources ($26.8 billion in cash and short-term investments as of December 31, 2000), skills in software development, brand name and distribution, plus partnerships with companies such as Intel. Weaknesses include slower-than-expected adoption of Windows 2000 and Office 2000, leading to the first profit warning in over a decade.[13]

Microsoft dominates the operating system and software markets so thoroughly that the U.S. government wants to break the company apart. The Justice Department action clearly represents a threat to the company as does a slowdown in personal computer sales and an increase in the use of the Internet for all types of computing and information tasks, leading to a slowdown in PC-based computing. On the other hand, there are significant opportunities to use the Web as a platform for software licensing and distribution, and in product categories such as video games.

Based on this SWOT assessment, one is not surprised to learn that Microsoft is on the cusp of unveiling an entirely new technology platform called .NET, which incorporates the key notion that programmers will write Internet software that runs on .NET instead of PC software that runs on Windows. Like Windows, .NET will provide the building blocks from which more software can be created, but will involve interactions between many machines connected via the Internet and providing services to each other. The idea of establishing a new Internet-based platform is to move Microsoft away from heavy reliance on the PC, and to position the company

Table 6-2 Situation analysis for Aprilia

Strengths	1. Worldwide exposure and a strong brand name in the racing community 2. Sevenfold increase in revenues since 1991, leading to strong cash position 3. Technology and know-how to produce higher-end, more powerful motorcycles
Weaknesses	1. Lack of brand awareness and market position in the United States and Asian markets
Threats	1. Slowing market growth in Europe, its major current market 2. Impending competition from Harley-Davidson, who is expanding in Italy
Opportunities	1. Manufacturing costs, including wage rates, are lower in some foreign markets 2. Expanding markets in the United States, Brazil, and Asia, and particularly Japan

to profit from the expected proliferation of non-PC devices such as smart telephones and set-top boxes. Microsoft will be able to sell subscriptions for messaging, project management, accounting, and other services, as opposed to relying strictly on sales and upgrades to maintain applications revenue.[14]

Using both its own competencies in software development as well as leveraging partnerships with Intel (for the central processor) and game developers Bungie Software and Digital Anvil, Microsoft plans to launch the Xbox video game console and Ultimate TV, to be powered by an interactive television receiver incorporating two tuners and a hard drive. Both initiatives are building blocks in Microsoft's strategy to build future home networks connecting multiple home devices and the Internet.[15]

Scenario Planning

Royal Dutch/Shell pioneered **scenario planning** before the oil crisis of the early 1970s. This technique is a tool to generate strategic alternatives based on varying assumptions about the future. One advantage of scenario planning is that it helps organizations prepare for different contingencies, including the unexpected.

Firms craft strategies that must be carried out in a world characterized by uncertainty, and therefore need some plausible notion of what shape the environment is likely to take. Scenario planning is a technique managers can use to formulate strategies and assess possible outcomes in different states of the environment. A *scenario* is a possible set of environmental circumstances, that is, what the environment may look like in the future.

A scenario is developed by positing a combination of events, conditions, and actions that together could materialize within the planning period. The analyst must identify key elements of the environment that potentially play a significant role in determining the outcomes of specific strategic alternatives, then make assumptions about the state or level of these key variables. The number of scenarios should be limited (perhaps three to five), consist of variables that have relevance to the potential outcomes of a strategy, and be specific to the company and industry. Steps for creating a scenario are presented in Table 6-3.

Table 6-3 Steps for developing a scenario

1. Identify the variables in the macro environment and in the task environment (see Chapter 5) that have the greatest potential impact on the firm's strategy.
2. Analyze the variables and develop assumptions about future trends and possible shifts in these variables.
3. Combine assumptions about individual trends or shifts into plausible and internally consistent scenarios.
4. Forecast/estimate the likelihood of each scenario.
5. Devise strategies for each scenario.
6. Monitor the environment to assess the likelihood of each scenario materializing, and have contingency plans in place in the event that the predicted scenario does not occur.

Strategic choice, using scenario planning, is based on the expected payoff under each scenario. Different decision rules may be used to make this choice. For example, we could choose the strategy with the highest expected payout (the expected value approach) or the strategy with the highest payoff in the scenario that is most likely to occur. The real value of scenario planning lies in the ability to test the robustness of a strategy given differing assumptions about the environment. In addition, scenario planning represents a form of contingency planning. As events unfold, we can gain a clearer picture of the environment and which scenario(s) are more likely to emerge. Having already asked the "what if" questions, that is, "what should be our strategic approach if we face a particular environment," we will have a strategic plan ready for each scenario that can potentially develop.

Identifying strategic uncertainties or environmental opportunities or threats can stimulate future scenarios.[16] For example, Microsoft can create alternative scenarios that posit different levels of household computer penetration, whether or not new communication technologies will significantly increase the response time associated with accessing the Internet, different levels of consumer price inflation, and different outcomes of the Justice Department's antitrust suit against the company. Different combinations of these factors, that is, different environmental scenarios, suggest different strategic choices for Microsoft, especially regarding the company's transition to Web technology.

As part of its strategy creation process, Duke Energy Corporation posited three alternative scenarios for the energy business:

1. the "Economic Treadmill," or a slowdown scenario, which projects U.S. economic growth at only 1 percent per year;
2. the "Market.com" scenario, which imagines an Internet revolution in the buying and selling of electricity and natural gas, possibly giving buyers a stronger position vis-à-vis sellers; and
3. a scenario called "Flawed Competition," which assumes continuing, uneven deregulation of the industry, price volatility, and a domestic growth rate of 3 percent or more.

Scenario one portends a problematic future for Duke Energy because the company has aggressively built up power plants, leading to too much capacity against weakening prices. Scenario two also creates great anxiety because it would render the ownership of hard assets, such as generating plants, less valuable than owning direct access to customers. Duke managers identified a number of indicators or signposts for each scenario and monitored these signposts to assess the likelihood of alternative scenarios materializing. Duke executives observed 11 of the 20 signposts of "Flawed Competition," as opposed to 3 of 23 for the "Treadmill" and 4 of 23 for "Market.com." Therefore, "Flawed Competition" is indicated as the most likely scenario and the firm has set strategy accordingly.[17]

Criteria for Strategic Choice

As we have seen, the search for strategic alternatives is guided and constrained, yielding a set of options, not all of which we either can or want to implement. Once we have generated the strategies we wish to consider, we are faced with the task of evaluating the options and selecting a strategy. To do so, we need a set of criteria to screen and test our strategic alternatives. As we have stated throughout the book, strategic choice criteria include:

- fit with company mission, vision, and objectives
- consistency with the realities of the external audit
- feasibility, given the firm's internal audit and its competencies and resources
- ability to leverage and build upon competitive advantage
- vulnerability to changes in the environment
- potential rewards (i.e., the return)
- appropriate level of risk for the company

Thus, our choice of strategy will be based, in part, on how well an alternative meets these criteria. In addition, behavioral factors will affect strategic choice, as discussed later in the chapter. Financial tools for evaluating and informing strategic choice are described in Chapter 7. These can be particularly helpful in assessing the risk and return criteria listed above.

GLOBAL DIMENSIONS OF STRATEGIC CHOICE

Firms that source, manufacture, or distribute in countries beyond their home base must employ either a global or a multinational strategy. A global strategy differs from a multinational strategy. A **multinational strategy,** also known as a *multidomestic* strategy, means that separate strategies for different countries or parts of the world are developed and implemented autonomously. A multidomestic operation involves a portfolio of independent businesses with separate investment decisions made for each country or region.[18] Historically, U.S. and European companies, faced with fragmented markets and cultures that encouraged local management of operations, have typically utilized multinational strategies.

A **global strategy,** by contrast, involves coordinated rather than independent strategies for different countries or parts of the world. This coordination can relate to the choice of target countries or regions; the degree of standardization of products, services, brands, and marketing campaigns across countries; and location of value-added activities such as research and development, production, and service, with global customers and worldwide competitors in mind. The global strategy's main focus tends to be the product or service while the primary focus of the multinational strategy is location or geography.

Verizon Communications Inc. was pursuing a global strategy when it announced creation of a worldwide network to serve large businesses, placing the company in direct competition with global long-distance companies including AT&T, British Telecommunications PLC, France Telecom SA, and WorldCom Inc. The declining consumer long-distance market has forced competitors such as AT&T and WorldCom to seek growth by providing services to business. These commercial markets are dominated by large firms requiring global services. Verizon plans to invest about $1 billion over 5 years installing its own transmission equipment and is buying capacity on undersea and underground cables so that it will be able to serve overseas business hubs directly.[19]

Why Firms Choose Global Strategies

Numerous forces exist today that make global competition a reality. Mature markets in developed nations exert pressure for companies in those countries to expand into foreign markets. The economic development of other countries may also create opportunities in these new markets. Many firms expand internationally to exploit current competitive advantages in new markets or locate activities in countries that offer lower costs (e.g., wage rates) or have favorable government policies or regulations.

A world made smaller by rapid, worldwide communication, merging of global consumer needs, emergence of global financial systems, and global technology transfer makes it both easier and more necessary for firms to compete globally. International agreements such as those brokered by the World Trade Organization (WTO) and the General Agreement on Tariffs on Trade (GATT), and regional alignments of trading partners such as the North American Free Trade Agreement (NAFTA) and the European Union (EU) have lowered trade barriers among participating nations. As a result, more and more companies seek offshore sources of supply, expand distribution into foreign countries, and have to fend off overseas as well as domestic competitors.

Firms employ global strategies for several reasons, which are summarized in Table 6-4.

Companies such as Coca Cola, Nike, and Disney create scale economies through standardization of products and marketing approaches. The global presence of Sony, Motorola, and McDonald's strengthens the brand and creates a cross-cultural understanding of what these brands represent. Global brand associations have become even more important with the growth of the Internet and consequent worldwide access to information. Of course, we must make sure that any words we use in advertising slogans translate properly. Numerous examples exist of slogans that when

Table 6-4 Reasons for choosing a global strategy

1. Scale economies, to the extent that firms can standardize product design, brands, production, distribution, and/or marketing programs across different countries or regions of the world
2. Global brand associations that communicate positive attributes such as innovativeness and product quality
3. Low-cost sourcing of raw materials and production due to lower labor rates and/or comparative advantage of the region
4. Investment and tax incentives in foreign countries
5. Cross-subsidization that allows for firms to use cash generated in one market to compete and build position in another
6. Avoidance of trade barriers by locating manufacturing or assembly plants in a host country
7. Competitors who already have or will soon globalize
8. Access to specific markets that demonstrate significant potential
9. Use of common technical platforms

translated take on unintended, unfortunate, and sometimes comical meanings. For instance, Chevrolet's "Nova," when translated into Spanish became "doesn't go," and Pepsi's slogan, "come alive," when translated into Chinese became "brings your ancestors back from the dead," creating significant challenges for truth in advertising.

The opportunity to source products from low-cost locations has been one of the prime reasons for the growth of global strategies. Major league baseballs and other sporting equipment are manufactured in countries such as Haiti and Korea where labor costs are significantly lower than in the United States. As we know from Chapter 1, ethical concerns may arise from offshore manufacturing. Nike has suffered negative publicity because of alleged problems in their contracted Asian manufacturing plants.

Countries such as Ireland have established significant economic incentives for companies to locate manufacturing, distribution, and sales operations. These incentives take the form of low-cost land acquisition, tax breaks, and even cash payments. Ireland is the number one location in Europe of pharmaceutical and health care companies, including Merck, Abbott, Pfizer, Pharmacia & Upjohn, Roche, Schering-Plough, and GlaxoSmithKline. Japanese auto companies have located production plants in the United States, staffed by Americans, not only to reduce transportation expenses but also to avoid tariffs on cars imported into the United States. Finally, companies in wireless communication have found Eastern Europe to be a particularly enticing market due to the relatively low level of penetration of wired telephones.

The growth of e-commerce has made a global marketing strategy easier for U.S. firms. Over 70 percent of the world's Web sites are in English (over 95 percent of secure Web sites are in English), and the combination of global media and the Internet are creating a global consumer culture.[20] Teenagers in France, for instance, have very similar tastes and preferences as compared to teenagers in the United States, and very different tastes and preferences to those French over the age of 50.

Standardization Versus Customization

Companies that compete globally face two types of potentially conflicting competitive pressures: pressures for cost reductions and pressures to be locally responsive.[21] Pressures for cost reductions cause companies to seek out low-cost locations for value-added activities, and to standardize products and marketing tactics across countries in order to achieve scale and experience efficiencies. Pressures for local responsiveness lead to differentiation of products and marketing tactics in order to meet individual country demand patterns as well as market and competitive conditions, distribution channels, business practices, and government policies. Differentiation involves greater duplication of activities, which in turn leads to higher costs.

As a result of the conflicting pressures toward both cost reduction and local market responsiveness, one of the key issues in global strategy is that of standardization or **globalization** versus customization or **localization.** Firms that standardize product design, production processes, brands, and marketing approaches can achieve significant cost savings. Research and development activities can be spread over a larger base of business. Standardized product design leads to efficiencies in the supply chain, manufacturing, and after-the-sale service. Use of the same brand name and advertising strategies from country to country helps create impact due in large part to the amount of international travel and global access to information.

While there has been an increasing convergence or homogenization of global tastes and preferences, customization is often mandated by significant differences in topography, climate, language, culture, customs, and regulations that exist between countries. For example, U.S. automobile companies must not only provide for increased fuel efficiency in overseas markets where gasoline prices far exceed those in the United States, but they must conform to local customs, such as driving on the left side of the road in Japan and the United Kingdom. The technology platform for VCRs and other electronics products differs between Europe and the United States. Companies that customize a brand name or marketing approach may find that the higher cost is more than offset by being perceived as a local player. Plus, products that deliver significant benefits in one country may not work at all in another country. Currently, any food manufactured from a genetically modified seed will have a very poor reception from the European Union or in Japan.

Certain guidelines exist to help managers make decisions on standardization versus customization. In general, commodity products, capital-intensive processes, and technology platforms favor some degree of standardization. At the same time, advances in the technology of design, manufacturing, distribution, and advertising have made it easier for companies to customize offerings without experiencing significant cost disadvantages.

A framework for assessing the globalization versus localization question is presented in Figure 6-7. The framework shows that some industries, such as aerospace, chemicals, and consumer electronics, are well suited for a global strategy. These industries are characterized by customers whose needs are relatively homogenous around the world. This means that products and services do not need to be customized for the local market. Other industries, such as food retailing, banking, and legal services, require products and services that are tailored to the needs of the local market, and are better suited for a multinational strategy. Some industries, such as pharmaceuticals and automobiles, require a mixed strategy to gain the efficiencies of a standardized approach and to adapt to and accommodate local market needs. For example, Lipitor, Pfizer's drug for elevated cholesterol, may be the same throughout the world, but how that drug is priced, promoted, distributed, and sold will depend on varying country regulations and market conditions.

In situations where pressures toward globalization are high and pressures toward localization are low, such as in high-technology products with high costs of

Figure 6-7
Global-local framework

Type of strategy	Global	Mixed	Multinational
Conditions and Forces Require	High standardization and low customization	Some need for both standardization and customization	Low standardization and high customization
Industry examples	Aerospace Electronics Chemicals	Pharmaceuticals Automobiles	Food retailing Banking Legal services

research and development, there is a strong argument for a global strategy. Hybrid strategies are also available. Dell uses a global strategy for sourcing and producing its computer products, but uses a localized sales and support strategy. Dell has announced creation of a wholly owned subsidiary to direct sales and support operations in India, plus a partnership with a local company, Tata Infotech, through which Dell will offer business services and operate spare parts depots in Indian cities.[22]

Where pressures toward globalization are low and pressures toward localization are high, such as in low-value consumer packaged goods that must appeal specifically to local tastes and preferences, there is a strong argument for a localized strategy. For other products, the strategic implications are not so clear. For example, McDonald's benefits by standardizing the back-of-the-house production and assembly of foods, but customizes specific items as well as the taste profile to appeal to local food preferences.

Pharmaceutical companies spend upwards of $500 million to develop a new drug and gain regulatory approval, but the cost of goods is minimal. So the key to profitability is to expand distribution globally in order to write off the investment over a larger market base. Local customs and medical practices affect the industry. For example, Japan is very concerned with safety and minimization of side effects, even to the extent that the Japanese will trade efficacy for safety, thus calling for lower dosages. Similarly, different countries with different cultures require different colors and shapes of both the pills and the packaging. Global pharmaceutical companies deliver these different products and packages, despite the inherent production and marketing inefficiencies, to both meet local needs and to help protect the brand against generics.

Competing on a global basis is complex and difficult. Differences in culture, language, business customs, economic and political systems, and regulations abound, and firms must gain insight into the far-reaching implications of these differences to understand and control the uncertainties inherent in global competition.

BEHAVIORAL ASPECTS OF STRATEGIC CHOICE

Strategic choice on any level (corporate, business, functional, global) requires the contribution and consideration of people inside the organization. As a result, human behavior has a profound influence on strategy. For example, the characteristics of the senior management team, the organization's culture, and its beliefs about ethics and social responsibility come into play in strategic choice, as they shape how individuals in the firm behave and what the firm seeks to achieve. Human behavior must also be considered when choosing strategies because, as explained in Chapter 8, people are a critical part of the implementation of any strategy.

In this section we turn to some of these key **behavioral aspects of strategic choice**—the senior management team, organizational culture, personal ethics and corporate social responsibility—and discuss how each factor relates to the strategic choice process.

Senior Management Team

The highest ranked executives of the organization, often referred to as the *senior management team,* are ultimately responsible for determining the firm's strategic direction. These individuals include the chief executive officer (CEO) and those individuals who report directly to him or her. In most cases this will include other chief officers such as the chief operating officer (COO), the chief financial officer (CFO), and the chief information officer (CIO), as well as any number of other senior executives such as senior vice presidents (Sr. VP) of the firm's various functional areas.

In a perfect world, the senior management team is omnipotent (knowledgeable about all facts related to the decisions at hand) and fully rational (able to process the information and make perfect decisions for the company) when choosing strategies. The reality is, however, that no person or team of people is perfect. It is impossible for the senior management team to possess all relevant knowledge and experience for every decision at hand, especially given that much of that information is based on expectations for the future. It is also unlikely that the senior management team, no matter how competent, will be able to process all information perfectly and make exactly the right decision for the firm. Herbert Simon, an economist and management scholar, referred to these limitations as "bounded rationality." He explained that because it is impossible for managers to be fully rational, managers are instead rational to the extent that they can be—they make decisions within the boundaries and constraints of the decision situation.[23]

Figure 6-8 depicts the various factors that influence a senior management team's decision making. These factors can be grouped into personal attributes, contextual conditions, and team dynamics. By impacting the team's strategic decision making, these factors ultimately affect organizational outcomes like the firm's strategy and performance.[24]

Personal Attributes.   Personal attributes include demographic characteristics of the senior management team members themselves. Factors such as a team member's age, education, gender, work experience, and firm tenure (duration of employment in the firm) affect how he or she gathers and processes information and ultimately makes decisions with other team members.

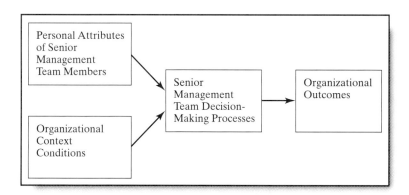

Figure 6-8
Model of senior management team decision making

The degree to which the senior management team members are similar or different from one another also impacts decision making. For example, a team made up of individuals who are very diverse will be more likely to generate different solutions for issues addressed, and will ultimately be more creative and innovative when making decisions. On the other hand, a team comprised of individuals who are more similar to one another will tend to be more efficient because team members will be inclined to look at issues similarly and thus need less time to debate alternative solutions.

Attitude toward risk affects strategic choice. The top management of any organization has a particular posture with regard to taking risks. Some organizations accept risk while others are risk-averse. Those organizations that have a risk-averse senior management will tend to stay "close to the vest" with strategic choice, investing to build the business in relatively small increments, not straying too far from existing product-market scope and adopting a conservative investment strategy. Companies that are more tolerant of risk will tend to encourage both innovation and entrepreneurial behavior within the organization, look to grow with both close-in and breakthrough innovation, and take on a much more aggressive position with respect to investing in existing in new businesses.

The Organizational Context. Senior management teams are also affected by contextual conditions when making strategic decisions. The impact of these conditions varies from one organization to the next, but some common examples are organizational resources (financial, physical, and human resources), the industry in which the firm operates, and the firm's performance record. For example, a senior management team cannot select a strategic course of action without the necessary resources to carry out that strategy, nor without considering the competition and perhaps regulatory constraints of the industry. Moreover, a firm's past performance tends to influence management when making strategic decisions. A history of poor performance puts pressure on management to choose a strategy that will turn the company around; whereas, a history of strong performance may lead to managers becoming overly confident and less inclined to change.

Another pertinent contextual condition is the organization's culture, which we take a closer look at next. Managers consider organizational culture when making strategic decisions because the culture will need to accept and commit to any strategic course of action for it to be properly implemented.

Decision-Making Process. When making strategic decisions, senior management teams, like any teams, must go through a process. As explained in Chapter 1, the strategic decision-making process involves several steps that require the senior management team to work together to identify and clarify strategic issues and then generate and choose among alternative solutions.

This process varies for each senior management team. Some process characteristics that distinguish one team from another are the comprehensiveness with which they cover issues, the level and type of conflict experienced by team members, the speed at which they make decisions, and the involvement of team members in the decision-making process. Sometimes this process can also involve *political maneuvering*, characterized by senior management team members trying to gain special advantage over other team members through actions such as gaining control over resources, granting favors, and bargaining.

Senior Management Team and Organizational Outcomes. Senior Management teams are interesting because, unlike other teams in the organization, they set strategy. In so doing, the team can have a long-term impact on organizational outcomes like financial performance, employee satisfaction, and societal well-being.

Organizational Culture

Every organization possesses a unique **organizational culture,** consisting of "shared values, beliefs, attitudes, customs, norms, personalities and heroes that describe a firm."[25] Culture is learned, shared, and passed down from generation to generation within the firm. Culture shapes the behavior of both individuals that make up the firm and the firm itself. For example, one can easily observe the differences in culture between a high-tech Silicon Valley firm and a major metropolitan bank in several dimensions: the appearance, dress, and language of employees, the schedules kept by employees, even the design and décor of company facilities.

Culture binds the organization and provides an identity for its people. Culture helps give meaning to the work that people do for the firm. People who do not share cultural values and norms find very quickly that there is a lack of fit or do not feel comfortable in the environment. On the other hand, those that share core values derive inspiration and a sense of commitment to move the organization ahead. As a result, culture is important to strategic choice as it impacts the organization's members' ability and willingness to carry out the strategy chosen by management.

No two organizational cultures are the same. Cultures differ from one another in a multitude of respects. Some common factors that distinguish cultures are the extent to which they exhibit the following characteristics:

- Innovation
- Risk taking
- Team orientation
- People orientation
- Technological sophistication
- Attention to detail
- Aggressiveness
- Stability

In fact, there is much evidence from the business world to support the notion that blending different organizational cultures, such as that of Chrysler and Daimler-Benz, proves to be one of the most vexing issues involved in mergers. A recent report noted that an Amazon and Wal-Mart partnership would be mutually advantageous, but cautioned, "their disparate cultures, size and target customers may present too wide a gulf to bridge."[26]

Strategies and other organizational initiatives that fall within the accepted range of behavior will likely be supported and embraced by managers and employees. Strategies that violate corporate norms will be very difficult to implement. Companies that experience a significant downturn in financial performance must often significantly alter organizational direction to adapt to a changing environment. One of the most difficult aspects of moving in a different direction is getting the people that make up the organization to respond positively to the change, because the change may not fit the existing culture.

UPS was founded in 1907, giving the firm a 64-year head start on FedEx. It was Frederick Smith, however, founder of Federal Express, who formed the idea of overnight package delivery in 1971, forever changing the package delivery business. UPS did not create its own overnight service until 1988. The explanation may lie in its corporate culture. UPS had a rigid, military-like culture from its earliest days as a messenger service. This culture did not breed risk-taking, but within the company, speed was valued above all other virtues. So while it took UPS a number of years to pull even with FedEx, UPS has moved ahead on many fronts, largely because UPS has created logistical systems for its customers that save time and money. For example, in a year, UPS has reduced Ford's delivery times by 26 percent and saved the car manufacturer $240 million.[27]

Because cultures are so multifaceted, they are difficult to understand. Ideally, a culture can be understood by spending time inside it and observing what the organizational members value and how they behave. Cultures can sometimes also be understood through classic stories told by people in the company. For example, it is an age-old legend in the Ford Motor Company that its founder, Henry Ford, used to remind his people when they disagreed with him that it was his name on the building. Company rituals can also give one a sense of its culture. For example, many companies have celebrations for employees like annual Christmas parties and company picnics.

Some organizations do not have a strong sense of culture; employees do not share common values. Often, these organizations have subcultures. *Subcultures* are smaller groups of people in an organization bonded together by a set of common values that are different than the values held by the majority of the people in the organization. An example of a subculture could be a sales team that focuses on customer needs and earning commissions.

As Microsoft attempts to transition to an Internet platform strategy, and as CEO Steve Ballmer exerts more influence, its culture is changing as well. Ballmer's emphases on sales, service, marketing, and reliability have displaced the technology-driven culture of Microsoft under the leadership of Bill Gates. The company is now more open and more willing to share, places more emphasis on getting things done as opposed to "being smart," and is more interested in pursuing sales to large corporations. This "version 2.0" Microsoft may be necessary to meet the demands of a changing information technology world.[28]

Personal Ethics and Social Responsibility

Organizations have a responsibility to serve the interests of customers, employees, and shareholders, but as we have noted, the responsibility does not stop there. The behavior of organizations impacts the communities in which they operate and the broader framework of society. For example, companies provide significant benefits to communities—employment, taxes, and intellectual capital, among others—but also can create issues such as traffic and congestion, pollution, and negative impact on the aesthetics of the community. What factors explain the various approaches organizations take with respect to their ethics and sense of responsibility to the broader society?

The organizational culture is influenced by the personal ethics of the people inside it. **Personal ethics** are the moral principles that define the behavior that a person believes is acceptable or right. One person's ethics often differ from another person's ethics, as people tend to consider situations differently. When assessing situations, individuals often adopt an ethical framework of reference. Some frameworks are:

- Utilitarian view—it is ethical if it represents the greatest good for the greatest number of people.
- The Golden Rule view—it is ethical if your behavior results in implications for others that you would not mind for yourself. In other words, "do unto others as you would want others to do unto you."
- Individualism view—it is ethical if it serves your own self-interests.
- Moral rights view—it is ethical if it protects and respects basic human rights.
- Justice view—it is ethical if it treats people fairly based on basic standards, rules, and laws.

Personal ethics are the foundation for a firm's business ethics and corporate social responsibility. *Business ethics* are the moral principles that define the behavior that the organization as a whole views as acceptable. Business ethics drive an organization's sense of **corporate social responsibility,** which is the obligation that it feels toward its stakeholders.

As in personal ethics, corporations differ in their sense of corporate social responsibility. All organizations tend to concern themselves with economic responsibilities. *Economic responsibilities* refer to an organization's obligation to be profitable and stay in business. This focuses on keeping jobs for employees and satisfying customers. Most organizations also concern themselves with *legal responsibilities,* which refers to an organization's obligation to obey the law and other external regulators.

Some organizations go beyond economic and legal responsibilities to emphasize ethical responsibilities. *Ethical responsibilities* refer to a company's obligation to respond to situations based on what it believes is right, just, and fair. A smaller number of organizations go even further and focus on voluntary responsibilities. Firms with *voluntary responsibilities* also focus on doing what is right, just, and fair. The difference, though, is that when an organization takes on voluntary responsibilities, it is not just responding to situations. The organization is proactively trying to be a good corporate citizen by attempting to advance the well-being of individuals, organizations, communities, and society.

In Chapter 3 we examined Merck's core values and organizational purpose. Merck is an example of a company whose core values and ethical standards ("medicine is for the people . . . it is not for the profits") guide its day-to-day operations. Ethics regulate but do not replace basic financial goals.[29] In order to maintain the confidence and trust of the public it is crucial that the public, and especially physicians and patients, recognize that Merck scientists are and have been guided in their research by ethical considerations and a focus on improving public health. Merck specifically trains and develops its corporate leaders with a process that incorporates a formal ethics component that is based on an updated global code of business conduct.[30]

Corporate social responsibility influences strategic choice because the strategy chosen will depend on an organization's sense of responsibility. For example, firms focusing on voluntary responsibilities will choose strategies that best improve the well-being of those people they affect, whereas firms focusing on economic responsibilities will choose strategies that focus on maximizing profits, regardless of how they affect others.

CONCLUSION

Strategies specify the actions organizations want to take in order to reach predetermined objectives. Objectives should be stated in terms that are actionable and measurable, and must be set so that the achievement of a sequence of short-term objectives will move the firm toward achievement of long-term objectives. For multiple business firms, strategies are established at the organizational as well as the business unit level. At the organizational level, portfolio models provide guidance for strategy creation. At the business unit level, techniques such as the SWOT Matrix and scenario planning help managers create strategies that are appropriate given the organization's situation analysis.

Microsoft is an example of a firm that operates beyond the boundaries of its home market and therefore must think globally in generating and choosing strategies. Global strategies involve choices regarding whether to standardize (globalize) or customize (localize) specific activities and processes. Firms must consider the various pressures toward both globalization and localization in setting strategy.

Strategic choice is subject to a number of behavioral influences including the characteristics of top managers, organizational culture, and both personal ethics and social responsibility. Financial tools for strategic choice are the focus of the next chapter.

KEY TERMS AND CONCEPTS

After reading this chapter you should understand each of the following terms.

- BCG Matrix
- Behavioral aspects of strategic choice
- Competitive advantage
- Corporate social responsibility
- GE-McKinsey Business Screen
- Global strategy
- Globalization
- Localization
- Long-term objectives

- Multinational strategy
- Organizational culture
- Personal ethics
- Portfolio models
- Scenario planning
- Short-term objectives
- SMART Format
- Strategic objectives
- SWOT Matrix

DISCUSSION QUESTIONS

1. You have just been appointed vice president of baseball operations for the most long-suffering franchise in major league baseball—the Chicago Cubs, a team that has not won a world championship since 1908. Using the SMART Format discussed in the chapter, develop a set of both long-term and short-term objectives for the franchise.
2. Compare and contrast the BCG and GE-McKinsey portfolio models in terms of (a) how they are constructed and (b) their implications for strategic choice.
3. Assume you are the president of a company with three major product divisions. Division A is in a low-growth market and has a low market share position. Divisions B and C are both market share leaders in their respective markets. Division C is in a high-growth market and Division B is in a market that is growing at a rate of 2 percent per year. Sales and income figures for the three divisions are shown in Table 6-5. Use the BCG Matrix to diagram your portfolio of product divisions and discuss the implications of your diagram (identify any assumptions you find necessary). Label your axes.

Table 6-5 Division sales and income

PRODUCT DIVISION	SALES (IN MILLIONS $)	OPERATING PROFITS (IN MILLIONS $)
A	250	25
B	200	35
C	50	10

4. Kodak is a company that exemplifies how fundamental change in technology can severely affect corporate performance. Using the business periodical literature, perform a SWOT analysis for Kodak's photography business, and use your SWOT matrix to generate four strategies that Kodak might pursue to enhance the firm's ability to create value for its customers, employees, and shareholders.
5. The genesis of Nike was collaboration between Bill Bowerman, who knew how to create high-performance running shoes, and Phil Knight, who understood how offshore production could yield a major cost advantage. Discuss Nike's current global strategy and the extent to which Nike is or should be globalizing/standardizing or localizing/customizing its strategies.
6. What is the relationship between the behavioral aspects of strategic choice and value creation for employees, customers, and shareholders?

EXPERIENTIAL EXERCISE

Microsoft has embarked upon a number of new strategic initiatives including .NET, Ultimate TV, and video games. Using the current business periodical literature, describe these and other new strategic initiatives of Microsoft. Assess each of these iniatives (1) with respect to the extent to which each leverages and enhances a competitive advantage and (2) according to the criteria for evaluating strategies specified in this chapter.

ENDNOTES

1. Hunger, J. D., and T. L. Wheelen. *Strategic Management.* 5th ed. Reading, MA: Addison-Wesley Publishing Company, 1996, 12.
2. Buckman, R. "With Its Old Playbook, Microsoft is Muscling into New Web Markets," *The Wall Street Journal,* June 29, 2001, A1.
3. Crockett, R. O., "Chris Galvin Shakes Things Up—Again," *Business Week* (May 28, 2001): 38–9.
4. Ben & Jerry's was acquired by Unilever in April 2000. Part of the acquisition agreement specified that Ben & Jerry's could continue their annual practice of donating a percentage of after-tax profits to charities.
5. Aaker, D. *Strategic Market Management.* New York: John Wiley & Sons, Inc., 1999, 4–5.
6. Boston Consulting Group, *Perspectives on Experience.* Boston: The Boston Consulting Group, 1974.
7. Paley, N. *The Manager's Guide to Competitive Marketing Strategies.* 2nd ed. Boca Raton, FL: CRC Press, 1999, 154.
8. Paley, N. *The Manager's Guide to Competitive Marketing Strategies.* 2nd ed. Boca Raton, FL: CRC Press, 1999, 155.
9. Hill, C. W. L., and G. R. Jones. *Strategic Management Theory: An Integrated Approach.* 3rd ed. Boston: Houghton Mifflin, 1995, 308.
10. Hill, C. W. L., and G. R. Jones. *Strategic Management Theory: An Integrated Approach.* 3rd ed. Boston: Houghton Mifflin, 1995, 171.
11. Weihrich, H., "The TOWS Matrix: A Tool for Situational Analysis," *Long Range Planning* 15, no. 2 (April 1982): 54–66.
12. Eridani, T., "Italian Motorcycle Maker Enters a New Race: U.S. Market," *The Wall Street Journal,* January 19, 2001, A19.
13. Anonymous, "Business: Microsoft's Cunning Plan," *The Economist* 358, no. 8203 (January 6, 2001): 53–54.
14. Anonymous, "Business: Microsoft's Cunning Plan," *The Economist* 358, no. 8203 (January 6, 2001): 53–54.
15. Clark, D., "Microsoft Advances on Game, TV Fronts," *The Wall Street Journal,* January 5, 2001, B2.
16. Aaker, D. *Strategic Market Management.* New York: John Wiley & Sons, Inc., 1999, 32.
17. Wysocki, B., Jr., "Power Grid: Soft Landing or Hard? Firm Tests Strategy on 3 Views of Future—Most Likely, Duke Energy Decides, Is a Growth Era of "Flawed Competition," *The Wall Street Journal,* July 7, 2000, A1.
18. Aaker, D. *Strategic Market Management.* New York: John Wiley & Sons, Inc., 1999, 255.
19. Young, S., "Verizon Plans Global Service for Business," *The Wall Street Journal,* February 7, 2001, B8.
20. Oliver, R. W., "New Rules for Global Markets," *The Journal of Businss Strategy* (May/June 2000): 7–9.
21. Hill, C. W. L., and G. R. Jones. *Strategic Management Theory: An Integrated Approach.* 3rd ed. Boston: Houghton Mifflin, 1995, 299.
22. Pai, U. L., "Dell Plans Subsidiary in India," *Electronic News* (August 21, 2000): 16.
23. Simon, H. A. *Administrative Behavior.* New York: MacMillan Publishing, 1947.
24. Hambrick, D. C., and P. A. Mason, "Upper Echelons: The Organization as a Reflection of its Top Managers," *Academy of Management Review* 9 (1984): 193–206.
25. David, F. R. *Concepts of Strategic Management.* 6th ed. Upper Saddle River, NJ: Prentice Hall, 1997, 196.
26. Hof, R., "Amazon+WalMart=Win/Win," *Business Week* (March 19, 2001): 42.
27. Haddad, C., and J. Ewing. "Ground Wars," *Business Week* (May 21, 2001): 65–68.

28. Swartz, J., "Ballmer Steers Microsoft down More Practical Path. Customer Solutions Take Precedence over Cool Technology." *USA Today,* June 26, 2000, 3B.

29. Koberstein, W. "The Inner Merck," *Pharmaceutical Executive* 20, 1 (January 2000): 44–58.

30. Gilmartin, R. V., "Innovation, Ethics and Core Values: Keys to Global Success," *Vital Speeches of the Day* (January 15, 1999): 209–213.

Chapter

7

Financial Tools for Strategic Choice

Chapter Outline
The Role of the Finance Function in Strategic Management
Financial Tools for Strategic Choice
Forecasting the Financial Results of Strategies
Sources of Funds for Strategic Initiatives
Conclusion
Key Terms and Concepts
Discussion Questions
Experiential Exercise
Endnotes

*T*he Walt Disney Company continually searches for growth opportunities. In 2005, Disney will open the doors of a new theme park—Hong Kong Disneyland. In Paris, Disney will add its second theme park, Disney Studios Paris, modeled after Disney/MGM Studios in Florida. Another new attraction is planned for Tokyo Disneyland, where the company is putting the finishing touches on Tokyo DisneySea.

Growth strategies such as these typically require a substantial investment of capital. This is certainly the case for Disney, which often spends millions of dollars to build a park before ever collecting a single dollar of revenue from ticket sales. The new Hong Kong Disneyland, for example, will have been in planning and development for about a decade before it opens.

Disney's CEO is well aware of the capital requirements of these strategic choices and has tried to allay any fears about them by stating: "From a creative standpoint, these new parks are incredibly exciting. But, from a hard, cold financial perspective they're pretty exciting as well. This is because Disney's total investment in all our new properties outside the United States is less than we have spent to build some individual theme parks in the past."[1]

The purpose of this chapter is to understand the critical role of the finance function in the strategic management process. We focus on three overriding issues: (1) financial tools for making strategic choices, (2) estimating or forecasting the financial results of a strategy, and (3) identifying ways to finance or pay for strategies. These issues are inherent in Disney's strategic choices described above. After reading this chapter you should be able to answer each of the questions listed in Figure 7-1. The figure shows that the questions posed for this chapter pertain to both strategic choice and to implementation, the third and fourth steps, respectively, of the strategic management process.

THE ROLE OF THE FINANCE FUNCTION IN STRATEGIC MANAGEMENT

Financial management is a subset of management that focuses on generating financial information that can be used to improve decision making, including strategic choice. As we know, strategic management focuses on value creation for key stakeholders of the enterprise. The finance perspective contributes to the focus of value creation by zeroing in on value for owners or shareholders.

What does The Walt Disney Company tell its owners and employees ("cast members") about its financial objectives?: "The company's primary financial goals are to maximize earnings and cash flow from existing business and to allocate capital profitably toward growth initiatives that will drive long-term shareholder value."[2] Sound financial management practices play a critical role in achieving these goals, and in contributing to the achievement of strategic objectives.

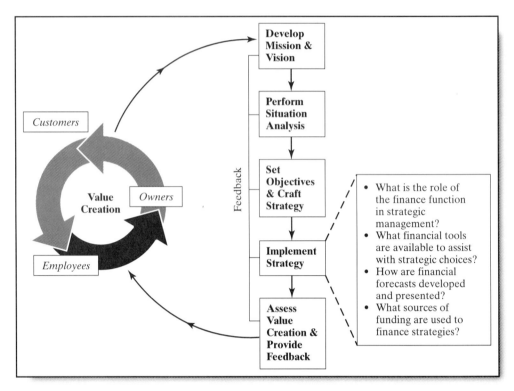

Figure 7-1
The strategic management framework

Consider an example. Suppose top management has identified the need in the marketplace for a new product. Should the project go ahead? Is it an attractive strategic choice? That decision cannot be made without a check on the project's long-term financial viability. But, before that can be assessed a more immediate question must be answered: How will the firm finance the project? Where will the money come from for retooling the machinery? How will the firm pay for the supplies, labor, and raw materials needed to manufacture the product? Who will supply the funds to package and ship the item? And, of course, marketing dollars will be needed to make consumers aware of the firm's willingness to satisfy their needs for this product. All of these issues are an important part of the finance function. No strategic initiative moves forward without consideration of financial management issues.

Before beginning our discussion of financial tools for strategic choice, let's consider some key financial concepts and terms that we will use throughout the chapter.

Capitalization of the Firm

The term **financial structure** typically refers to the total of all the sources of funds that the firm has acquired for its operations. The term **capital structure** is generally used to describe the permanent or long-term sources of financing used by a company. As we will describe in more detail later in this chapter, firms use both internal funding sources and external funding sources to satisfy their needs for cash; they draw on cash from operations as well as debt and equity sources.

Does capital structure and the mix of financing sources make a difference in creating value? Certainly! As we will note below, acquiring funds to implement strategic plans (as well as to carry out day-to-day operating activities) costs money and adds an inherent element of risk to the firm's very existence. There is uncertainty in nearly every strategic choice, just as there is risk in the choice of financing the enterprise.

Capital Budgeting

Managers make decisions every day that involve the fundamental trade-off between cash flows now and cash flows in the future. For example, Disney must evaluate the trade-off between negative cash flow created by the costs of building new theme parks and the expected future positive cash flow that should result from gate receipts. Disney managers must determine whether the cash outflow is justified by the anticipated inflows from future revenues. These are simple examples of **capital budgeting** decisions.

Cost of Capital.   It is critical at the outset to recognize that acquisition of financing is not a costless event. Regardless of the type, source, or timing of acquiring funds, somebody will demand compensation for being without their own money or property. It is beyond the scope of this text to deal extensively with the problems involved in determining the firm's *cost of capital,* but a common theme in any discussion of strategic choice is the cost/benefit trade-off associated with obtaining financing and compensating suppliers of funds.

We deal with the cost of capital in this chapter as if it were a known commodity and one that is fixed. That is a simplification adopted only so that we can focus the discussion on the models and tools used by the strategic management team in making choices and assessing outcomes. Suffice it to say that the firm's *weighted average cost of capital* is an important consideration in strategic choice.

FINANCIAL TOOLS FOR STRATEGIC CHOICE

Before describing the various financial tools used in strategic choice, we must set the stage with a review of four basic components common to all business investment decisions. To judge the value-creating attractiveness of a strategy, we must consider:

- the amount expended—we'll call this the *net investment;*
- the potential benefits—the *net operating cash inflows;*
- the time period involved—the strategic initiative's *economic life;* and
- any end-of-project recovery of capital—the *net salvage value.*

These four elements are not difficult to understand, but our analysis must consider both the dynamic and interactive effects of them. We will see this through a discussion of and examples using several related techniques that can assist us in making strategic choices.

Payback Period

How soon will I get my investment back? That's not an unreasonable or uncommon question for any investor to pose. The strategic manager is an investor. She or he (more likely "the team") proposes to allocate some of the firm's scarce resources to an initiative that is expected to create value for the firm. A simple, unsophisticated rule of thumb we can use to help answer this question is the **payback period.** This technique compares forecasted cash inflows from a strategic initiative to the project's net investment. Let's look at a simple example.

Suppose that the strategic management team is presented with a proposal to acquire a new product-distribution warehouse. This state-of-the-art facility would be located at a new site, which will significantly reduce the cost of processing orders and getting the product in the hands of customers. The net investment is $10 million. Annual net savings of $1 million in distribution expenses are expected. (We ignore here, for the sake of simplicity, the obvious potential for more or larger orders that could result from better customer service.)

We can say that as long as the expected savings from the warehouse last for 10 years, we ought to consider implementing this strategic investment. How do we know that? Because the payback period is 10 years.

Payback = Net investment/Annual cost savings.
In our case: $10,000,000/$1,000,000 = 10 years.

The result of this uncomplicated exercise is the number of periods required for the initial outlay to be repaid. It's a rough-and-ready test of whether the cost of a strategic initiative can be recovered within its expected economic life span.

Unfortunately, recouping the net investment really isn't enough for our value-creation-minded strategic management team. Their concern is with payback that *exceeds* the input cost. Furthermore, they must consider the basic fact that dollars of payback that arrive in future years are not equivalent in purchasing-power value to those dollars invested in a strategic initiative today.

There is also a third consideration. The payback period is not really a breakeven position, for if the net investment in the chosen project had been placed instead in a secure savings account, at least a minimal amount of interest above the initial investment would have been earned. Note, too, that this simple payback period analysis implicitly assumes level annual operating cash inflows. This insensitivity to variations in cash flow can be a serious shortcoming for certain new product introductions and physical asset replacement decisions.

All of this is not to say that payback period is not usable, just that its shortcomings limit the weight we ought to assign to its output in making strategic choices. Payback is easy to understand and compute. As long as we understand its limitations, payback will suffice as a quick way to decide whether a strategic initiative should be given more sophisticated analysis. Some of the pros and cons of using payback period as a strategic choice tool are listed in Table 7-1.

Rate of Return

The **rate of return** technique, like payback period, is a quick and easy financial tool for evaluating a proposed strategy.

Table 7-1 Payback period

ADVANTAGES	LIMITATIONS
• Easy to compute and understand • Provides a preliminary quantitative analysis of strategic alternatives	• Does not account for the time value of money • Assumes a constant level of forecasted cash inflows • Does not account for other opportunities forgone by choosing the strategy in question.

First, let's call the average annual net operating cash inflows expected from a strategic initiative the *return on investment.* Then, all that is needed is to convert this absolute indicator of a project's benefit to an understandable ratio. For example, the rate of return on investment is easily computed as follows:

Rate of return = Average annual operating cash inflow/Net investment.

The proposed strategy is attractive if the calculated rate of return exceeds a *hurdle rate* set by managers, that is, a minimum rate necessary to accept the strategy.

Time Value Concept

These two simple methods of making financial decisions on strategic projects are just that: simplistic techniques that give first-cut indications. They are useful to set the stage for analysis by making a connection between a strategy's cost (net investment) and benefit (net operating cash inflows or net savings in cash outflows).

As we have stated, strategic choices entail trade-offs that weigh economic consequences of current costs against probable future cash flow benefits (i.e., inflows or cost savings). Given an appropriate period for analysis, this assessment requires an understanding of the **time value of money.** Before moving to the several techniques used in helping strategic managers analyze the time value of money, we need to review this important concept.[*]

Strategic decisions are always forward looking—they are an investment in the future. Given this future orientation, the simple axiom that a dollar received today is worth more than a dollar received 1 year from now takes on added relevance. The chance to profitably invest the dollar received today is postponed, or forgone, in anticipation of cash inflow later. This lost opportunity is the cost (*opportunity cost*) involved in the strategic choice to trade investment today for operating cash inflows in the future.

A dollar spent now cannot be invested to earn any additional return. Similarly, spending a dollar 1 year from now means that dollar can earn a return in the meantime. So the time value concept relates to both the investment (outflow now or later) decision and the opportunity to earn a return (current inflows or future inflows).

Let's consider an illustration. In Figure 7-2, concentrate on the timing of the cash flows generated by the initial strategic investment.

---

[*] You have undoubtedly encountered the concept of time value during your study of basic accounting principles and fundamental corporate finance. If, after the discussion of the topic in this chapter, you are still uncomfortable with its application, review a contemporary text in managerial accounting or corporate finance.

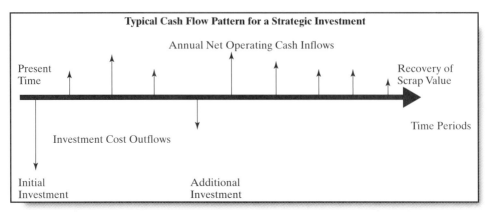

Figure 7-2
The time value of money

The figure shows that the initial outlay for a strategic initiative takes time to earn a return: Nike might spend $2 million this year to design a new shoe that will not generate any sales until 18 months from now. Campbell Soup's development of a new line of snack crackers by its Pepperidge Farms group might cost $1 million now, but not yield any sales for 1 year. Merck might spend $200 million to create and test a new pharmaceutical product that will require 7 years from initiation to market introduction, and, it will take Disney 6 years of construction before the gates open at the new Hong Kong theme park.

It is not enough to ask, as we did in the previous section, "When do I get my initial investment back?" For every period in which any portion of that initial outlay is not available, earning potential is lost. As important as getting back the initial outlay is, the timing of that return—the inflows of cash in the future—is critical to the strategic choice. Those dollar inflows in the future have less value than the dollar spent today.

All of the future cash inflows have to be "brought back" in time to the present so they can be matched fairly—that is, in the same purchasing power units—with the present cost of the strategic initiative. The methodology to do this is called *discounting*. It is the standard practice for expressing future dollars in the form of equivalent present dollars. It is the basis for all modern techniques of investment and valuation. Determining the *present value* of expected future inflows (or cost savings) is the foundation for any serious financial analysis applied to inform strategic choice.

To be certain that you understand the time value concept, consider the following example.

Step 1: Suppose you have $1,000 to invest and choose to place this sum in a bank savings account that earns interest at the annual rate of 5 percent. In 1 year, you will have $1,050. The amount of your return would be $50; the rate of return is the previously stated 5 percent. (You can compute this rate just as we did: amount of return/initial investment, or, $50/$1,000—that's 5 percent.) Suppose, also, that your friend had $1,000 to invest, but being uncertain about the financial viability of local banks, simply put the cash in a shoebox under the bed. For your friend, the chance to earn $50 was lost. This is the opportunity cost described.

Step 2: The *future value* of your $1,000 investment in our example is its initial cost, $1,000, plus the interest earned, $50 ($1,000 at 5 percent for 1 year), or $1,050. The future value of your friend's investment (or, in this case, non-investment) is just $1,000: there was no return on that initial amount.

Step 3: Looking into the future from the time (today) when you and your friend made the decision on how to invest, you expect to have $1,050 of future value and he/she expects to have $1,000. Certainly, you expect to be better off. Surely, your friend's strategic choice entails a missed opportunity to be better off.

Step 4: The present value of your strategic choice is known to be $1,000. How is that related to the future value of $1,050 (see Step 2)? Consider that the future value is the initial value plus the return: $1,050 = $1,000 + $50. Note that the future value divided by the initial investment is nothing more that 1 plus the earnings rate: $1,050/$1,000 = 1.05. If we *discount* the future value by the factor of 1.05, we convert that future value into the present value: $1,050/1.05 = $1,000. In other words, the present value of $1,050 received 1 year from now when the interest rate is 5 percent is the same $1,000 initial investment with which we started this example.

Step 5: But, what about your friend? The method of analysis does not change—the promise to receive $1,000 from the shoebox in a year, when we could earn 5 percent in the bank, is $952.38: nothing more than the future value discounted by 1.05 ($1,000/1.05 = $952.38).

Let's summarize. Without question the sum of $1,000 offered to someone (your friend) 1 year from now is less valuable than $1,000 offered today. The simple reason is that with the money in hand now, you can invest it to have a future value that is larger than the initial sum available, and certainly larger than the promised $1,000 1 year hence.

This exercise demonstrates that with an assumed earnings rate of 5 percent, the expected receipt of $1,000 1 year from now is "worth" only $952.38 today. The analysis is meant to reflect the economic reality of the trade-off between dollars received today and ones to be received in the future. In addition it is meant to show that, in the context of strategic choices, a dollar committed today will have to be returned at a larger absolute amount if a positive rate of return is expected. Conversely, strategic managers will commit fewer present-value dollars to receive the same number of future-value dollars. How much less will we pay for a dollar in the future? That all depends upon the earnings rate involved and the time at which the future dollars will be received.

Net Present Value

Strategic managers must decide what dollars to commit *today* with the expectation of receiving dollars in the future. The senior management team at Southwest Airlines has to choose whether to commit $50 million for two new Boeing jetliners to serve new markets. What justifies today's dollar outlay for jets? Future cash inflows from ticket sales. But those future ticket sales dollars are not equivalent to the current cash outlay. Today's dollars are worth more than the promised dollars of the future. We know that from the simple shoebox example in the prior section. What's the strategic manager to do when faced with this situation? He or she must convert future dollars to equivalent present-day dollars. In other words, the future inflows must be discounted to today's dollars. The future value must be translated into present value.

The **net present value (NPV)** technique weighs the cash flow trade-off among initial investment outlay, future benefits, and potential net salvage value in equivalent present value terms. This will allow the strategic manager to see whether the net balance of these values is favorable or not.

To use this tool, a rate of discount that represents the normal earnings opportunities of the firm must first be specified. Then the present value of each and every cash outflow and inflow associated with the strategic initiative over its entire expected useful economic life can be computed. With everything in time-adjusted terms, the present value of inflows (positive amounts) and outflows (negative amounts) can be combined. The result will be the NPV.

The NPV number indicates whether the strategic initiative, considered over its economic life, will achieve the earnings rate applied in its calculation. A positive NPV indicates that the cash flows generated by the strategic initiative over its economic life will:

- recover the initial outlay;
- recover any additional capital costs included in the analysis;
- earn the desired/required rate of return on the investment; and
- provide a cushion in case the future differs from expectations.

Conversely, a negative result suggests that the strategic initiative will not achieve an outcome that meets the earnings standard expected of new strategies and is likely to create an opportunity loss if implemented. In other words, it is not a value-creating strategy.

NPV is quite sensitive to the assumptions upon which is calculated. Timing of cash inflows, needs (and timing) of additional capital outlays beyond the initial one, and the magnitude of the amounts involved, all impact the model's outcome. Some of these factors are "nearly certain," while others are subject to conjecture and estimation. Probably the most important variable involved, though, is the rate of discount (or expected earnings rate) employed.

From an economic standpoint, the discount rate chosen ought to be the rate of return that the strategic management team has come to expect will satisfy owners. This is likely the rate of return investors normally enjoy from similar investments of equivalent risk. In short, this is the opportunity rate of return.

This may sound simple, but in the corporate setting the choice of discount rate—so essential to the NPV analysis—is complicated by the variety of strategic initiatives available and the types of financing that might be provided by owners and creditors. The rate used to discount cash flows associated with strategic alternatives should reflect the minimum return requirement that will produce the normally expected level of shareholder return, appropriately adjusted for any special circumstances that apply to the firm in its ability to acquire funds to initiate the project.

The standard most commonly used for discounting in NPV analysis is the overall corporate weighted average cost of capital (see the previous discussion). Shareholder value cannot be created if strategic choices are not made in such a way that earnings on the choices exceed the cost of capital needed to implement the strategies.

Net present value analysis is so important and prevalent in guiding strategic choice that we should focus on some examples of its application. The examples used are simplified to get at the heart of the analytical techniques and the logic underlying the use of the NPV technique.

Consider the following example: Nuprod Co. managers propose the introduction of a new and improved version of one of their existing products. An initial outlay of $100,000 for new equipment is required to produce the new product. Sales are expected to provide after-tax cash inflows of an additional $25,000 in each of the next 6 years, without any significant annual fluctuation. Although the equipment will not be completely worn out after 6 years, as a consequence of technological obsolescence it is unlikely to be worth more than the scrap value for which it can then be sold. Removal costs will approximately equal this residual value.

The total initial outlay needs to be recovered over the 6-year period and earn a reasonable rate of return—let's assume that rate is set at 8 percent. This will be our discount factor for the future cash inflows.

We know that the payback period technique suggests that this is a worthwhile project. The initiative is expected to last 6 years, and the payback of initial outlay occurs in 4 years. (Remember: initial investment divided by annual net cash inflows yields the payback period measured in years. Here: $100,000/$25,000 = 4 years.) So, further assessment of the project is warranted. Payback, as you will recall, does not take into account the time value of either the $100,000 initial outlay or the $25,000 annual net inflows over 6 future years. Table 7-2 contains the detailed analysis.

What does the analysis tell us? For one thing, we certainly were correct in looking at more than the simple payback analysis, for as seen in the table's last column, and payback period notwithstanding, this strategic initiative was still "in the red" from a net present value viewpoint at the end of the 5th year. Look at the present value numbers. They tell us what each year's net cash inflow is worth in today's dollars. The further away in time the inflow occurs, the smaller its present value. Another way to approach this is to recognize that when the earnings rate requirement is 8 percent, a rational investor will pay only $17,025 for the promise of a $25,000 cash inflow 5 years from today.

Table 7-2   Net present value (NPV) example

TIME PERIOD	PROJECT COST	BENEFITS CASH INFLOW	PRESENT VALUE FACTOR	PRESENT VALUE	CUMULATIVE NET PRESENT VALUE
0	$100,000	—	1.000	−$100,000	−$100,000
1		$25,000	0.926	23,150	−76,850
2		25,000	0.857	21,425	−55,425
3		25,000	0.794	19,850	−35,575
4		25,000	0.735	18,375	−17,200
5		25,000	0.681	17,025	−175
6		25,000	0.630	15,750	15,575
	$100,000	$150,000		$15,575	

Note the slight similarity of the analysis to the simple payback approach discussed earlier. The recovery of initial investment occurs within the assumed economic life and there is something to spare. Remember that the critical difference between simple payback and NPV is the fact that the time value analysis has a built-in earnings requirement in addition to the initial investment recovery. In fact, this project will return an excess economic value beyond the required earnings—if all the estimates turn out to be true—of $13,375 in net present value terms. The project exceeds the criterion for earnings that was set by management. From a strategic standpoint, then, it's a worthwhile, value-adding strategic choice.

Before moving to the next financial tool for strategic choice, let's consider the sensitivity of this model to the earnings standard that management might impose. Suppose that management has been presented with a competing strategic alternative of the same level of risk and a similar operating time horizon, that earns 12 percent. Under these circumstances, how does our new product initiative stack up? This is just a question of changing that built-in earnings requirement, which NPV handles with ease. Here the discount rate is 12 percent, and as expected, all of those yearly net present value numbers will decline. The full analysis is in Table 7-3.

The project, being forced to compete for scarce resources and return a higher rate than previously indicated, barely meets the criterion for selection. It would not be difficult to show that were management to ask for a 14 percent return on this initiative, it would fail the NPV test.

Notice, in addition, that the higher earnings requirement has the added impact of lengthening the time before the project's NPV turns positive. Thus, actual economic life, always a matter for supposition, becomes more critical. Changes in the marketplace, the technical environment, or the physical production process may intervene and upset the planned outcome.

NPV is a technique that can easily accommodate changes in initial outlay (maybe the firm can negotiate a discount on the new equipment) or length of life (possibly patent protection can be acquired on a new product). Even the assumption about invariant cash inflows can be adjusted without difficulty in the model.

Table 7-3 Sensitivity of NPV analysis

TIME PERIOD	PROJECT COST	BENEFITS CASH INFLOW	PRESENT VALUE FACTOR	PRESENT VALUE	CUMULATIVE NET PRESENT VALUE
0	$100,000	—	1.000	−$100,000	−$100,000
1		$25,000	0.893	22,325	−77,675
2		25,000	0.797	19,925	−57,750
3		25,000	0.712	17,800	−39,950
4		25,000	0.636	15,900	−24,050
5		25,000	0.567	14,175	−9,875
6		25,000	0.507	12,675	2,800
	$100,000	$150,000		$2,800	

The best use of the net present value technique is as a screening device that indicates whether a stipulated minimum earnings standard (our discount rate, which may well be the firm's cost of capital) can be met over the strategy's economic life. When NPV is positive, there is potential for earnings in excess of the standard and, therefore, economic value creation. On the other hand, a negative NPV puts management on notice that the project cannot achieve capital recovery and the required earnings standard with the projected cash flow scheme.

While net present value is a valuable tool in assessing strategic alternatives, it doesn't answer all the questions management might have regarding the financial attractiveness of a strategy. For example, when comparing different projects, how does one evaluate the respective size of the "excess" NPV calculated with a given earnings standard when investment outlays differ significantly? To what extent is achieving the expected economic useful life a factor in such comparisons? Also, how does one quantify the potential errors and uncertainties inherent in the future cash flow estimates? And, if all the estimates are realized, what is the specific return earned by a project? Let's take up these additional questions as we look at other financial tools used in strategic choice.

Profitability Index

After using the net present value technique to evaluate several alternative strategies, managers may be faced with a choice that involves projects of different investment size. Decision makers, in this case, cannot ignore the fact that even when the NPV analyses are nearly equal, different projects involve initial investments that are significantly different.

In other words, it does make a difference whether a strategic alternative promises a present value of $2.5 million from an initial investment of $2 million, or whether in another case—with equivalent risk and economic life—a $2.5 million present value results from a $2.25 million investment. In the first instance, the excess benefit or NPV cushion is a much larger fraction of the net investment. All other things equal, this first alternative is much more attractive to management even though the expectation is that its net return in current dollars is no different than the other choice. The benefits from the projects may be the same, but the costs to carry them out are not.

We have a simple way to express this important relationship—the *profitability index.* This indicator may be used to evaluate strategic alternatives with different required levels of investment. You might think of this as a mechanical way of standardizing the projects to get at the heart of the value-creating issue: it's not how much absolute value (here, NPV) management creates, it's how much it creates with the investment outlay made. In effect, we want a rate of earnings. Thus, we use the profitability index idea to level the playing field.

The formula to compute the index is:

$$\text{Profitability index} = \frac{\text{Present value of operating inflows (\textit{benefit})}}{\text{Present value of net investment outlay (\textit{cost})}}$$

The technique tells us what the rate of return is for a dollar of initial investment, making it easy to compare strategic choices when the input dollars differ in amount.

Let's apply this tool to these examples. First, here are the profitability index numbers:

$$\text{Profitability index} = \frac{\$2,500,000}{\$2,000,000} = 1.25$$

$$\text{Profitability index} = \frac{\$2,500,000}{\$2,250,000} = 1.11$$

The higher the profitability index, the more attractive the project. While both of these strategic initiatives are expected to return a $2.5 million value in present dollar terms, the first one earns 25 percent on the initial investment and the other yields 11 percent (not a bad return, but not 25 percent). This surely helps in the decision-making process.

If the benefit-to-cost ratio is 1.0 or less, the strategic initiative is just meeting or is actually below the minimum earnings standard used to derive the present value. An index number of 1.0 corresponds to an NPV of zero. Remember, though, that because net present value already implicitly accounts for a required rate of return, zero is not a totally bad situation. We simply have no cushion or excess to account for changed conditions or assumptions that do not reflect reality accurately.

Let's try this exercise again with our previous example for the Nuprod Co. In the case where management would accept an 8 percent return as the standard (see Table 7.2), we can compute the profitability index to be 1.156. Recall that the net present value of the strategy was $15,575, so the present value would be this number plus the cost of the strategy ($100,000).

$$\text{Profitability index} = \frac{\left(\$100,000 + \$15,575\right)}{\$100,000} = 1.156$$

When the project was required to compete against an alternative at a 12 percent return, you will recall that the NPV dropped to $2,800 (see Table 7-3 for details). Of course, as the benefits decline so will the index of profitability.

$$\text{Profitability index} = \frac{\left(\$100,000 + \$2,800\right)}{\$100,000} = 1.028$$

The profitability index provides valuable additional insight for the strategic manager. As noted and in the examples, it allows us to make better-informed judgments when we are presented with strategic choices of varying investment size.

Internal Rate of Return

Most strategic managers are familiar with the concept of internal rate of return, and students of strategic management ought to understand this financial tool also. The *internal rate of return (IRR)* is simply the discount rate that, when applied to both the cash outflows and cash inflows over a project's economic life, yields a zero net present value. That is to say, IRR is a rate of discount that sets the present values of inflows and outflows equal.

The idea of an inflow–outflow equalizing discount rate is predicated upon letting the IRR become a variable that is dependent upon the cash flow pattern and viable economic life of the strategic initiative. In the cases we presented previously of net present value analysis and the profitability index, we specified an earnings standard to discount the investment's cash flows. Here, we turn the problem around to find the discount rate that makes cash inflows and outflows equal. The derivation of IRR can be relatively complex and is best left for another learning venue. Suffice it to say that with a standard financial or business calculator and the appropriate inputs, the IRR can be determined directly.

Why do we want to determine IRR? What is gained by its use? IRR is another convenient *investment-ranking device.* The internal rate of return is the earnings rate delivered by a project. This makes it particularly attractive when several alternatives need to be compared in the strategic choice process. In addition, when evaluating a single strategic alternative, the IRR is easily compared to the firm's cost of capital to see whether the alternative is worthwhile (i.e., value-creating).

Present Value Payback Period

The payback period approach discussed above can be modified to consider the issue of risk inherent in strategic choice. Furthermore, we can enhance this technique so that it considers the time value of money.

Present value payback establishes the minimum economic life necessary for a strategic alternative to meet the predetermined earnings standard. In other words, present value payback can be achieved at a specific point in time when the accumulation of positive present value inflows equals the cumulative negative present value of all the outlays for the strategic initiative. If you like, that's the present value breakeven point in the project's life. Remember, this breakeven, because it is in present value terms, actually includes the normal earnings standard required of the project. Many managers think of this as the point at which the strategic initiative becomes attractive. In a larger sense, we might consider this the beginning of value creation for owners.

If a strategic initiative is a straightforward combination of a single initial investment followed by a series of level annual net operating inflows, the present value payback analysis is quite simple and can be readily done on a financial calculator or spreadsheet program. Consider again the Nuprod Co. project that we have used as an example throughout this chapter.

Let's use the facts of the Nuprod Co. case to modify the simple payback period analysis. The unadjusted payback period is:

$$\text{Payback period} = \frac{\$100,000}{\$25,000} = 4 \text{ years}$$

Using the time value concept we have stressed throughout our discussion, we need to interpret the $25,000 yearly amount of net inflow as an annuity. When we convert that stream of inflows to a present value context, it is clear that those amounts are not worth $25,000 each in today's value terms. In fact, using an 8 percent discounting factor, it will take five of these $25,000 yearly net payments to pay back the initial investment—while earning the required rate.

To see this, note that the present value of a $25,000 annuity for 5 years is:

$$\$25,000 \times 3.993 = \$99,825^*$$

---

*Note: The figure 3.993 in this equation is taken from an annuity table, and is based on the 8 percent discount rate and 5-year life of the project.

To show one final instance of why it is important to consider the ever-shrinking worth of dollars promised in the future, consider this same payback example from the perspective of a higher required standard for earnings. The simple payback tells us to go with the Nuprod Co. strategic plan because its economic life (6 years) exceeds the payback period (4 years). At an 8 percent earnings standard, every indication is still go: payback is 5 years and the project should return nice excess value by continuing to produce net value for another full year.

However, what if the earnings standard for the project is nudged up (reasons: cost of capital is higher than 8 percent or there are competing projects of similar size, risk, and economic life that earn more) to 12 percent? Now, present value payback will not occur (keeping this as simple as possible) until 5 years and 9 months pass. You might want to say that this is now too close to call. With only a cushion of three months of earnings, management may be wary of implementing this strategy—the future cannot be known well enough to guarantee that all of their estimates will be on target and on time.

The present value payback period is a means of establishing a minimum life for a strategic initiative. This tool becomes one more way to assess the margin for error in managers' analyses. Also, it sharpens the analysis team's understanding of the relationship between economic life and acceptable performance. Clearly, it is an improved version of the simple payback tool that we first considered. As such, it is a useful companion to the standard net present value technique.

Summary. These examples illustrate how important it is for strategic managers to be adept at applying fundamental tools of financial analysis. Strategic choice is difficult. These techniques help managers array and compare their strategic alternatives when making decisions. In addition, they provide a common language and basis for understanding when managers from different functional areas talk about strategic choice. The tools of analysis discussed in this section are an important part of the manager's skill set.

We do not want to overstate the case, however. Keep in mind that strategic choice is not exclusively a matter of number-crunching analyses. In the end, strategic choices are based on a variety of factors, including financial and nonfinancial considerations. These include the financial tools discussed here and summarized in Table 7-4, as well as factors discussed in the previous chapter, including fit with the organization's mission and situation analysis, the ability to leverage and build competitive advantage, the experience and risk tolerance of the strategic managers, the organizational culture, and concerns about ethics and social responsibility.

FORECASTING THE FINANCIAL RESULTS OF STRATEGIES

An important concern for strategic managers is the question of exactly what the organization's financial reports—its accounting statements—will look like if a particular strategic choice is made. In effect, we are interested in estimating the future financial position of the firm under alternative scenarios regarding strategic initiatives. This requires a future-looking process of turning prospects for profit into actual value creation. That course of action starts with development of pro forma financial statements.

Table 7-4 Financial tools for strategic choice

FINANCIAL TOOL	WHAT DOES IT TELL US?
Payback period	How long it will take before the initial cost of the strategic choice is returned through new net cash inflows.
Rate of return	The strategic choice's investment yield.
Net present value	Value, in today's dollars, of the stream of future net cash inflows reduced by the initial outlay incurred to implement a strategic choice.
Profitability index	Ratio of the present value of net inflows to the present value of net investment outlay.
Internal rate of return	The unique rate of discount that sets the present value of a strategic choice's net inflows equal to its outflow.
Present value payback period	Minimum economic life required to recover a strategic choice's initial outlay—stated in present value terms.

Pro Forma Financial Statements

The heart of the firm's financial plan is contained in its **pro forma financial statements.** These statements are estimates or forecasts of the firm's financial picture. Pro forma statements—the balance sheet, income statement, and statement of cash flows—are enormously versatile accounting reports that can serve at least three very important purposes:

- estimate future free cash flows and cash needs;
- project financing requirements for new projects;
- set targets for performance and assessment of achievements.

Financial projection is a useful simulation of the likely results of both management's broad assumptions about the future and the consequences of strategic plans. The relative ease with which pro forma financial statements and cash flow projections can be developed makes them quite attractive as tools for decision making.

Assumptions About the Future.   To be begin the process of assessing where the firm will be in the not-too-distant future, strategic managers must develop a realistic and supportable set of assumptions about how the factors that impact the firm's performance are expected to change.

Think back to our discussion about the external environment in Chapter 5. Before we can honestly deal with how our company will fare in the future, we must ask questions about the forces in the external environment that affect us. For example, is there specific governmental regulation on the horizon that will impact our business (or that of our near competitors)? Do changing demographics have important effects on our ability to generate revenues? Will technological change, consumer tastes, or general economic conditions impinge on the firm's ability to accomplish its mission and create value? The external audit process will help us answer these questions and identify the factors that we will need to consider in the process of estimating the firm's financial future.

Our projection of the firm's future financial health depends on the validity of the assumptions we make about the external environment. These assumptions must be fully developed and assessed.

Financial and Operating Relationships. The most important ingredient for successful projection of the firm's financial position into the future is a thorough understanding of the fundamental relationships that drive the financial outcomes. While the use and sophistication of computer models and planning spreadsheets is a great boon to the process discussed here, nothing takes the place of management's insight and expertise regarding the actual operation of the firm.

Projecting the Income Statement. There is no magic formula that assures we will be successful in developing projected financial statements. The pro forma income statement, however, is normally the first to be developed for a number of reasons. The operating lifeblood of every business is dollars from sales revenue. Furthermore, the bottom line, net income, is of the utmost concern to business owners. Finally, the connection between sales and all the items that intervene and shrink top-line revenue into bottom-line profit are the major focus for the estimation process. All of this suggests that we tackle the income statement first in the development of pro forma statements.

Sales Forecasts. To begin the process we need to project sales. This figure is crucial because many items in the pro forma are derived from the sales forecast based on their historical relationship to sales as well as assumptions about the future. Deriving the numbers from sales is known as the *percent-of-sales method.*

Sales can be estimated in a number of ways—from sophisticated market and customer studies to extrapolation of prior trends—but the best guide will be past experience adjusted for the expected changes in the external environment and anticipated results of the strategic choices being considered. The sales forecast will need to reflect anticipated changes in both volume and price.

Expense Forecasts. Next we turn to expenses, beginning with cost of sales. The essential elements here are direct labor, direct materials, and overhead. Cost of sales is typically estimated as a percentage of sales (i.e., the percent-of-sales method).

Fortunately, the relationship between sales and cost of sales is typically rather stable, with changes occurring only slightly over time. Much of this stability has to do with the fact that the firm may be able to control the mix of input factors, but can rarely have any significant effect on the prices it pays for these inputs. In the longer run (not generally relevant to this pro forma estimation exercise, unless it is the actual focus of the strategic initiative under consideration) substitution of basic input factors—capital for labor, as an example—may alter the sales to cost of sales relationship, and therefore deserves consideration.

Typically, the percent-of-sales method is applied to obtain the estimates for nearly all the operating expenses described on the income statement as "general and administrative." There tends to be much more variability and discretion, though, with selling expenses. These items may need a projection method that is not a linear extrapolation of the current or prior periods' association with sales.

Below the line of net income from operations, there are two important elements for consideration. Interest costs will depend on the choices made in financing the enterprise and the firm's specific rate structure for credit. There is no expected relationship of these interest costs to dollar volume of sales. Income taxes, on the other hand, tend to be estimable with relative ease because changes in tax rates occur infrequently.

Before attempting to connect the income statement and balance sheet, the issue of distributions of profits to owners should be considered. For contemporary U.S. corporations, there tends to be a very stable, almost rigid, view taken toward dividend policy. In the projection process, unless there is substantial evidence to the contrary, most strategic managers expect that the *payout ratio* (i.e., the proportion of earnings distributed to owners) will change little over time. Certainly, this proposition will not hold for "new economy" companies.

Forecasting the Balance Sheet.   With the income statement projected, we can move to the balance sheet. The link between the company's income statement and its balance sheet is net income. It is still beneficial to project the basic elements of assets and liabilities on the basis of prior proportions as well as relationship to sales. For example, if the firm routinely sells only on credit and historically collects 95 percent of its receivables within 30 days, we have a straightforward way of estimating the balance sheet number once the sales are projected. Likewise, if the company's payables are mainly related to material inputs, and are typically paid within 20 days of purchase, the elements for estimation based on sales are available. As a final example, if there is no plan to change the financing structure of the firm in the near term, then the future debt structure in the projected balance sheet will be known.

When we turn to the balance sheet in this projection process, we have the freedom to solve for either a cash balance or a financing component item (typically, long-term debt). In other words, the balancing nature of this accounting report provides us with the opportunity to have the pro forma statements generate the cash or debt requirement. As we noted above, this is one very useful purpose served by a set of pro forma financial statements.

Cash Flow Projections.   The statement of cash flows is a report that highlights the results of management's financing, investing, and operating decisions by showing the results of cash movements over a period of time. The cash flow statement also is extraordinary in its ability to act as a bridge between the operating statement and the balance sheet. Of course, the best part of all this is that once the other two pro forma statements are completed there is no additional projection work to do—just the conversion of operating, financing, and investing activities to the cash basis for display.

To summarize, pro forma statements are a convenient and relatively easy way of projecting expectations of the company's financial performance. They can be helpful in determining cash and financing needs. To create these statements requires reasonable assumptions about the external environment's impact on the firm and solid reasoning about the financial relationships among the categories in the accounting reports. The reward for developing pro forma statements is a view of the future that strategic managers can use to plan the path for achieving value creation.

Format and Presentation of Pro Forma Statements

Let's consider two additional important questions about the development and presentation of pro forma statements. First, how far ahead should we estimate with our pro forma statements? General rules are difficult to handle in this circumstance, but most analysts would like to project 5 years and are willing to settle for three. As the future unfolds it tells us about the validity of the assumptions that underlie our forecasts. That means that pro forma statements require adjustment, refinement, and revision as the unknown future turns into the certain present and as the present becomes unchangeable history.

The second question is: How will we present the expected impact of new strategies on the pro forma statements? Most strategic managers want to see an estimation of the future without changes compared to each of the viable strategy alternatives being considered for implementation. For example, top management needs to know what the financial staff projects profit will be if no changes are made, if strategy A is implemented, and if strategy B is chosen. Strategies A and B might be complementary, mutually exclusive, or scaleable in a way that both can be implemented. Today's desktop computing capabilities allow managers to consider many "what if" scenarios before a choice is made.

Figure 7-3 shows the format and presentation of a pro forma income statement for the S. T. Mater Company, a hypothetical company operating in the United States. The pro forma is based on the assumptions identified in the notes to the statement. For the sake of simplicity, we make the assumption that S. T. Mater expects stable growth in revenues and expenses until year 3, when a new market development strategy is implemented. The strategy is to expand beyond the domestic market for the first time, entering Mexico. This new strategy means added growth in sales, but also higher selling expenses and new debt, as reflected in the year 3 figures.

Notice the format of Figure 7-3. It begins with actual numbers from S. T. Mater's current period. It is helpful to express these numbers both in units (e.g., dollars) and as a percentage of sales (i.e., common size). Another useful way to present the pro forma is in percent change format, which is not shown in Figure 7-3. From the actual figures, S. T. Mater analysts have projected 3 years into the future. A remarks column or detailed set of footnotes also accompanies the pro forma to identify and explain the assumptions underlying the projections.

The pro forma helps us to evaluate the strategic choice of expanding into Mexico. If our estimates are reasonable, the pro forma suggests that expansion into the Mexican market does not create value, at least not right away. We come to this conclusion not only because our net income declines in year 3 (from $529,000 to $507,000), but also because our net profit margin drops from 11 percent to 9.8 percent. This does not mean we should reject this strategic alternative, however. Notice that we have projected only the first year revenues and expenses for our expansion strategy. Many strategies do not pay off in their first year, as we know. We need to evaluate this strategy over a longer time horizon. The financial tools described previously in this chapter will assist us in this task.

SOURCES OF FUNDS FOR STRATEGIC INITIATIVES

As if strategic managers didn't have enough to do, they also have to be concerned with financing strategic choice, that is, paying for the strategic initiatives. What financial resources will be needed? How much will those resources cost? How will

	S. T. Mater Pro Forma Income Statement				
	Current Year (C)		**C + 1**	**C + 2**	**C + 3**
	Amount	Common Size	Amount	Amount	Amount
	'(000)	(%)	'(000)	'(000)	'(000)
Sales revenue	$4,350	100%	$4,568.00	$4,796.00	$5,180.00
Cost of goods sold:					
Labor, materials, and overhead	$2,536	58.3	2,663	2,796	3,020
Depreciation	144	3.3	151	158	171
Gross profit	1,670	38.4	1,754	1,842	1,989
Selling expenses	$430	9.9	452	475	622
General and administrative expenses	352	8.1	370	388	420
Net operating expense	888	20.4	932	979	947
Interest expense	0	0.0	0	0	8
Profit before taxes	888	20.4	932	979	939
Income taxes	408	9.4	429	450	432
Net income	**480**	**11.0**	**503**	**529**	**507**

Figure 7-3
A pro forma income statement

Notes: Sales growth is forecasted at a rate of 5 percent in years 1 and 2, followed by 8 percent in year 3 when a new market (i.e., Mexico) is entered (these forecasts would be supported by research and analyses).

Cost of goods sold remains constant. Therefore, gross profit margin does not change (38.4 percent of sales) over the 3 years.

Selling expenses increase to 12 percent of sales in year 3 due to the added costs of entering the Mexican market. All other operating expenses remain constant.

To finance expansion into Mexico, a $100,000 loan will be taken in year 3 to defray the costs of purchasing new vehicles for product distribution. The vehicles will have a 10-year useful life. All of this amount could be financed at 8 percent interest. Prior to year 3, S.T. Mater has no debt.

The effective income tax rate holds at 46 percent.

that cost be covered in the short term? In the long term? These and other questions are addressed as part of financial management of the firm. They are also questions that have a bearing on strategic choice.

Because our focus is on strategic management, we concentrate in this section on the long-term, or permanent, financing needs of the firm. We make this decision because the nature and pattern of long-term funding sources is related to the types of strategic initiatives that we have been considering. It is important to recognize that there is a *maturity matching* at work in corporate finance: long-lived resources are financed from long-term sources. In Figure 7-4 we use balance sheet categories to depict the relationship between sources of funds (liabilities and equity) and corporate resources (assets).

Business firms continually seek new financing. At times this is additional financing. Other times this activity is focused on rearranging the financial structure of the

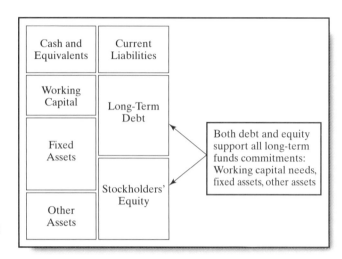

Cash and Equivalents	Current Liabilities
Working Capital	Long-Term Debt
Fixed Assets	
	Stockholders' Equity
Other Assets	

Both debt and equity support all long-term funds commitments: Working capital needs, fixed assets, other assets

Figure 7-4
Long-term funds commitments and sources

firm to change the risk posture (e.g., reduce debt), adjust the maturity profile (e.g., reduce long-term obligations), or reduce the cost of funding the enterprise.

All firms must consider several key elements when facing decisions on how to finance their growth. Paramount among these are (1) cost considerations and (2) risk exposure, and to a lesser extent, (3) flexibility and (4) timing. Obtaining and servicing funds to operate the firm comes at a cost. No holder of wealth will relinquish that holding without compensation of some sort. Banks charge interest on loans and stockholders acquire a share of ownership in the firm. The firm's risk profile—if assessed by the standard of variability of earnings—is impacted directly by the specific cost commitments that each alternative funding source entails. Thirdly, the range of future funding sources (the flexibility element) changes as each new financing decision is put into place. For instance, acquiring more long-term debt today may constrain our ability to borrow in the future. Finally, shifting conditions in the funds markets—most of which are beyond the control of those seeking financing—have an enormous potential to impact the first two elements considered here, namely cost and risk exposure.

Alternative sources of financing are available for firms. Some firms, because of their size, industry or other special attributes, will not be able to avail themselves of every possible source. In general, however, firms use both *internal funding sources* and *external funding sources* to satisfy their needs for cash.

Internal Funding Sources

The most common way for the firm to finance its continuing and incremental activities is through **internal financing.** For simplicity, we define internal sources as any means that management can tap into on its own without going to the financial marketplace for funds. After making any additions desired to working capital, excess internally generated funds are either distributed to owners or used to finance additional long-term productive assets. We consider three main categories for internally generated funds: earnings retention, reallocation of business resources, and deliberate retrenchment.

Recycling Free Cash Flows.   Funds from internal financing are primarily the result of free cash flow from operations. Basically, this is net income plus non-cash charges like depreciation. We say that cash flows are recycled because these excess dollars come from sales that were generated by prior investments in strategic initiatives and productive assets.

Choosing to retain net income and not distribute it to owners in the form of dividends is a conscious decision made by top management. Dividends paid to owners are not available for reinvestment in the business. Certainly, investors' expectations and historic payout policies are important considerations. By and large, though, more funds are raised for financing by this somewhat effortless method than in any other way. Consider the following examples:

- **Lexmark International:** "The [$300 million] capital expenditures are expected to be financed primarily through cash from operations."[3]
- **R. J. Reynolds Tobacco Holdings, Inc.:** "RJR Tobacco plans to spend $70 million to $80 million for capital expenditures during 2001 funded primarily by cash flows from operations."[4]
- **Nabisco Group Holdings Corp.:** "Management also expects that cash flow from operations will be sufficient to support its planned capital expenditures in 2000."[5]
- **Phillip Morris Companies Inc.:** "The 2001 [capital] expenditures are currently expected to be funded from operations."[6]
- **SBC Communications Inc.:** "Net cash provided by operating activities exceeded our construction and capital expenditures during 2000, 1999, and 1998."[7]

Divestment Followed by Reinvestment. Financing for a new strategy can be obtained by selling off a division or piece of the company. Instead of generating sales from consumers, the business raises cash by selling a piece of its operations.

PepsiCo used this financing scheme when it sold its food service division (Pizza Hut, Taco Bell, and KFC) and used some of the funds generated from the sale to purchase Tropicana. We know from Chapter 3 that this is a divestment strategy. In a sense, PepsiCo reallocated its resources. Notice that PepsiCo's management team chose to finance this decision internally by selling part of the firm and reinvesting the proceeds to carry on the mission with a different operating configuration.

Retrenchment. Contrast this divestment-reinvestment strategy with the retrenchment-downsizing one. Here, at least in the short term, the strategic path taken involves actually getting smaller. This shrinking of the firm may be for defensive purposes, as when a division is sold, with the proceeds distributed to owners to fend off an unwanted corporate suitor; the proceeds may be used to pay down debt; or there may be a genuine interest in closing down a piece of the business, as has been seen in financial services industry companies. Increased risk, government regulation, or some other external force may press the strategic management team to adopt this type of plan. Whatever the driving force, retrenchment may result in internally generated funds.

External Funding Sources

There are times when internally generated funds will be insufficient to finance all the firm's strategic alternatives. When this occurs, the firm must either ignore some profitable projects (possibly putting the corporate strategy at risk) or turn to **external financing** for long-term funding.

The strategic managers of most firms choose the latter course of action with the objective of growing the business. Companies that must raise funds externally can turn to investors and lenders to satisfy their needs.

Investors give a company money when they buy securities it issues. These securities, which are generally negotiable, usually take the form of publicly issued debt instruments, equity, or some hybrid combination of these two (such as convertible notes and debentures).

Alternatively, firms may turn to lenders to satisfy their financing needs. The typical vehicle in this case is a commercial bank loan for short- and medium-term credit, and privately placed bonds when long-term borrowing is intended.

Regardless of whether it is derived from securities markets or financial intermediaries, external financing has diminished over the past 25 years as a source for corporate cash needs. Internal financing represents more than 60 percent of all financing sources of U.S. corporations.

Debt Financing Options. Choosing debt as a financing option means adding a clear element of risk to the business. Whether acquired from a financial institution or in the securities market, the cash-for-debt (i.e., cash now for promises to repay in the future) swap creates a legal obligation to pay regardless of the financial health of the firm. The debt servicing cost (interest) is a fixed one that must be met regardless of the firm's ability to generate revenues.

On the other side of this financing-with-debt issue, though, is the highly advantageous opportunity to boost returns by leveraging. In effect, if the firm earns a higher rate of return on borrowed money than the cost of acquiring and using that cash, owners will be rewarded with the spread between these two rates. For example, if the firm can return a profit of 10 percent on every dollar it puts into a strategic initiative, but need only pay a lender 5 percent for use of that dollar, owners will be pleased with management's decision to finance the activity in that way.

Here are some examples of major companies that acquired external financing for their strategic choices through various debt arrangements:

- **Verizon Communications:** "The net cash proceeds from increases in our total debt during 2000 of $5,058 million was primarily due to the issuance of $5,500 million of long-term notes issued by Verizon Global Funding Corp."[8]
- **Crestline Capital Corporation:** "In July 2000, the Company entered into five loan agreements totaling $92.4 million secured by mortgages on eight senior living communities."[9]
- **Visteon:** "Cash provided by financing activities in 2000 included primarily proceeds from the issuance of commercial paper. Cash provided from financing activities in 1999 included primarily additional debt associated with acquisition activities."[10]
- **Host Marriott:** "In October 2000, the Company issued $250,000,000 of 9 ¼ percent Series F senior notes . . . to partially fund the acquisition of Crestline Lessees Entities."[11]

Equity Financing Options. We noted before that most financing for strategic initiatives is from internal sources. Most external financing is in the form of debt. In fact, for nearly all of the period from 1980 through the turn of the century, net new equity issues—stock sold minus stock repurchased by its issuer—was at or below zero.

The predominance of internal financing versus external financing is not accidental. Firms could easily pay out net profits in cash and raise new cash by selling securities to investors in the market or turning to lending institutions. The preference for debt over equity when external financing is used is, likewise, not unintentional. Without regard to the obvious increased risk created by debt, the fact that there is a tax advantage for debt servicing charges easily explains the preference pattern: interest paid on debt is tax deductible, dividends paid to shareholders are not.

Large-scale issuance of new equity in mature industries and by other than start-up enterprises is the least likely means of financing strategic initiatives. When economic activity is high and profits are peaking, it is not unusual to see major corporate acquisitions accomplished with the use of equity as the currency, but firms do not issue new equity whenever the strategic management team selects a new product or process or location for operations. Equity financing tends to be reserved for the big deals that change the whole strategic path of the enterprise.

A summary of the financing options for strategic choice is presented in Table 7-5.

Table 7-5 Financing options for strategic choice

SOURCES OF FUNDS	FUNDS ACQUISITION OPTIONS	
Internal Funds Generation	Retention of net income Divestment with reinvestment Retrenchment	
External Funds Acquisition	Debt incurrence	Financial institution borrowing Public debt securities sale
	Issuance of equity securities	

CONCLUSION

Value creation is ultimately what the strategic management process is all about. The financial management function supports this value-creating focus. In this chapter we have reviewed the finance function in the firm and the various tools that are available to assist managers in making strategic choices. An important part of strategic choice is to project a financial view of the firm as it might appear under alternative strategic choices. Pro forma financial statements are an effective way to do so.

As always, benefits come at a cost. Financing for the strategies selected might come from internal or external sources. External financing sources will involve public and private securities sales. More likely than not, when external financing is sought it will be from creditors—either individual investors or financial institutions—or private lenders.

Once our strategies have been selected, we face the challenging task of implementation. This is the focus of the next two chapters.

KEY TERMS AND CONCEPTS

After reading this chapter you should understand the following terms.

- Capital budgeting
- Capital structure
- External financing
- Financial structure
- Internal financing
- Net Present Value (NPV)

- Payback period
- Present value payback
- Pro forma financial statements
- Rate of return
- Time value of money

DISCUSSION QUESTIONS

1. What is the role of the finance function in strategic management?
2. What financial tools are available to assist with strategic choices? What are the pros and cons of the various tools?
3. What is the purpose of pro forma financial statements? How are they developed and presented?
4. What sources of funding are used to finance strategies? How has demand for the various sources shifted over the past 2 decades? Why?
5. Do you agree or disagree with the following statement: The present value payback technique is the best way to assess the attractiveness of a strategic choice.
6. Use the textbook's Web site to learn more about the current condition of Disney. What recent sources of financing have been used by Disney? Do you think the decisions to use these sources were effective? Explain.

EXPERIENTIAL EXERCISE

Developing a Pro Forma Income Statement. Develop a revised pro forma income statement for S. T. Mator, Inc. (STM) based on the following information.

S. T. Mator, Inc. (STM) is a manufacturer of air filters for lawn mowers. The company has developed the following pro forma income statement for the period ending June 30, 2003 based on the assumption of no new products and a continuation of current trends and growth rates.

Assume that the strategic management team is considering a strategy to extend STM's product line by manufacturing fiber elements for truck and automobile oil filters, and wants to know the projected impact of the strategy on next year's financial results. The new product would be done on a contract basis for a manufacturer of one of the leading oil filter brands now in the marketplace.

The project team provides these data and assumptions on the proposed strategy:

1. A contract could be negotiated for initial yearly output of 1 million fiber elements at 60 cents per unit.
2. New equipment, with a 10-year useful life, would be needed for production. Installed cost would be $400,000. All of this amount could be financed at 9 percent interest.

S. T. Mator, Inc.
Pro Forma Income Statement
For the Period July 1, 2002 to June 30, 2003

	Amount (000)		Common Size (%)	
Sales revenue		$4,350		100.0
Cost of goods sold:				
Labor, materials, and overhead	$2,536		58.3	
Depreciation	144	2,680	3.3	61.6
Gross profit		$1,670		38.4
Selling expenses	$430		9.9	
General and administrative expenses	352	782	8.1	18.0
Profit before taxes		$888		20.4
Income taxes		408		9.4
Net income		$480		11.0

3. Based on engineering and manufacturing estimates, labor, material, and overhead costs of the new product would be approximately 55 percent of the unit selling price.
4. To handle the additional administrative burden of this contract, another office worker would be hired. The yearly employee cost (wages, benefits, taxes) would be $45,000.
5. Unless otherwise stated, assume all historical cost relationships are constant.

ENDNOTES

1. *Annual Report 2000,* Los Angeles: The Walt Disney Company, 2000, 6.
2. The Walt Disney Company, "Investor Relations and Shareholder Services," October 31, 2001, www.disney.go.com/corporate/investors/index_flash.html.
3. Lexmark International, "Year 2000 Form 10-K," March 20, 2001, 18.
4. R. J. Reynolds Tobacco Holdings, "Year 2000 Form 10-K," March 1, 2001, 29.
5. *Annual Report 1999,* New York: Nabisco Group Holdings Corporation, 1999, 34.
6. *2000 Annual Report,* New York: Philip Morris Companies, Inc., 2000, 31.
7. *Annual Report 2000,* San Antonio, TX: SBC Communications, 2000, 18.
8. *Annual Report 2000,* New York: Verizon Communications, 2000, 23.
9. Crestline Capital Corporation, "Year 2000 Form 10-K," March 29, 2001, 35.
10. *Annual Report 2000,* Dearborn, MI: Visteon Corporation, 2000, 18.
11. *Annual Report 2000,* Bethesda, MD: Host Marriott Corporation, 2000, 38.

Chapter 8

Strategy Implementation: Leading People and Change

*K*nown by many as "Big Blue" because of the color of its corporate logo, IBM dominated the computer mainframe business for many years. Big Blue practically owned the market and the IBM name was synonymous with quality and dependability, but IBM lost its stronghold and its success slipped away in the early 1990s as market demand shifted from mainframe computers and IBM was slow to respond. Today, however, Big Blue is back.

The story behind IBM's recovery is the story of a company that transformed itself. It is a story of a company that met the

IBM

IBM (International Business Machines), established as a manufacturer of business machines, today develops and manufactures computer systems, software, networking systems, storage devices, and microelectronics. In recent years consulting has grown to become IBM's second-largest source of revenue. Today IBM is the world's largest information technology (IT) consulting company, with more than 80,000 people providing consulting, systems integration, and solution development services worldwide. To learn more about IBM visit www.ibm.com.

challenge not only by developing a new strategy but also by being able to *implement* the new strategy.

Up to this point in the book we have emphasized the importance of strategy formulation—the steps for developing and choosing good strategies. The success of the strategic management process depends in large part on effective strategic choice, but that is not the end of the process. A well-conceived strategy must also be implemented or put into action, and this is often where strategic management breaks down and fails. According to research, the inability to get things done, to have ideas and decisions implemented, is widespread in organizations today. It is, moreover, a problem that seems to be getting worse in both public and private sector organizations. [1]

Many factors influence the success of strategy implementation. It is possible to group the factors into two broad categories: the human or people issues and the organizational issues. The purpose of this chapter is to discuss the implementation phase of strategic management, focusing on the people issues of managing change. This includes the management style and skills of the leaders, the role of middle managers in the process, overcoming resistance to change, and aligning the culture of the organization with its new strategy. We will examine common reasons for failure of strategy implementation and identify principles of effective implementation. After reading this chapter, you should understand the human side of implementation and be able to answer each of the questions listed in Figure 8-1. The organizational side of implementation will be discussed in Chapter 9.

WHO IS RESPONSIBLE FOR STRATEGY IMPLEMENTATION?

One of the prime functions of a strategic manager is to cope with changes in a firm's external environment in order to ensure its survival and long-term growth.[2] Changes in the organization are often necessary to adapt to these external changes. Hence, the

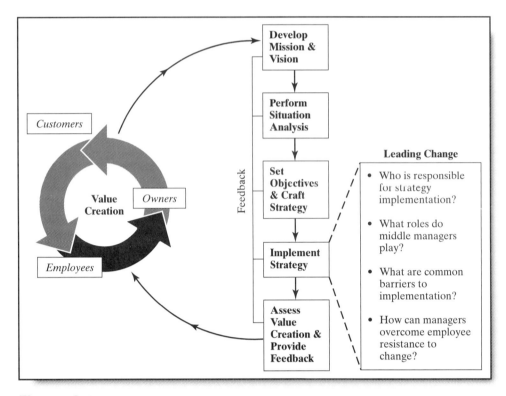

Figure 8-1
The strategic management framework

simple answer to the question of who is responsible for strategy implementation is—everyone. In most organizations, just about everyone plays a role in implementing strategy and creating change within the firm.

In large and diversified companies, corporate strategies at the top of the organization must be supported by business level strategies, which in turn are bolstered by functional level strategies. From top to bottom of the organization, everyone contributes in some way to the effort. Corporate executives team up with vice presidents or senior managers of the divisions to translate corporate objectives into business level priorities. The division managers, in turn, will work with their direct reports (subordinates and peers) to take business level objectives to the functional level. Plans will be developed, programs established, and budgets created. Within each division, functional managers, supervisors, and operating employees have specific goals and responsibilities. Although the strategy may have been formulated by a select group of top managers or by a team of representatives of several or all levels of the organization, the task of implementation usually rests on the shoulders of all employees.

The Roles of Middle Managers

Middle managers play a particularly important role in strategy implementation for two reasons: (1) they are a key source of information for top managers regarding the internal and external environments of the organization, and (2) they are often most directly responsible for overseeing the implementation process within their functional areas. In recent years the number of middle managers in organizations has been reduced due to the advent of new information and communications technologies and the corresponding flattening of organization structures.[3] As organizations become flatter and less hierarchical, however, the strategic importance of middle managers in the implementation of strategies is likely to increase.

Figure 8-2 identifies four roles played by middle managers in strategic management. As the link or liaison between corporate officers and frontline workers, middle managers have the opportunity to exercise their influence either upward or downward in the implementation process. This is reflected in the "direction of influence" column in Figure 8-2. The second column of the figure focuses on the "expected activities of middle managers." These activities are categorized as either *traditional*, whereby middle managers focus on their conventional roles as senior management's agents for strategy implementation, or *entrepreneurial*, whereby middle managers are more active and creative in both developing and implementing strategies and essentially become change agents.[4]

Using these dimensions we obtain four roles played by middle managers. Synthesizing information and implementing deliberate strategies are both traditional roles of middle managers. In the *synthesizing information* role, middle managers assist top managers in constructing the world around them through data gathering and labeling the data as either opportunities or threats[5] so that top managers can analyze the situation in a strategic fashion. *Implementing deliberate strategies* is the most traditional role of middle managers where they take a master strategy created by top managers and lead the frontline workers to execute the envisioned strategies.

In the role of *championing strategic alternatives*, middle managers act more proactively and help to shape the strategies and direction of the organization by using upward influence on senior managers. This role allows middle managers to experiment with new ideas among frontline employees. Similarly, in the *facilitating adaptability* role, middle managers take the strategy from top managers but become innovative in fostering the implementation. They encourage broad-based participation by employees and seek ways to overcome employee resistance to change. These entrepreneurial activities and roles are further discussed later in this chapter.

Figure 8-2
Strategic roles of middle managers

Direction of Influence	Expected Activities of Middle Managers	
	Traditional	Entrepreneurial
Upward	Synthesizing Information	Championing Strategic Alternatives
Downward	Implementing Deliberate Strategies	Facilitating Adaptability

Source: Adapted from Floyd, S. W., and B. Wooldridge, "Dinosaurs or Dynamos? Recognizing Middle Management's Strategic Role," *Academy of Management Executive* 8, no. 4 (1994): 47–57.

Implementation is a complex and sometimes muddled process. It may require major changes in the systems, structure, leadership style, employee behaviors, and resources of the organization, as well as the identification and creation of new core competencies and organizational culture. These change efforts may require a considerable length of time.

Implementation is commonly viewed as a mechanical process where action plans are deduced and carried out by middle managers from a master strategy conceived by top management. Research suggests that the reality is considerably more complex: "Even in fairly stable situations, priorities must be revised as conditions evolve and new information unfolds. Implementation, therefore, is best characterized as an ongoing series of interventions which are only partly anticipated in top management plans and which adjust strategic directions to suit emergent events."[6]

Let's consider an example of successful implementation before introducing a strategy implementation model.

The Transformation of IBM: An Example

For decades IBM sailed along as an undisputed industry leader in manufacturing mainframe computers and creating related software, but during the 1980s and early 1990s, IBM was thrown into turmoil by back-to-back revolutions. First, "the PC revolution placed computers directly in the hands of millions of people. And then, the client/server revolution sought to link all of those PCs with larger computers that labored in the background (the "servers" that served data and applications to client machines). Both revolutions transformed the way customers viewed, used and bought technology. And both fundamentally rocked IBM."[7]

The focus of the market shifted from corporate buyers interested in business applications across the organization to personal productivity and desktop computing. IBM was slow to respond to the shifts, perhaps because it was lulled into complacency by decades of success. IBM seemed locked into an obsolete understanding of the market and an antiquated business strategy. Unable or unwilling to change, IBM's financial performance began to slip.

IBM had difficult years in 1992 and 1993 as shown by the trend analysis of operating margins in Figure 8-3. By 1993 the company's annual net losses reached a record $8 billion. At this point, senior managers gave serious consideration to a strategy that would have split divisions into separate independent businesses. In retrospect it is fortunate that this strategy was not enacted because IBM has successfully reinvented itself and regained its former position as an industry leader.

Once viewed as a conservative and bureaucratic manufacturer known primarily for computer hardware, today IBM is a more responsive and nimble company, known not only as a hardware company but also as a versatile information technology (IT) consulting firm and a leading provider of e-business solutions. These changes reflect a dramatic realignment of IBM's strategy and corporate culture. Table 8-1 reveals the extent of the transformation at IBM. By the end of the 1990s, consulting

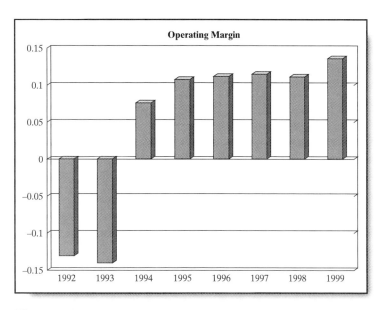

Figure 8-3
IBM operating margins

Source: PriceWaterhouseCoopers, "Edgar Scan Database."
http://edgarscan.pwcglobal.com, accessed March 7, 2001.

was IBM's second-largest source of revenue, up from 11 percent of total revenue in 1992 to 37 percent in 2000. In dollar terms, consulting revenues jumped almost 500 percent during this period, from about $7 billion to $35 billion. Today IBM is the world's largest IT consulting company, with more than 80,000 people providing consulting, systems integration, and solution development services worldwide.

To achieve this transformation, IBM needed to formulate and implement new strategies. What were the keys to successful implementation for IBM? As we will see, IBM needed to address and realign both people and organizational issues to support the new strategy.

Table 8-1 Sources of revenue for IBM

IBM BUSINESS SEGMENTS	1992 % OF TOTAL REVENUE	2000 % OF TOTAL REVENUE
Hardware	52	43
Consulting services	11	37
Software	17	14
Financing	8	5
Other	12	1
Total	100	100

A Strategy Implementation Model

Implementation is like a puzzle. The challenge is to fit the pieces together to support the organization's strategy. Figure 8-4 is a model of the strategy implementation process and illustrates the challenge. A strategy is set first, and people and organizational factors are fashioned around it. For instance, employees are hired or promoted based on their ability to contribute to the strategy. The design of the organization takes shape around the strategy. When the strategy and objectives are changed to take the organization in a new direction, there may be a clash between the old structure and systems and the new strategy. This clash creates a tension in the organization that may result in administrative problems and weakening organizational performance. As employees, structure, and systems adjust and adapt to the new strategy, performance improves and implementation is enhanced.

The case of IBM illustrates the importance of the concept of "fit" or alignment in the implementation process. One of IBM's new strategies was to seek aggressive growth in the IT consulting market, with an objective of becoming the leading worldwide IT consulting company and a powerhouse in providing e-business solutions. Implementing this strategy necessitated changes in staffing—more IT specialists were hired and layoffs were announced in the hardware/mainframe area. These layoffs were particularly difficult for IBM because of its history of promoting and following a no-layoff policy. Furthermore, in 1993 for the first time in its history, IBM hired an outside person as CEO. The corporate culture of IBM was transformed from a rather conservative and even staid, tradition-bound climate to be more nimble, responsive, and flexible. Other changes were made in IBM's structure (to support the growth of consulting) and systems, to name just a few. Failure to realign these implementation factors would have undermined the strategy and perhaps exacerbated

Figure 8-4
An implementation model

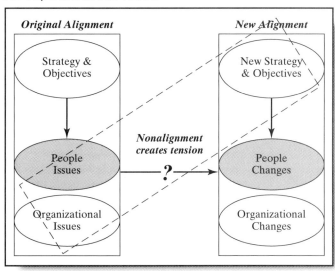

IBM's financial problems. Instead, the realignments were made and IBM's strategy has succeeded.

The Role of Organizational Culture in Implementation

Recall from Chapter 6 that an organization's culture represents the shared values of its members. Culture expresses the underlying beliefs and attitudes of the organization's members and drives their behavior. In Chapter 6 we emphasized the behavioral impact of culture on strategic choice.

Organizational culture also plays an important role in strategy implementation. For example, consider the case of a merger or acquisition, where the results of the strategy depend on whether the merging firms can successfully integrate their cultures. When the two cultures clash, implementation is very difficult. Such was the case when AT&T acquired NCR Inc. (National Cash Register) for $7.48 billion. This acquisition was resisted by NCR management and preceded by an acrimonious relationship. AT&T felt, however, that NCR fit nicely into its long-term strategy of becoming a major force in the information processing industry. Due in part to the clash of cultures, many NCR managers resigned from the merged firm. Five years and more than $3 billion later, AT&T continued to struggle to absorb NCR into its fold. Finally, in 1996 NCR was spun off as an independent firm.

This example illustrates that culture can be a barrier to implementation—but culture can also be a facilitator. A strong organizational culture, where norms, values, and beliefs are clear and shared widely, may make it easier for firms to get the employee buy-in needed to implement strategic changes. Employees are often more willing to embrace the new strategy because a broad consensus within the firm already exists concerning the direction of the firm.[8] On the other hand, when a strong culture becomes rigid and inflexible, it is unable to accommodate change and becomes an impediment to implementation. The implication for managers is that culture is a key implementation variable that must be monitored, managed, and aligned with the strategy to improve its likelihood of success.

Why Does Implementation Fail?

Between the ideal of strategic alignment described above and the reality of successful implementation lie many difficulties. Research shows that some of the most common barriers to implementation are related to people issues, including:[9]

- Unclear strategy or poor communication of strategy
- Top-down or laissez-faire senior management style
- Poor coordination across functions, business activities, or national borders
- Employee resistance to change or inadequate preparation for change

Any one of these factors can be an implementation killer. Let's examine each one and some remedies for avoiding or overcoming the barriers.

Unclear Strategy or Poor Communication of Strategy

Lacking a clear vision and/or strategy and not effectively communicating a strategy are two different problems, but they both can result in failed implementation. In either case, employees are confused and uncertain about what really matters. Priorities are muddled or inconsistent and no clear sense of direction and purpose exists.

An example of this barrier to implementation was described by John Kotter, an expert on managing organizational change. One company developed a four-inch-thick notebook describing its strategic change, complete with procedures, goals, and deadlines. What was lacking, however, was a clear and compelling statement of where this new strategy was leading—the new vision of the future. Instead of inspiring change and rallying the employees, the notebook of details created confusion and frustration.[10]

The problems of miscommunication can take several forms. A common example is when top management believes that one meeting or one announcement of the new strategy is sufficient. This is rarely the case. This mistake is based on the assumption that if top management pronounced the change, it is understood and will be supported. Another common example is when top management fails to "walk the talk." In this case the number and variety of communication efforts may be sufficient to get the message across, but senior managers undermine the power of the message by decisions and actions that fail to support the new strategy. When this occurs, actions speak louder than words, and the real message being sent is antithetical to the new strategy.[11]

To overcome these implementation barriers, strategic managers need to use a variety of communication channels to promote the change—memos, meetings, public speeches, the company newsletter, formal and informal interactions, press releases, and e-mail announcements. In short, strategic managers should look for every opportunity to broadcast and reinforce the message of change and the underlying need for change. Repetition and variety are important.

In addition, managers must lead by example. As we know, communication comes in both words and deeds. Behavior from senior managers that is incongruent with the new strategy can overwhelm all other communication efforts.

Two-way communication is also an important principle of successful strategy implementation. This is discussed in the next section.

Top-Down or Laissez-Faire Senior Management Style

Another barrier to implementation of strategy can be the management style of senior executives. Two common obstacles are a top-down style, which imposes strategic change on employees without adequate attempts to get their buy-in, and a laissez-faire style whereby executives are too isolated and disengaged from the implementation process. Change is a process that needs to be managed. It takes time. Implementation almost always requires the support of employees to carry out the new strategies. Fiats from corporate executives to "change or else" can be an abdication of management's responsibility to take the time to manage change as a process. The same point is true of a hands-off style of management.

Consider the example of a successful mid-sized consulting firm that recently hired a new division manager. The new manager came from a competitor where he had established a strong and successful track record. On arriving at his new company, the division manager (DM) was instructed by the company president to seek growth opportunities for the division. Revenue growth was strong in some segments but had fallen drastically, by almost 50 percent, in one of the division's core markets.

To achieve the growth expected by the president, the new manager embarked on the development of a series of new consulting services and programs based on his experience in the industry and his knowledge of emerging trends. At first the changes were supported by employees, albeit somewhat reluctantly. But when the manager continued to push for more and more new programs, employees began to push back. They resisted for a variety of reasons, but one of the most important ones was their sense of frustration with the manager's top-down style. They felt they had no voice in the strategy process and believed their legitimate concerns about rapid or undisciplined growth and inadequate resources to support the growth were either unheard or ignored. The division manager was astute enough to recognize the warning signals being sent, and he stepped back, slowed down, and listened. This recognition marked the beginning of a change in his management style.

Building a shared vision of the future and an organization-wide commitment to strategic change is not a simple task, nor a task that can usually be accomplished by mandates from senior managers. Two-way communication in the planning process and involvement by employees throughout the organization, and not just at the top, helps to overcome this barrier to implementation. Peter Senge, a leading author and management thinker, contends that the task of designing ongoing processes in which people at every level of the organization can speak openly and participate meaningfully in the planning process is critical because it ultimately determines the quality and the power of the results. "A true shared vision cannot be dictated; it can only emerge from a coherent process of reflection and conversation."[12]

High-Involvement Strategic Planning.   These notions of employee participation make sense in theory, but are they practical? Is it really possible to involve middle managers and operating employees in the strategic management process? New planing tools and techniques are an attempt to do just that. For example, **high-involvement planning,** also known as *direct participation,* is an inclusive approach to the strategic management process.[13] The approach is achieved by moving away from the top-down, control-oriented model of planning to a process that encourages the participation and ideas of middle managers and frontline employees such as sales representatives, engineers, and operating employees.

By engaging larger numbers of employees in the planning process, high-involvement planning seeks to achieve the goals of better strategy by tapping into the creative ideas of employees, and better implementation by fostering employee buy-in to the outcomes of the process. Furthermore, the process views frontline employees as vital strategic resources instead of mere factors of production. It is based on the premise that corporate executives cannot afford to be isolated from the people in their organizations if they are to compete in today's ever-changing world of business.[14]

Including all employees in the process may not be realistic due to the prohibitive costs in time and money of full participation, and the lack of enthusiasm for participation by some employees. Instead, the goal is to create a **hierarchy of imagination.**[15] The conventional view is that strategic decision making is the domain of top management but the hierarchy of imagination concept stresses the importance of including key people from each level of the organization in the planning process, as shown in Figure 8-5. This process can only work with a management style based on information sharing and two-way communication.

Several models of high-involvement planning exist, many involving large numbers of employees in a planning conference that extends over a few days, usually at an off-site location. These models tend to follow a three-stage process of planning the conference, conducting it, and following up after the completion of the conference. Typical steps within each stage are identified in Figure 8-6.

Successful high-involvement approaches normally have the following characteristics:[16]

- A compelling need for change within the organization
- Clearly defined goals, problems, issues, or opportunities to address
- Involvement of employees from all levels and functions of the organization
- Visible commitment and active participation of senior executives
- Availability of relevant information to make informed analyses
- Follow-up and accountability for action plans that are generated

High-involvement planning does not mean that strategic choice becomes a shared responsibility or that all employees will make strategic decisions. That is still the ultimate responsibility of senior managers. What it does mean, however, is that through their participation, employees have a voice in the process and a clearer understanding of how and why strategic choices were made.

A specific model of high-involvement planning is the *Future Search Model,* developed by Marvin Weisbord.[17] This technique is further described in the appendix to this chapter.

In summary, high-involvement planning is important not only as a way to tap into the innovative ideas of employees, but for its ability to foster real-time strategic change. The openness, two-way communication, and active participation of employ-

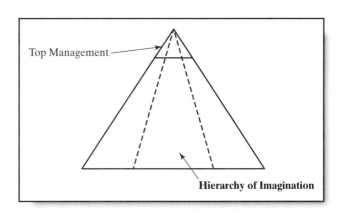

Figure 8-5
The hierarchy of imagination

Source: Hamel, G. "The New Context and Conduct of Strategy," August 11, 1997. (paper presented at the national meeting of the Academy of Management, Boston, MA, 1997). Used with permission of Dr. Gary Harmel of the Academy of Management Presentation.

Figure 8-6
The stages of high-involvement planning

STAGE 1: PRE-CONFERENCE PREPARATION	STAGE 2: CONDUCT CONFERENCE	STAGE 3: FOLLOW-UP
• Form a steering group to design and lead the conference	• Open the conference by framing the issues and encouraging active participation	• Communicate the outcomes of the conference
• Define the purpose of the conference	• Create a sense of openness, community, and trust	• Define the roles and responsibilities for the changes
• Define the boundaries of the discussion, including what is off limits	• Use planning techniques designed to engage the whole group	• Make resources available to support change efforts
• Select, invite, and prepare participants	• Define the changes needed in the organization	• Stress accountability
• Arrange for logistics of the conference		• Monitor change, communicate ongoing process, and call for more change

ees, which characterize the process, are important approaches for overcoming the barriers to implementation associated with a top-down management style.[18]

Poor Coordination Across Functions, Business Activities, or National Borders

A third barrier to implementation is a lack of coordination within the organization. Strategy implementation is a cross-functional endeavor requiring different parts of the organization to work in harmony. For example, a new product launch depends on the coordination of efforts between the R&D function that develops the new product prototype, the manufacturing function that adjusts its systems to produce the product, and the marketing and sales functions that promote and sell it. This cooperation is known as horizontal alignment and is discussed in detail in the next chapter.

In this chapter we focus on another type of required coordination that is particularly important in the case of international companies—cooperation across national borders. As companies grow and as the business environment becomes increasingly global, transactions across national borders are very common. As this trend continues, the ability to work effectively with people from other cultures is paramount. This skill depends on the ability to understand and adapt to differences in *national culture,* reflected in how people from other parts of the world think, work, and what they value. Failure to be culturally competent is a recipe for disastrous strategy implementation.

An example will help to clarify this point. A product manager for a large pharmaceutical company based in the United States had global responsibility for various aspects of a new over-the-counter health care product launch.[19] This project included working with an affiliate company in the Netherlands to prepare a marketing campaign. The project was urgent because it was known that a competitor was developing a similar product and each company wanted the first-mover advantage.

Because time was short, the American manager worked long hours and expected her counterpart in the Netherlands to do the same. The harder she worked the more frustrated she became with the seemingly slow pace and lack of responsiveness of her Dutch partner. Finally, one morning she became enraged when she was unable to get a critical piece of information from her colleague who had left the office for the day and was not answering his cell phone.

Why did this happen? What was the reason for the apparent disconnect between the two colleagues? Perhaps the American's expectations were unreasonable. Perhaps the Dutchman was unmotivated. Perhaps the explanation was simply the time difference between the two countries. These are all plausible explanations and there are others, but what about the possibility of a cultural clash? Could this be the result of two people dealing with the same situation from two completely different sets of cultural values? Let's look at the research data.

Studies have shown that management concepts and theories are not universal. What works in one country or region (e.g., the United States) may be completely ineffective in another (e.g., the Netherlands) due to the cultural differences of the people involved. Culture is a constraint that impacts the practice of management. Geert Hofstede, an authority on the subject, has completed a series of studies on cultural variables in management and found that cultural values differ along several key dimensions, including:[20]

- **Power distance**—the degree of inequality between people in a culture that is considered normal and acceptable. This might be reflected in the extent to which differences in power and decision-making authority exist within organizations in a particular culture.
- **Individualism**—the degree to which people in a country prefer to act as individuals rather than as members of a group. *Collectivism,* the counterpart of individualism, is evident in cultures that value loyalty to the group.
- **Competitiveness**—the extent to which tough values like aggressiveness, results, assertiveness, and performance are emphasized versus more nurturing values like service, care for the disadvantaged, quality of life, and personal relationships. Cultures high in competitiveness are more task oriented than relationship oriented.
- **Uncertainty avoidance**—the degree of discomfort associated with risk-taking and ambiguity. Cultures high in uncertainty avoidance are risk averse and prefer clear rules and structure. Low uncertainty avoidance suggests a greater willingness to take a chance, to explore, and to accept change.

Hofstede's research shows that these variables differ from one culture to another and help to explain why certain management practices may work in one culture and not in another. Of course, not all differences can be accounted for by cultural variations. Individuals within cultures have their own unique ideas and experiences that impact their behavior. Furthermore, there is the impact of corporate culture, as mentioned above, on behavior. Nevertheless, these cultural dimensions are important factors in understanding how to manage across national and regional borders.

Table 8-2 lists the scores of several countries and one region on the cultural dimensions. This data is important because cultural competence is not based simply on being aware that cultural differences exist or that there are various dimensions of culture, but on being able to pinpoint the differences and then take the steps necessary to adapt. Cultural competence depends on this three-step process: (1) awareness of differences in cultural values and norms, (2) positioning one's own culture relative to your counterpart, and (3) adapting to the differences to facilitate exchange and cooperation.

Let's return to the example involving the American and Dutch colleagues working on the new product launch. Recall that the American manager was frustrated by her Dutch counterpart who seemed to lack her sense of urgency to beat the competitor to the market. We can use the data from Table 8-2 to diagnose the potential impact of cultural differences in this case. The data suggests that the United States and the Netherlands are similar on three of the four cultural dimensions, but very different on the dimension of competitiveness. This difference might account for the contrasting approaches taken by the colleagues—an aggressive and task-oriented approach versus a more relaxed and relationship-oriented style. Let's assume for now that it does, and that we'd like to apply the three-step process of cultural competence from the perspective of the American. What could she do to work more effectively with her counterpart?

Step one is *awareness*—being cognizant of the potential impact of culture. Step two is *positioning*—examining the data and pinpointing the specific areas were the American and Dutch cultures are most likely to clash, in this case on the dimension of competitiveness. Step three is *adapting*—deciding how to adjust to the differences to increase the chances of an effective and productive working relationship. The three-step process encourages the American to realize that culture matters and that she may be well served by taking the time to first establish a good personal rapport and working relationship with her Dutch counterpart.

Knowledge of Hofstede's cultural dimensions is important but not necessarily sufficient for **cultural competence.** Other cultural variables may also play a role in

Table 8-2 Dimensions of culture

	PD	ID	CO	UA
United States	40 L	91 H	62 H	46 L
Netherlands	38 L	80 H	14 L	53 M
Germany	35 L	67 H	66 H	65 M
Japan	54 M	46 M	95 H	92 H
France	68 H	71 H	43 M	86 H
West Africa	77 H	20 L	46 M	54 M

Notes: PD = power distance; ID = individualism; CO = competitiveness; UA = uncertainty avoidance; H = top third; M = middle third; L = bottom third (among 53 countries and regions).
Source: Adapted from Hofstede, G. "Cultural Constraints of Management Theories," *Academy of Management Executive* 7, no. 1 (1993): 91.

achieving cross-cultural cooperation. Take the case of Germany. The American and German managerial models are very different in some ways, although these differences are not reflected in the cultural dimensions in Table 8-2. The German model of "codetermination" requires employee participation on the company's board of directors and representation in the board's decision making. As a result, German managers must eschew autocratic directives in favor of consensus among bosses and workers. Mergers, acquisitions, strategic alliances, and other forms of partnership between German and U. S. companies must take these differences into account.

Employee Resistance to Change or Inadequate Preparation for Change

The fourth and final barrier to implementation discussed in this chapter is employee resistance to change or lack of preparation for change. This problem may be the result of an autocratic, top-down management style, the second barrier discussed above, or it may surface despite senior management's best efforts to involve employees using a more participative management style. In any case, the end result is the same—incomplete and flawed implementation.

Research suggests that employee resistance is not an inevitable by-product of change. It is, however, a common response, especially when the change is large scale, ambiguous, or threatening. Reasons for resistance are many and include:

- loss of control,
- fear of the unknown,
- lack of confidence to adapt to the new demands of the change,
- an ever-increasing workload,
- past resentments and distrust toward management,
- loss of status or job security for the employee.[21]

Consider the following example. Robert was an accountant specializing in corporate tax for a large firm. He had been with the same firm for 8 years, since his college graduation. He was a respected employee who had steadily advanced within his firm. One night after a tiring day at work, he sat down to relax and watch the late news. What he learned was anything but relaxing—it was reported that his firm had agreed to merge with an equally large competitor. The consolidation of the industry was an ongoing trend and mergers were commonplace, but this was different. For the first time it was his firm and involved him personally. Furthermore, the announcement was completely unexpected; he had no prior knowledge of the merger.

Robert felt numb. "It couldn't be true," he told himself. "We're a strong and successful firm. We don't need to merge. It's all a mistake. It won't happen. I'm sure it will fall through." It didn't take long for Robert to realize that it wasn't a mistake—it was real. It was several days before he overcame his initial shock. When he did he was angry. "How could they do this?" he muttered to himself. "Can't they see they're going to ruin the firm? This is ridiculous!" After a few weeks Robert's anger and frustration eventually dissipated and were followed by a period of reflection. His mind-set changed from anger to questioning. "What will I do? What does the merger mean for me and my future here at the firm? Is there still a place for me and can I continue to advance? Should I update my resume and explore new opportunities?"

Robert's reaction to the merger is an example of resistance to change and inadequate preparation for change. It is also a typical reaction to unwanted change. Research shows that people often experience a predictable emotional and psychological response to threatening change. This four-phase response—avoidance, resistance, exploration, and commitment—is shown in Figure 8-7.[22]

Of course, not all change is resisted. In fact, it is sometimes welcomed and embraced. But when it comes to threatening and unexpected change, this four-phase response is common. The first phase is **avoidance.** As in our example of Robert above, avoidance is characterized by withdrawal and by a feeling of numbness and a sense of denial. Avoidance is a passive form of opposition while the second stage, **resistance,** is more active. Negative emotions run high in the resistance phase, including anger, frustration, disgust, anxiety, and in extreme cases, even hostility. During these first two phases, the individual continues to focus on the past, on what was and how it might be preserved. A breakthrough occurs in the third stage when the employee begins to accept that the future will be different and trying to cling to the past is a fruitless effort. Robert entered the **exploration** phase when he began to question the impact of the merger on his future with the firm. Confusion and a lack of clear focus remain but at least an awakening to a new reality has set in. During resistance and exploration the individual's focus turns inward on the personal impact of change. During the final phase, **commitment,** the focus shifts outward to the causes and effects of change throughout the organization. The employee's focus is much clearer and broader. He or she is now ready to accept the change, adapt, and move forward.

When faced with threatening change, most people will move through each of these stages, though not necessarily in strict sequence or at the same pace. Some people will bounce back and forth between stages. Furthermore, the timing of the movement may be different for each person. Some will transition through rather quickly in days or even hours, while others may get bogged down for weeks or more in a particular

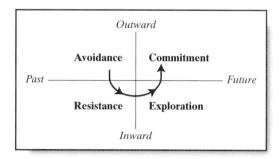

Figure 8-7
A four-phase reaction to change
Source: Adapted from Scott, C. D. and D. T. Jaffe. *Managing Organizational Change: A Practical Guide for Managers.* Menlo Park, California: Crisp Publications, Inc., 1989, 26.

phase.[23] To complicate the transition even further, the manager(s) in charge of leading the change may be struggling with the same emotional reactions.

Leaders of strategic change, at all levels of the organization, play a key role in determining how quickly the transition from avoidance to commitment occurs. Fortunately, there are actions managers can take to facilitate the process. For example, during avoidance, communicate openly and often with employees. Let them know that the change will happen, what to expect, and how they might adjust. Provide as much information as possible, as soon as possible. Lacking information, employees often assume the worst. Anxiety, stress, and frustration will only build if information is withheld.

During the resistance phase, give employees some freedom to express their concerns and fears. Talk to them in person; do not rely exclusively on memos, e-mail, and other impersonal means of communicating during a difficult change. Listen carefully and respond with empathy as employees work through their anxieties. Insist that employees understand the reasons for the change and its expected benefits.

In the third phase, exploration, employees begin to realize their need to adjust and adapt, but they may be unclear about how to do so. Managers of change can help by working with employees to establish priorities and short-term goals. Seek ways to regain the team's focus. If the change means that employees need to acquire new skills and knowledge, programs for training and development should be discussed and planned. Involving employees in these discussions may help to allay their fears and send the message that the company wants to invest in their future.

Finally, in the commitment phase, employees have moved on to accept the change. New behaviors and practices have been established; cooperation and teamwork are evident. This is a victory worth celebrating. Recognize and appreciate the employees who have made the transition. They have learned and adapted. They have successfully overcome one of the most difficult barriers to implementation—employee resistance to change.

Leaders of change need good coaching skills. With good coaching and appropriate training programs (if necessary), most employees will adapt to change, even major and threatening change. It may be necessary, however, to hire new employees and/or replace those who cannot or will not commit to change. Organizations must learn and adapt to survive. Employees who refuse to change despite appropriate efforts by leaders of change are jeopardizing the organization and their own future in it. They do so at their own risk.

Successful Strategy Implementation: The People Issues

In the previous section we emphasized a variety of barriers to strategy implementation and mentioned several ways to deal with the barriers. Strategy implementation is a bad news–good news scenario. The bad news is that implementing change can be a complex, time-consuming, and challenging process, as we have stated. Even successful change efforts are fraught with surprises and frustrations, but the good news is that there are principles for managing people through the change process that leaders can rely on to facilitate implementation. In this section we discuss those principles.

Organizational change is typically viewed as a three-part process known as unfreezing, changing, and refreezing.[24] During the **unfreezing** phase, the organization must disengage from its past, understand the reasons for change, and prepare itself for transformation. Next, the organization creates and embraces a new vision of the future and takes steps necessary to achieve that new vision. In the **refreezing** state, new policies, practices, systems, and structures are put into place to institutionalize the change.

A stream of research studies over a period of decades has resulted in a set of principles or steps for managing the transition from unfreezing to refreezing.[25] These principles have become recommended procedures for any organization attempting to implement significant strategic change. Let's take a closer look at several of the principles (see Table 8-3).

Because change is inevitable in today's dynamic and competitive business environment, managers would do well to understand and practice these principles for implementing change. While the list is not exhaustive, it does identify many steps that can mean the difference between implementation success and failure.

Table 8-3 Principles for implementing change

- Establish a sense of urgency: Analyze and explain the need for change. If the situation is urgent, let people know. Identify and discuss crises, potential crises, or major opportunities. If it is not urgent, however, don't attempt to create a false sense of urgency.
- Communicate early, often, and in person: Whenever possible, communicate openly. Full disclosure may not always be possible but it is the ideal.
- Involve people in the process: Form a guiding coalition with enough power to lead the change effort. Encourage the group to work together as a team. Give employees a personal stake in the outcome of the change and provide employees with the training they need. Consider using a high-involvement planning process.
- Create and communicate a shared vision of the future: Develop a statement of strategic direction that articulates the links between the organization's competitive environment, its new strategies, and the organizational changes needed to realize the goals of the strategies. Use every vehicle possible to communicate the new vision and strategies.
- Develop an implementation plan: Define roles, responsibilities, deadlines, and resource requirements for change. Work with employees to establish the plan and to develop a sense of partnership.
- Anticipate and remove barriers to change: Encourage new ideas and behaviors and change systems, policies, and structures that undermine the new strategies. Hire, promote, and develop employees who can implement the new strategies.
- Reinforce and institutionalize new approaches: Articulate the connections between the new behaviors and corporate success. Plan for and create short-term wins. Recognize and reward employees involved in the improvements.

Source: This list was adapted from three sources: Kotter, J. P., "Leading Change: Why Transformation Efforts Fail," *Harvard Business Review* (March–April 1995): 59–67; Kanter, R. M., B. A. Stein, and T. D. Jick, "The Challenge of Execution: Roles and Tasks in the Change Process," *In the Challenge of Organizational Change,* New York: Free Press, 1992, 369–394; and Beer, M., and R. A. Eisenstat, "The Silent Killers of Strategy Implementation and Learning," *Sloan Management Review* (summer 2000): 29–40.

In applying the principles to their organizations, leaders of change will need to consider the unique circumstances they face and adapt accordingly. For instance, consider the first principle in Table 8-3—creating a sense of urgency. There are many ways this can be accomplished. One way is to circulate data about customer satisfaction and financial performance to more managers and employees, especially information that demonstrates weaknesses. Similarly, organizations can insist that more employees speak directly with dissatisfied customers or disgruntled stockholders. Providing people with information on future opportunities and on the organization's current inability to pursue those opportunities, or exposing organizational weaknesses relative to key competitors can also raise the sense of urgency within the organization.[26] As we have consistently emphasized, value creation is the barometer of successful strategic management. Failure to create value should trigger a sense of urgency in the organization.

CONCLUSION

IBM continues to transform itself by accelerating its growth in consulting services and e-business solutions and cutting back in other less profitable areas such as retail sales of PCs. IBM's new vision and strategies have been supported by a large-scale realignment of both people and organizational factors within the company. In this chapter we have identified and discussed the people issues of implementation. In the next chapter we turn our attention to the organizational issues.

KEY TERMS AND CONCEPTS

After reading this chapter you should understand each of the following terms.

- Avoidance
- Commitment
- Competitiveness
- Corporate culture
- Cultural competence
- Exploration
- Hierarchy of imagination

- High-involvement planning
- Individualism
- Power distance
- Refreezing
- Resistance
- Uncertainty avoidance
- Unfreezing

DISCUSSION QUESTIONS

1. Who is responsible for strategy implementation? What roles do middle managers play in implementation?
2. Discuss the importance of alignment in strategy implementation. Identify the people factors to be aligned.
3. Discuss how the management style of senior executives can be a barrier to implementation and what can be done to overcome this barrier.
4. What is high-involvement planning and under what conditions is this approach most likely to succeed?

5. Identify and explain Hofstede's four dimensions of culture and how they may be used to facilitate implementation across national borders.
6. Why is employee resistance to change a common implementation barrier? What can be done to address this barrier?

EXPERIENTIAL EXERCISE

Managing Strategic Change. Research a company that attempted—either successfully or unsuccessfully—to transform itself by developing and implementing a major change in strategy. Provide all relevant details. Critique the implementation efforts and approach used by the company. What does your analysis tell you about effective strategy implementation?

ENDNOTES

1. Pfeffer, J. *Managing with Power.* Boston, MA: Harvard Business School Press, 1992, 7.
2. Chandler, A. D. *Strategy and Structure: Chapters in the History of the American Industrial Enterprise.* Cambridge, MA: MIT Press, 1962; Lawrence, P. R., and J. W. Lorsch. *Organization and Environment: Managing Differentiation and Integration.* Homewood, IL: Richard D. Irwin, 1969.
3. Floyd, S. W., and B. Wooldridge, "Dinosaurs or Dynamos? Recognizing Middle Management's Strategic Role," *Academy of Management Executive* 8, no. 4 (1994): 47–57.
4. Joshi, M. P. "Implementing Strategic Change: Styles Used by Middle Managers." Unpublished Dissertation, Fox School of Business and Management, Temple University, Philadelphia, PA, 1996.
5. Floyd, S. W., and B. Wooldridge, "Dinosaurs or Dynamos? Recognizing Middle Management's Strategic Role," *Academy of Management Executive* 8, no. 4 (1994): 47–57.
6. Floyd, S. W., and B. Wooldridge, "Dinosaurs or Dynamos? Recognizing Middle Management's Strategic Role," *Academy of Management Executive* 8, no. 4 (1994): 51.
7. IBM, "IBM Archives: A History of Innovation," November 2, 2001, www.ibm.com/ibm/history/story/era4.html.
8. Joshi, M. P., and R. D. Hamilton. "The Use of Participative Style by Middle Managers in Implementing Strategic Change: The Role of Organizational, Economic, and Individual Perceptual Factors," working paper series # 01-03, 2001, Saint Joseph's University, Haub School of Business.
9. Beer, M., and R. A. Eisenstat, "The Silent Killers of Strategy Implementation and Learning," *Sloan Management Review* (summer 2000): 29–40.
10. Kotter, J., "Leading Change: Why Transformation Efforts Fail," *Harvard Business Review* (March–April 1995): 63.
11. Kotter, J., "Leading Change: Why Transformation Efforts Fail," *Harvard Business Review,* (March–April 1995): 63.
12. Senge, P. M., C. Roberts, R. Ross, B. Smith, and A. Kleiner. *The Fifth Discipline Fieldbook: Strategies and Tools for Building a Learning Organization.* New York: Doubleday/Currency, 1994.
13. For a good description of how one large company, Chevron Corporation, used the direct participation approach, see Ellis, C. M., and E. M. Norman, "Real Change in Real Time," *Management Review* (February 1999): 33–38.
14. Bartlett, C. A., and S. Ghoshal, "Changing the Role of Top Management: Beyond Systems to People," *Harvard Business Review* (May–June 1995): 142.

15. Hamel, G. "The New Context and Conduct of Strategy," August 11, 1997. (paper presented at the national meeting of the Academy of Management, Boston, MA, 1997).
16. Ellis, C. M., and E. M. Norman, "Real Change in Real Time," *Management Review* (February 1999): 36.
17. Weisbord, M. *Discovering Common Ground.* San Francisco: Berrett-Koehler, 1992.
18. Jacobs, R. W. *Real Time Strategic Change: How to Involve an Entire Organization in Fast and Far-Reaching Change.* San Francisco: Berrett-Koehler, 1994. Robert Jacobs published a book entitled *Real-Time Strategic Change,* which extols the benefits of high-involvement planning. The book emphasizes that high-involvement planning is built on principles that address several of the keys to successful change management.
19. This example is based on a case study found in Brake, T., and K. Sullivan, *Doing Business Internationally: The Cross-Cultural Challenges.* Princeton, NJ: Princeton Training Press, 1992, 2–26.
20. Hofstede's research on the cultural dimensions of management has extended over many years. His studies include Hofstede, G., "National Cultures in Four Dimensions: A Research-Based Theory of Cultural Differences Among Nations," *International Studies of Management & Organization* 13, no. 1–2 (1983): 46–75; and Hofstede, G., "Cultural Constraints in Management Theories," *Academy of Management Executive* 7, no. 1 (1993): 81–94.
21. Kanter, R. M., B. A. Stein, and T. D. Jick. *The Challenge of Organizational Change.* New York: The Free Press, 1992, 380.
22. This pattern is illustrated and described in video and text form by Scott, C., and D. Jaffe, *Managing Organizational Change: A Practical Guide for Managers.* Menlo Park, CA: Crisp Publications, Inc., 1989.
23. Scott, C., and D. Jaffe, *Managing Organizational Change: A Practical Guide for Managers.* Menlo Park, CA: Crisp Publications, Inc., 1989, 26.
24. The three-part model was originally developed and explained in Lewin, K., "Frontiers in Group Dynamics," *Human Relations* 1 (1947): 5–41. Since the time of this publication the model has been developed and expanded and new terminology has been used to describe the three parts of the process. The essence of the model, however, has remained relatively unchanged.
25. For a good overview of this stream of research on change management, see Kanter, R. M., B. A. Stein, and T. D. Jick. *The Challenge of Organizational Change.* New York: The Free Press, 1992.
26. Kotter, J., "Leading Change: Why Transformation Efforts Fail," *Harvard Business Review* (March–April 1995): 63.

Appendix 8A
*The Future Search Model**

Described, in outline form, is the *Future Search* model. This approach has been used in many settings with many different types of organizations (business, nonprofits, education, health care, etc.). The approach is designed to involve multiple stakeholders, both internal and external to the organization, in the planning process. As described, the process takes place over 2.5 days, although this can be modified to suit the needs and constraints of the organization. Weisbord has found that the approach works best with 25 to 60 participants when the organization is in a period of transition and organizational leaders are visible and engaged in the process.

A diagram of the process is shown in Figure 8A-1. Keep in mind that the diagram is an outline not a prescription; the specific design of the process will need to be adapted to the organization's unique circumstances.

DAY I: AFTERNOON
Focus on the Past

Who we are, where we have been, how we view world trends, what we want for the future.

Typical tasks: Three lists written on newsprint and posted on the wall: Self, World, Organization (or Sector, Community, etc. as appropriate).

Each person notes milestones and trends over a given number of years and records their items on the newsprint. Mixed stakeholder groups analyze the items and report (1) similarities, differences, and values, (2) probable and ideal futures (world, sector). Agreed upon conclusions are noted (look for "common ground").

Purposes of Phase: (1) Promote shared leadership. Every person in the room is writing on flip charts within 45 minutes of the start, thus making real that all have contributions to make. All flip charts remain on the walls throughout. (2) Build community quickly (people appreciate facts of each others' lives, recognize common needs, etc). (3) Establish global context for local issues (e.g., Think globally, act locally).

DAY 2: MORNING
Focus on the Present (External)

Make a group "mind map" of world trends as they affect the organization/issue being studied (e.g., ask the question: What external factors are affecting our organization's ability to achieve excellence?). Each person indicates on the map his/her own priorities. Then, stakeholder groups (i.e., groups with common interests or roles) analyze the map for (1) important priorities to us, (2) what we (i.e., the organization) are doing now, and (3) what we need to do in the future. All groups report and similarities and differences in perception are noted and discussed.

Purposes of phase: (1) Discover impact of current world trends on stakeholders, how each group is responding, and what they want for the future. (2) Establish future priorities and discern interdependencies.

Focus on the Present (Internal)

Each stakeholder group lists current "prouds" (i.e., what we feel good about) and "sorries" (i.e., recent regrets) regarding the organization.

---

*Marvin Weisbord, author of *Discovering Common Ground* (San Francisco: Berrett-Koehler, 1992), describes the practice and pitfalls of "Future Search" conferences. I am indebted to consultants Rod Napier and Pat Sanaghan for introducing us to this, and many other, interactive planning models. Napier and Sanaghan, along with Clint Sidle, have published a book on the topic (*Tools and Activities for Strategic Planning,* New York: McGraw-Hill, 1997).

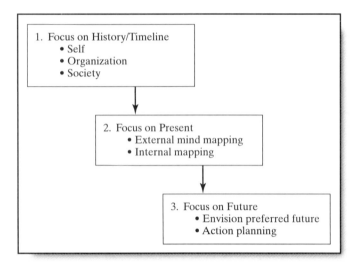

Figure 8A-1
The future search process

1. Focus on History/Timeline
   • Self
   • Organization
   • Society

2. Focus on Present
   • External mind mapping
   • Internal mapping

3. Focus on Future
   • Envision preferred future
   • Action planning

They indicate which they want to continue, drop, or enhance in the future. Lists are posted and discussed.

Purposes of phase: (1) Discover values (what's important) for each group. (2) Discern "current reality" (our perceived pluses and minuses).

DAY 2: AFTERNOON
Focus on the Future

Mixed stakeholder groups imagine ideal future scenarios. They travel into the future and choose a way of dramatizing what they find (e.g., a *60 Minutes* segment, or a play, or a *Fortune* cover story that features their organization and its accomplishments). They report concrete details as if they have already happened or are happening right now. They build in values, practices, and policies derived from earlier phases.

Volunteers observe common and unique features of all scenarios and present them for group discussion and validation.

Purposes of phase: (1) Provide value-based, hopeful foundation for immediate action plan-

ning. Discover what people really want to spend their time on now ("Today is yesterday's future"). (2) Think systemically about the whole, rather than the problems. (3) Engage in purposeful dialogue across all boundaries.

DAY 3: MORNING
A Consensus Scenario

Common features are highlighted and validated by the whole group. Groups are asked to consider which unique features they would like to incorporate into the common scenario. This document becomes the ideal preferred future.

Action Planning: Volunteers or stakeholder groups make long- and short-range action plans to start implementing the ideal strategic future. Their plans are reported to the conference before closing and plans are made for collecting and disseminating the learning and documents.

Purpose: To act together now on whatever common ground has been discovered leading to the ideal futures.

Chapter

9

Strategy Implementation: Managing the Organizational Issues

*S*outhwest Airlines is America's most efficient and profitable major airline. The airline has grown from 195 employees and three planes that flew between three cities within Texas in 1971 to the fourth largest U.S. domestic carrier with over 30,000 employees and a fleet of more than 340 planes. Southwest is the only major airline to make a profit every year for the last 28 years.

Southwest's success in being a lean, mean flying machine[1] is attributed to its ability to successfully implement its low cost strategy and provide a service that customers value. This chapter will help you understand Southwest's success in implementing their strategy.

In the previous chapter we examined the people issues of strategy implementation. The purpose of this chapter is to focus on the *organizational* side of implementation, emphasizing the need for project planning, strategy-systems alignment, and the role of organizational structure and design. International aspects of strategy implementation are also examined.

We proceed by first discussing the importance of project management in strategy implementation. Next, we consider the importance of various functional areas in carrying out the programs, policies, and plans that support a company's overall strategy and help in creating value for customers. The concepts of vertical (across levels) and horizontal (across functions) alignment and their role in successful strategy implementation are discussed. Later we look at how strategy is successfully implemented through a compatible organizational design that helps coordinate activities effectively throughout the organization. The relationship between strategy and structure is emphasized. Lastly, we examine different ways of creating international alliances for successful implementation of strategy. After reading this chapter, you should be able to answer each of the questions listed in Figure 9-1 regarding strategy implementation.

KEYS TO SUCCESSFUL IMPLEMENTATION: THE ORGANIZATIONAL ISSUES

In Chapter 8 we introduced the model of implementation shown in Figure 9-2, emphasizing the people issues of the process. As Figure 9-2 suggests, successful implementation also requires attention to organizational issues, the focus of this chapter. Let's take a closer look at these issues.

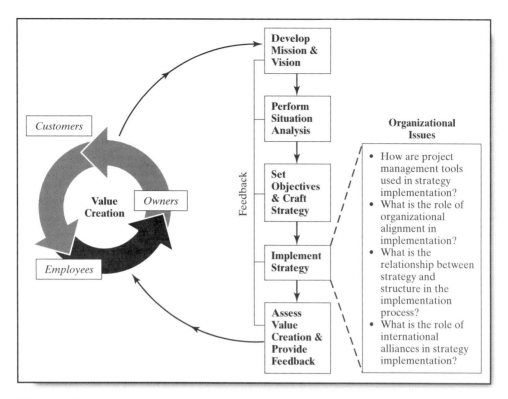

Figure 9-1
The strategic management framework

Consider the example of Federal Express (FedEx). What organizational systems and arrangements does FedEx use to achieve its strategic goal of providing fast and reliable service to its customers? Careful choice and deployment of technology, effective design of package delivery systems, and tight coordination across the company, among other things, support the FedEx strategy.

To achieve a record of more than 99 percent accurate, next-day delivery, FedEx designed its package handling system after a hub-and-spoke network arrangement. The hub was located in Memphis, Tennessee—an airport with a near-perfect record for good flying conditions. To achieve speed and accuracy in package tracking, FedEx drivers use "SuperTracker" devices to note changes in the status of packages entrusted to them. Data from these devices is fed into the computers on board each of Federal Express's radio-controlled vans, and then transmitted via cell phone to local FedEx offices. The local offices then transmit data via satellite to a central database, which also receives data from sorters.

Of course, people (FedEx employees) also play a key role in successful implementation. The company's human resources department recruits and retains highly energetic, enthusiastic, and intelligent employees who sort over a million pieces of mail in a short period of 4 hours.

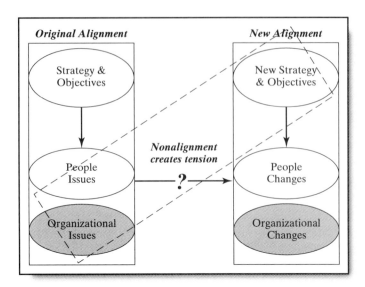

Figure 9-2
An implementation model

As the FedEx example suggests, successful implementation depends on effective management of both people and organizational issues. In this chapter we emphasize the organizational side of implementation, emphasizing three factors:

- project management—planning, scheduling, monitoring, and control
- organizational alignment
- organizational structure and design

PROJECT MANAGEMENT

The task of strategy implementation can be viewed as a project with a specific purpose and desired results. Like any project, strategy implementation requires a cross-functional group of employees to implement a logical sequence of interrelated activities within a time frame and without exceeding the available resources. The successful execution of such a project involves project planning, scheduling, monitoring, and control or **project management.**

Project planning is required to establish a set of directions in sufficient detail to tell the implementation team exactly what must be done, when it must be done, and what resources to use for successful implementation. The purpose of planning is to facilitate successful implementation or accomplishment of the goals. Project planning requires organizing the team and linking needs with timed project activities.

Project plans are constructed by identifying the activities, in a logical sequence, that are necessary to execute the project from start to finish. Kodak's new Advantix photographic system, introduced in February 1996, was the end result of extensive planning by not only the cross-functional teams within Kodak, but also four major film and camera manufacturers worldwide. The main project plan consisted of a four-stage process.[2] Stage 1 involved defining and refining the project concept, including identifying consumer needs and potential benefits to Kodak and other film and camera manufacturers, and developing intended strategies, product descriptions, and manufacturing processes. Stage 2 consisted of designing the product and market launch, including project commitment and design readiness. Stage 3 focused on marketing and manufacturing implementation, and Stage 4 on market introduction and sales.

The project plan, as the Kodak example shows, needs to specify exactly what is to be done, by whom, and when. A simple method to assist in planning all this detail in a hierarchical manner is called an *even planning process*,[3] which starts with making a list of major activities, in a general order, to complete a project. Each of the first-level activities is then broken down into second-level tasks ranging in number between two and 20. Each of the second-level tasks is then split into two to 20 subtasks. The end result of this planning process is an **action plan** that identifies the set of required activities to meet the project objectives, the person(s) responsible for each activity, the time required to complete each activity, the predecessor activities, and the resources. *Predecessor activities* are tasks that must be finished before a new task can begin. An action plan for the launch of a sample new product is presented in Table 9-1.

Project scheduling involves placing an action plan on a time scale with relative and specific times for activities. Some commonly used techniques for project scheduling are Program Evaluation and Review Techniques (PERT) and the Critical Path Method (CPM). PERT was developed in the late 1950s through the joint efforts of the U.S. Navy Special Projects Office, Lockheed Aircraft, and a consulting firm (Booz, Allen, and Hamilton) to manage the Polaris missile project. During the same time period, Du Pont, Inc. and Remington Rand Corporation developed CPM to manage maintenance projects in chemical plants. PERT has been credited with delivering the Polaris missile project 2 years ahead of its planned completion date.[4]

A major difference between the two techniques is their orientation to the time elements of projects. For example, PERT was designed to handle *probabilistic* time estimates of activities, and to aid in determining the probability of completion of a project by a given date. The probabilistic time estimates are subject to variation. CPM, on the other hand, used *deterministic* time estimates—time estimates that are fairly certain.

Both techniques help identify the *critical path* in the project—the set of tasks that control the duration of the project. Every project has at least one critical path. The tasks or activities on the critical path are called *critical activities*—any delay in these activities will result in a delay for the entire project. Managers find it extremely helpful to know which activities are critical and which activities have slack, so they can concentrate on the critical activities to ensure a timely completion of the project. If an organization could implement its intended strategies ahead of time, it would start reaping the benefits sooner.

The use of scheduling techniques has increased with the proliferation of project management software packages such as Microsoft Project, Primavera, Project Scheduler, CA-Superproject, and Time Line. A project schedule serves as the basis for monitoring and controlling project activity.

Project monitoring and control includes collecting information about project performance, comparing actual progress to the plan, and taking action to bridge any difference between the desired plan and the actual results. The common formats used to present a schedule and monitor progress include Gantt charts and network diagrams.

Table 9-1 Action plan

STEPS	TIME (DAYS)	RESPONSIBILITY	PRECEDENT
OBJECTIVE: LAUNCH THE NEW PRODUCT BY JUNE 15, 2002[a]			
I. Preliminary Investigation			
1. Market assessment	60	Marketing	
2. Technical assessment	90	Production	
II. Evaluate Sales and Customer Reaction	15	Marketing	1.1, 1.2
III. Detailed Investigation			
1. Market research	30	Marketing	2
2. Technical appraisal			
a. Manufacturing appraisal	45	Production	2
b. Financial analysis	15	Finance	2
IV. Development Stage			
1. Prototype	15	Marketing, Production	3.1, 3.2
2. Customer feedback	15	Marketing	4.1
3. Develop market launch plans	30	Marketing	4.2
4. Develop production plans	40	Production	4.2
V. Testing and Validation			
1. In-house product tests	15	Marketing, Production	4.1
2. Field trials	15	Marketing	4.2
3. Pilot production	15	Production	4.2, 5.1,5.2
4. Trial sell	20	Marketing	5.3
VI. Pre-commercialization Analysis			
1. Review operations plan	7.5	Finance, Production	4.4, 5.4
2. Review marketing plans	5	Marketing, Distribution	4.3, 5.4
VII. Full Production and Market Launch	30	Purchase, Production, Marketing	6.1, 6.2

[a]Based on the information in Brody, A. L., and J. B. Lord, eds. *Developing New Products for a Changing Marketplace.* Lancaster, PA: Technomic Publishing Co. Inc., 2000 and Cooper, R. G. *Winning in New Products.* 2nd ed. Reading, MA: Addison Wesley, 1993.

A **Gantt chart** is a horizontal bar chart with an embedded time scale that helps identify the start and completion of activities. It is a useful tool for indicating the current status of activities compared to the planned progress for each. A network diagram is composed of a number of arrows and nodes. The arrows represent the activities and the nodes indicate the start and completion of an activity. A network diagram better illustrates the interdependence of activities as compared to a Gantt chart.

From the information in the action plan a Gantt chart, as shown in Figure 9-3, was produced using Microsoft Project 2000, a project management software. Task names for summary activities, such as preliminary investigation, are in bold. The critical tasks are shown in red and noncritical in blue. The red vertical line in the chart is the project status line. As of December 23, 2001, preliminary investigation, including market and technical assessment, evaluation of sales and customer reaction, market research, and financial analysis have been completed. Technical appraisal is partially completed since manufacturing appraisal, a subtask scheduled to end by December 20, 2001 is incomplete (see Figure 9-3). This is a critical task and any delay in its completion is going to affect timely completion of the entire project.

Resource Allocation

The task of managing a project involves deploying resources to achieve the desired goals. The Gantt chart in Figure 9-3 has resources noted for each task. Resources are usually limited and can have a significant effect on the timely completion of a project. In our product launch example, the marketing department seems to be heavily engaged in the first quarter of 2002. To know the exact requirement of the marketing group in that quarter on a daily or weekly basis, we could obtain a time-based resource usage profile from the project management software. If the time-based profile indicates the project needs more resources than are available, the management has the option of either making additional resources available or pushing back the completion date of the project. In some cases, it may also be possible to transfer resources from noncritical to critical activities.

THE ROLE OF ORGANIZATIONAL ALIGNMENT IN STRATEGY IMPLEMENTATION

Organizational alignment is the process of linking and coordinating discrete activities within the organization. Alignment requires a shared understanding of organizational goals and objectives by managers at various levels and within various units of the organizational hierarchy. A firm's ability to seek and maintain a competitive advantage rests upon its ability to acquire and deploy resources that are in line with the organization's competitive needs. The two forms of organizational alignment are:

- Vertical alignment
- Horizontal or lateral alignment

Vertical Alignment

Vertical alignment refers to the alignment of strategies, objectives, action plans, and decisions throughout the various levels of the organization. Recall from Chapter 1 that there are three levels of strategy—corporate, business, and functional—which we refer to as Levels 1, 2, and 3, respectively, in Figure 9-4. In addition to coordinating activities and priorities across each of these three levels, vertical alignment depends on coordination at a fourth level—the decision areas within each function. Figure 9-4 shows this hierarchy of relationships. Strategic management is an iterative process that starts with the development of an overall strategy at the corporate level to guide the entire organization. Strategy implementation is effectively carried out in a bottom-up fashion, with an aim to make lower-level decisions consistent with the decisions at the upper levels. When this consistency is achieved, vertical alignment has been realized.

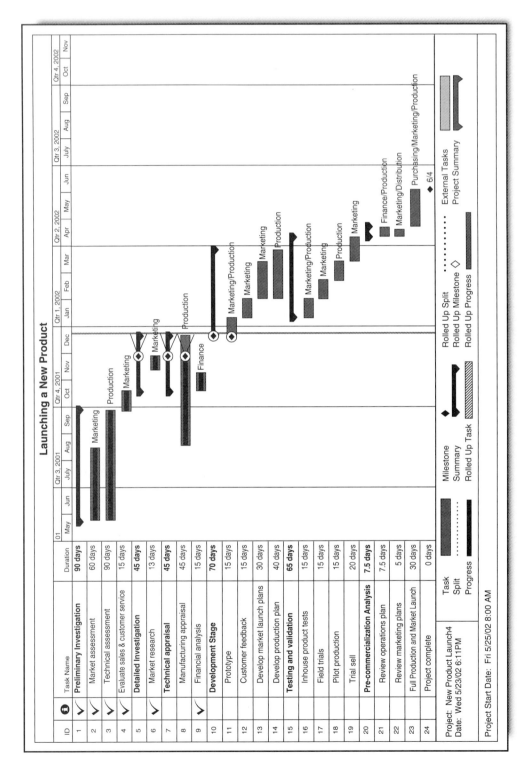

Figure 9-3
Gantt chart for launching a new product
This file was created with Microsoft Project software.

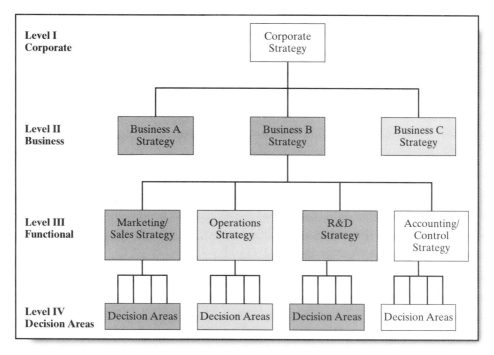

Figure 9-4
Vertical alignment of strategy

At Level 4 the specific actions or decisions made within each function should support that function's strategy. For example, the decisions made in the operations function (e.g., production capacity and scheduling, technology utilization, plant location, workforce management, performance measures) should be made in line with the Level 3 operations strategy of the company. Similarly, the promotion or pricing decisions should be consistent with the marketing strategy. Further, each functional strategy should support the competitive advantage (overall low cost or differentiation) pursued by each business unit (Level 2). Each business unit, division or SBU (Strategic Business Unit), in turn, supports the company's overall mission and corporate strategy (Level 1).

Consider an example. General Motors (GM) has made a conscious corporate level decision (Level 1) to be in the automobile manufacturing and financing business, and not in airplane manufacturing. Consistent with the corporate strategy, GM has established various SBUs (Level 2)—Pontiac, Oldsmobile, Saturn, Cadillac, and GMAC, a financing division. Each of the SBUs focuses on a specific market segment or a subsegment with minimal overlap. For example, Cadillac targets the high-end, older, "Be American Buy American" type of customer, whereas Saturn goes after the safety- and environment-conscious younger generation that does not want to haggle over price. Its GMAC division deals with the financing of all types of automobiles made and sold by GM. At Level 3, within each of GM's SBUs, different functional areas—marketing, operations, finance, HR, and R&D—implement functional strategies that support the corresponding SBU strategy.

Vertical Alignment and Cost Leadership. A manufacturer pursuing a business level strategy of cost leadership should focus on establishing tight cost control, strictly enforcing rules to control product or service costs and ensuring proper utilization of resources in various functional areas.[5] Each functional area will then translate these objectives into function-specific action plans so as to support the business strategy.

For example, to align with the low cost strategy of an SBU, the decisions made within the operations function regarding technology, capacity, location, and workforce management should support the functional strategy objectives of efficiency, machine utilization, and labor productivity. An SBU with an emphasis on low cost should opt for a line type of process technology if it is a discrete product manufacturer, such as a TV manufacturer, or a continuous process technology for products like fertilizer, sugar, oil, or cement. A *line process* is characterized by a product-focused grouping of machines and workstations set up in a sequence dictated by the steps required for manufacturing the product. When a line process is used to manufacture non-discrete products in bulk, such as sugar and fertilizer, it is termed a *continuous process.* Further, the SBU would locate its plant(s) near resources to minimize transportation costs, among other things. The management practices used by the operations manager(s) would stress monitoring and control,[6] to make sure the resources (people, materials, machines, and equipment) were being efficiently utilized.

Vertical Alignment and Differentiation. The approach used to achieve vertical alignment for a business strategy based on differentiation would look much different. Suppose an SBU sought competitive advantage based on delivery speed and product flexibility in a make-to-order setting. Operations managers in this case should opt for a job or batch process technology with multipurpose machinery that can handle varying needs of its customers. A *job process* is characterized by a function- or process-focused grouping of machines and workstations. A job process is well suited for the production of a wide variety of small-size (low volume) customer orders. A *batch process* is an intermittent production process like a job shop, but can handle relatively large quantities of a set mix of products. The quantities produced per batch are generally predetermined based on the proportion of set-up costs to inventory holding costs.

Even though developments in information technology have rendered distances less consequential, such plants should be located near customers or near freeways and airports to lend easy and fast access to customers. Operations managers should demonstrate participative and relationship-oriented workforce management practices, such as consulting, delegating, and team building.[7] For example, managers may often need to consult with employee teams before making delivery commitments or promising an alteration or a design change to their customers. To ensure a speedy delivery, the employee teams would be empowered to make certain decisions on their own. These decisions and approaches to achieve vertical alignment are summarized in Table 9-2

Is Vertical Alignment a Reality? Despite the numerous anticipated benefits of aligning decisions within an organization, not all organizations manage to achieve vertical alignment. In fact, research shows mixed evidence regarding the prevalence of vertical alignment. One study[8] involving 39 manufacturing managers found a close match between business strategies and manufacturing priorities. In two other

Table 9-2 Achieving vertical alignment: Cost leadership versus differentiation

STRATEGY/ DECISION AREA	COST LEADER	DIFFERENTIATOR: DELIVERY SPEED/PRODUCT FLEXIBILITY
Operations strategy	Strictly enforce rules to control product or service costs Focus on efficiency, machine utilization, labor productivity.	Reduce rigidity in systems Promote ability to switch from one product to another quickly Reduce processing lead time
Process choice or technology	Line or continuous	Job or batch shop
Workforce management practices in operations	Monitoring, controlling, problem solving	Consulting, delegating, team building
Location	Near raw materials	Near customers

studies of manufacturing strategy,[9] however, perceived strategies across the business and functional levels were found to be misaligned. Researchers in the marketing field also observed misalignment between marketing executives and their sales managers with regard to specific product strategies.[10] One of the factors related to misalignment, identified in a study[11] of 98 manufacturers, was the length of association between managers. As years of association between managers increase, misalignment decreases. Another misalignment factor was found to be the differing responsibilities and perspectives of managers at different levels of the organization. For example, senior managers seem to emphasize externally focused priorities such as meeting customer demand and counteracting competitive challenges. Functional managers seem to have an inward focus on issues such as cost control and manufacturing flexibility.

These studies suggest the need for organizations to foster more interaction and exchange among managers at different levels and across functions. Organizations should develop new and better ways to communicate so that strategies and competitive priorities are understood uniformly across all levels and the benefits of vertical alignment may be achieved.

Horizontal Alignment

Horizontal alignment refers to coordination of efforts across the organization and is primarily relevant to the lower levels in the strategy hierarchy. Horizontal alignment can be defined in terms of cross-functional and intra-functional integration. **Cross-functional integration** implies the consistency of decisions across functions (Level 3) so that activities and decisions across marketing, operations, HR, and other functions complement one another. **Intra-functional integration** is achieved through coherence across decision areas (Level 4) so as to achieve synergy within each function. For successful implementation, decisions within a function (Level 4) should be aligned vertically with that function's strategic objectives, and laterally across decision areas within a function.

The process of horizontal alignment requires exchange and cooperation among various functional activities, as depicted in Figure 9-5.

Horizontal Alignment and Cost Leadership. Let's consider a business, such as Southwest Airlines, that strives to be a cost leader. As mentioned before, a cost leadership strategy requires establishment of tight cost control and strict rule enforcement throughout the organization to control product or service costs. Cost leaders should also ensure proper utilization of resources in various functional areas. Each functional area needs to translate these objectives into function-specific action plans to support the business strategy. The operations function, for example, will attempt to cut costs through efficiency, machine utilization, and labor productivity. R&D will strive for standardized product designs to contain costs. Marketing will offer a limited variety of products and promise minimal options or design changes to accommodate customers' desires. Human resources will focus on job specialization.

Horizontal Alignment and Differentiation. On the other hand, an SBU that seeks to differentiate itself on product flexibility would seek to promote the ability to offer several products and to easily modify them to accommodate customer needs. To achieve its intended business strategy, overall, the business unit should work toward reducing rigidity in its systems, promoting the ability to switch from one product to another quickly, and reducing the processing lead time.

To support the above business objectives, the R & D function should consider a custom design approach. If this objective is combined with delivery speed, the strategy could include the ability to put quickly together a wide variety of products through various permutations and combinations of the basic product modules. For example, some watch manufacturers use this approach by having a few common

Figure 9-5
Horizontal alignment through cross-functional integration

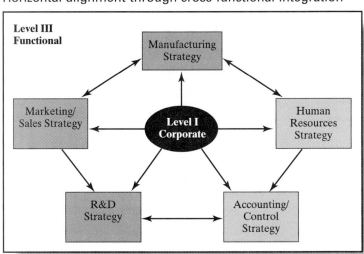

base designs, and a variety of dials, straps, and colors to create several combinations that appear different to the customer.

The R&D department and the marketing department should work in unison to lead in new product development and new product introduction. Marketing's promotion plan should be based on product variety and could use a price premium for customization. Manufacturing should develop the ability to produce in small batches and to switch quickly from one product to another.[12] The SBU's assembly operation should be able to process a wide variety of products in a short period of time without having to spend too much time in changeovers. Human resources should focus on hiring multiskilled workers and should foster job rotation. Purchasing may need to develop a base of reliable suppliers in the vicinity so it can procure materials in small quantities quickly and reliably. Table 9-3 summarizes these relationships.

Horizontal Alignment at JM Mold.   JM Mold of Piqua, Ohio, a small tooling manufacturer, is an excellent example of cross-functional coordination and exchange, not only within the organization but also with its customers and suppliers. The tooling manufacturer competes on the basis of delivery speed and flexibility. JM, primarily an automotive tooling manufacturer, has the ability to swiftly handle changes in the form of new customers, new markets, engineering changes, and delivery changes. When Encor Technologies of Mt. Gilead, Ohio, bid on a project to produce dryer lids for Whirlpool on a very tight time schedule, it contacted JM for the tooling.[13] JM was able to seize the opportunity because it has geared its systems so it can accommodate design changes swiftly.

Table 9-3   Achieving horizontal alignment: Cost leadership versus differentiation

FUNCTIONS	COST LEADER	DIFFERENTIATOR: DELIVERY SPEED/PRODUCT FLEXIBILITY
Operations	Focus on efficiency Machine utilization Labor productivity	Promote ability to switch from one product to another quickly Reduce processing lead time
Marketing	Offer a limited variety of products Promise minimal options or design changes to customers	Offer product variety Price premium for customization Lead in new product introduction
R&D	Standardized product design	Custom design approach Lead in new product development
Human Resources	Job specialization	Foster job rotation Focus on developing multiple skills

JM uses a software package for remote access to a home computer that is able to hold "concurrent design meetings," says Ed Kinsella, a JM Mold manager. When a customer calls to request a customized mold, the mold design in JM's computer system pops up on the customer's screen. They can both make changes to the mold as desired and get feedback in real time. This technology helps JM accomplish its strategic objectives of flexibility and timeliness by eliminating the need for meetings, and by letting customers view the mold progress report complete with video stills from their offices.[14]

In the particular case of Encor and Whirlpool, JM even had its engineer work directly with Whirlpool's marketing, safety, and production people, who were making changes until the third day before the completion of this 14-week job. Thus, even when Whirlpool outsourced some of its operations—design, tooling, and prototyping—it sought to align its objectives and activities with those of its suppliers and subcontractors.

Consequences of Weak Horizontal Alignment. The lack of cooperation and exchange across functions, on the other hand, can lead to suboptimal decisions. Consider the example of a supermarket that competes on the basis of price and encourages cost cutting throughout the organization. Accordingly, the purchasing manager decides to save money for the organization through bulk purchase of sugar. He orders two truckloads of sugar to take advantage of a 10 percent price discount. He fails to consult with other functional managers, however, about the ramifications of his decision. When the sugar arrives, the operations manager is asked to unload and stack it in the store warehouse. Due to limited space availability, the operations manager is unable to unload the sugar, and, in turn, decides to rent and keep the trailers in the parking lot for a couple of weeks, thus incurring rental expenses. When the accounting department is presented with an invoice from the trucking company for rental, it summons the operations manager. After hearing the operations manager's side of the story, the accounting manager decides to get rid of the sugar fast to save on truck rental, and contacts the marketing department to launch a half-price sale on sugar. Thus, a cost-saving strategy without adequate cross-functional consultation on the part of a purchasing manager turned out to be a loss-making endeavor for the organization.

Horizontal Alignment within a Function. Coordination across decision areas within a function is also important for effective implementation. As shown in Figure 9-6, alignment across decision areas within a function, such as operations, contributes to improved performance. The decision areas in the operations function are broadly classified under structural and infrastructural decision areas.[15] The *structural decisions* relate to the physical structure of the facility, such as location, technology, and capacity. The *infrastructural decisions* are about the operating systems, such as manufacturing planning and control, workforce management, quality management, organizational design, and performance measurement system.

Let's examine how decisions in various areas within a function, such as operations, can be coordinated. To develop the ability to produce in small batches and to switch quickly from one product to another, a company has opted for a batch manufacturing process. To facilitate production in batches, the company should buy general-purpose machinery and equipment that offers the ability to switch quickly from one product

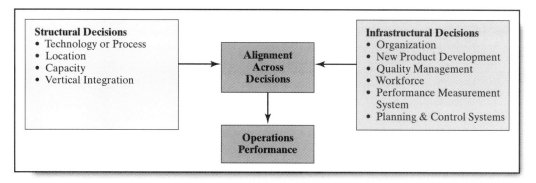

Figure 9-6
Horizontal alignment within the operations function

to another with minimal set-up time. To support the ability of the manufacturing process (to offer variety and still deliver on time) the company should use a *lead capacity strategy,* that is, it should have surplus capacity, some of which will be necessary because of the underutilization due to changeovers.

The decisions regarding infrastructure, such as organization structure and workforce management, should also complement the structural decisions—technology and capacity. Thus, in the above example, the workforce management practices that complement technology and capacity decisions would include encouraging employees to work in self-managing teams that are empowered to make routine decisions and to fix problems as they arise without having to wait for approvals and intervention from the bosses.[16] Researchers contend that linking decisions within a function leads to improved performance.[17]

Enterprise Resource Planning (ERP): A Way of Achieving Horizontal Alignment. An **enterprise resource planning (ERP)** system integrates decisions and resources across various functional areas using a common database. Enterprise-wide integration is possible through the use of a common database, which reduces duplication of effort and forces various functions to coordinate their activities. For example, in an ERP system, marketing and production work together to develop a common forecast, which is then used by the finance department as a basis for raising capital or making funds available, and by the HR department to make available the required number of people with requisite skills.

In the absence of an integrated system, various functions might have generated their own forecasts, perhaps, using different approaches and arriving at different conclusions. The integrated ERP systems eliminate redundancy and duplication of information, while making real-time information accessible to the entire organization. These systems also facilitate coordination on a global basis, with customers, suppliers, or other units of the same company, through the availability of current information on a common database that is accessible anywhere in the world at any time. Managers in various functions or in different geographic regions can take a business perspective rather than a functional perspective, and make sure that their decisions are aligned with the decisions of others in the organization.

A successful implementation effort also hinges on a compatible organizational design, that is, the structure and control systems that help a company achieve its intended strategy. Organization structure is a key component of design.[18] The *organization structure* specifies the reporting relationships between different offices and employees, the lines of authority, the channels of communication, and information flow.

The organizational design provides a vehicle to coordinate the activities of various functions and ensures that they are in line with the overall strategy of the business unit and the corporation. Because each function develops and pursues its own strategy, of course, in unison with the business strategy, it needs a structure to exploit the skills and capabilities of its employees, and to control and coordinate activities of its employees to achieve the desired functional goals and objectives. An organization needs to create a mechanism that coordinates the activities of different functions and divisions to effectively pursue the organizational strategy, yet affords sufficient autonomy to various functions in achieving their goals.

The elements of organization structure include chain of command, span of control, and form or degree of centralization. The principle of **chain of command** suggests that an employee should report directly to one supervisor. Early researchers argued that employees reporting to two or more bosses might have to cope with conflicting priorities. The principle is easy to follow in traditional organizational structures and many contemporary organizations as well. There are some specific situations, discussed later in the section, when strict adherence to the principle creates some inflexibility in the organization, and it has to be violated.

Span of control pertains to the number of subordinates directly reporting to a supervisor. Some studies suggest that a supervisor can effectively manage six direct reports,[19] but in practice span of control varies depending upon several factors, such as the managerial level in the organization, training and experience of subordinates, and task complexity. The span of control for managers at General Electric is nearly twice as much as it was about 15 years ago.[20] At Southwest, eight or nine frontline employees report to a supervisor as compared to 30 to 40 at American Airlines.[21]

The *degree of centralization* refers to the distribution of decision-making authority at various levels in the organization. In a highly centralized organization, decisions are mostly made at the top, whereas in a more decentralized organization, employees at lower levels are empowered to make decisions. In organizations that have a relatively simple task structure and a focus on cost control, such as a fan assembly operation, a greater degree of centralization affords efficient use of employees and control. An organization that competes on the basis of delivery speed or product flexibility is better served through employee empowerment, that is, higher decentralization. Authorizing employees to make decisions on the spot reduces the need for unnecessary approvals by senior managers, which hinders speed.

Five Components of an Organization Structure

An organization can be divided into five distinct components as in Figure 9-7.[22] The top management is called the *strategic apex*, which is primarily responsible for creating a vision for the organization. The employees that do the frontline work of the

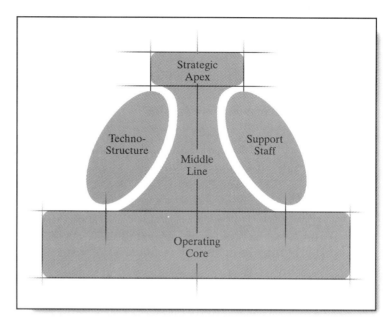

Figure 9-7
The components of an organization
Source: Mintzberg, H., "Organization Design: Fashion or Fit?" *Harvard Business Review,* (January–February 1981): 105.

organization constitute the *operating core*. The managers who mediate between the top management and the working core form the *middle line*. The staff people responsible for the planning and control of the organization form the *technostructure*, and the staff personnel who provide indirect services to the entire organization, such as secretaries and mail room employees, form the *support staff*. The configuration that results from putting these components together is called an *organization structure*.

The Structure–Strategy Relationship

Organizational design decisions are not static, but dynamic in nature. An organization needs to revisit and perhaps change its structure as it changes its strategy. As seen in Figure 9-8,[23] changes in strategy may lead to administrative problems. For example, as an organization grows or expands as a result of its opportunities and needs (created by changing population demographics or technological advancements) the new strategy may present additional administrative burdens for the existing structure. The organization's neglect of the administrative challenges could lead to inefficiency or ineffectiveness, and have financial implications for the organization.

Types of Organization Structure

The need and relative importance of the five components of structure varies from organization to organization depending upon the nature of the work being done and the degree and type of coordination of activities required. The components may be

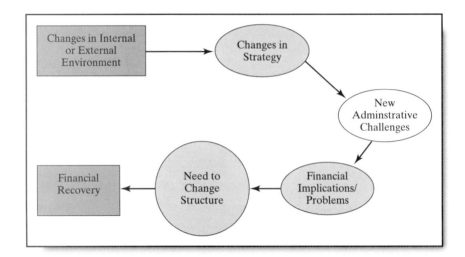

Figure 9-8
Structure and strategy
Source: Adapted from Chandler, A. D., Jr., *Strategy and Structure: Chapters in the History of the American Industrial Enterprise.* Cambridge, MA: M.I.T. Press, 1962. Reprinted by permission of Harvard Business Review.

configured into any of several distinct types of organizational structure, which have been found to be suitable in different situations. The types of structure are:

- Simple
- Functional
- Divisional
- Matrix
- Network

Simple Structure. In a young and small entrepreneurial firm, the top manager— often the owner and president/CEO—creates a vision for the organization and carries it out by directly supervising the operating core with little or no need for any staff or middle line managers. Such an arrangement is called a *simple structure*.[24] It offers flexibility for simple innovation, low overhead, and high responsiveness to customers. There is little formalization or standardization of tasks and processes. The control is centralized with almost all decision-making power resting at the strategic apex with the chief executive. Some examples of simple structures include dot.com companies, and Mom and Pop stores.

Functional Structure. As a business grows, so does its range of activities, which become increasingly difficult to manage through a simple structure. One way to manage the expanded range of activities is to group employees based on their specialization or the task they perform. For example, all information technology specialists are grouped together, as are all accountants, human resource specialists, and so on. This way of grouping specialists together is called a **functional structure,** and leads to hierarchies within each function. Figure 9-9 shows a generic functional struc-

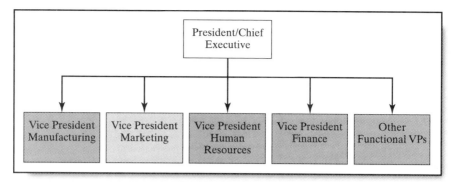

Figure 9-9
A functional organization structure

ture. Such hierarchies provide a clearly defined career path for individuals within each function, and afford managers greater control of activities.

A functional structure facilitates information sharing and learning among specialists. For example, if a tool and die specialist discovered a more efficient way of exchanging dies for a plastic molding machine, the same knowledge could be easily disseminated to other specialists in the manufacturing function. Such structures promote a high degree of standardization and formalization, which leads to efficiency and consistency. A functional structure is, therefore, well suited for an organization pursuing an overall low cost strategy.

Divisional Structure. Another way to solve the coordination problem associated with the expanded range and scope of tasks associated with growth and diversification strategies is to use a **divisional structure.** The divisions could be formed on the basis of products, geography, or customers served. Each division may have functional subdivisions, but divisional lines separate functional specialists from one another. Top management, through its headquarters managers, maintains control over the divisions by setting quantifiable goals for each division. The divisional managers are held responsible for the performance of their units, which is measured through performance and control systems. The organization typically creates a small technostructure to design and implement these control systems, and a central support staff to provide common services, such as public relations and legal counsel, to the divisions.[25] Top management also maintains a degree of direct supervision through periodic visits to each division.

A divisional structure facilitates functional integration or horizontal alignment within each division. For example, an R & D engineer is more likely to learn quickly about the feasibility of a design and the availability of materials from a manufacturing manager and a purchasing manager, respectively, if they are in the same division than he or she would in a functional organization.

Figure 9-10 presents a divisional structure of a large automobile company such as General Motors. General Motor deploys a product division approach at Level 2. Each of its automobile divisions—Buick, Cadillac, Chevrolet, Oldsmobile, Saturn, etc.—enjoys considerable autonomy in their management of day-to-day affairs. In

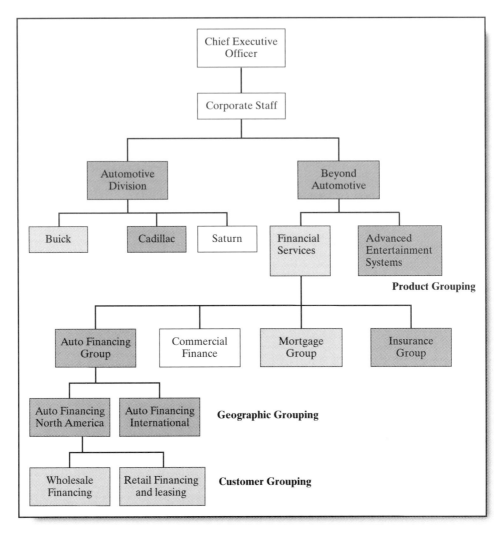

Figure 9-10
Divisional structure of an auto manufacturer (modeled after GM)

the auto-financing group, within GMAC Financial Services, the divisions are based on geographic regions of operation—North America, and International. Under each of the geographic divisions, the grouping is based on the type of customer—wholesale financing, and retail financing and leasing.

The major advantages of the divisional structure include its focus on results, better allocation of corporate resources and enhanced control, ease of accommodating growth and diversification, and freeing up of corporate staff from operating responsibilities so they can focus on strategic issues.

The major disadvantages of the divisional structure are the duplication of resources and activities and competition among divisions for corporate resources. For example, each division may have its own human resources department. If the human resources function were centralized as in a functional organization, those activities could be done at a fraction of the cost. The second problem of competing for resources may lead to rivalry among divisions and reduced interdivisional coordination.

The internal competition fostered by the divisional structure has a positive side; it forces divisions to consider differentiating from one another. For example, the Cadillac division differentiates itself from Chevrolet based on product design, product performance, and customer service (various dimensions of quality). Further, as the divisional managers enjoy a considerable degree of autonomy, it makes it easier for them to pursue the differentiation strategy. For example, a division could easily pursue delivery speed strategy for its products or services because it does not have to consult with the headquarters on operating decisions. Employee empowerment and having to deal with fewer administrative layers within a division speeds up the decision-making process and reduces the processing lead time.

Matrix Structure.   The **matrix structure** combines the advantages of specialization that a functional structure offers with the focus and accountability that a divisional structure affords.[26] Figure 9-11 illustrates a matrix structure. This kind of structure has a dual focus on functional and product or project considerations. Employees in this structure have at least two bosses: a product or project manager, and a functional manager. The project manager has the responsibility and commensurate authority to coordinate the project team's activities to achieve the project's goals. The functional manager is responsible for the team member's annual reviews, salary, and promotion recommendations. The two managers, however, must communicate regularly to effectively coordinate the work of product or project team members drawn from various functions.[27]

A primary advantage of the matrix structure is that it affords the flexibility to handle complex and interdependent projects while maintaining the benefits that result from keeping experts grouped under various functions. A potential disadvantage of this type of structure arises from the violation of the chain of command principle. If the product or project managers fail to coordinate the demands upon employees with their respective functional bosses, the resulting confusion and ambiguity may lead to power struggles among managers.

Network Structure.   A **network structure** results from linking a central group of core staff with loosely coupled partners, such as subcontractors. The core group sets a strategic direction of the organization and provides operational support to sustain the network.[28] The key operational activities are, however, subcontracted to various organizations or individuals. Figure 9-12 presents a network structure for a computer manufacturer such as Dell.

Dell Computer Corporation uses a network of organizations (suppliers) specializing in various areas: surface-mount technology, semiconductor manufacturing, motherboard building, electrical assemblies, etc. By *outsourcing* component parts (i.e., not building the components in house), Dell can choose among the best suppliers in the world. As new processes are developed that further improve product quality, as is common in the electronics industry, Dell partners with the supplier who has taken advantage of them. Because Dell has not made an investment in the components

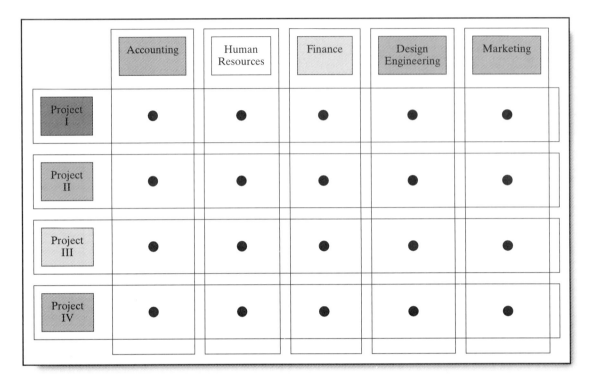

Figure 9-11
Matrix structure

manufacturing business, it is free to select the best suppliers at all times. Yet, it believes in dealing with as few suppliers as possible so it can maintain close relationships with them.

Dell's network structure affords a competitive advantage of product and volume flexibility, and speed. If one supply partner experiences trouble keeping up with the demand, Dell can work with others to augment capacity.[29] Despite Dell's heavy reliance on suppliers for various components and technologies, it still plays a leadership role in keeping track of customer preferences and market trends. Dell effectively translates customers' desires into relevant technology and proactively communicates with suppliers to seize opportunities. Dell takes the lead in setting company goals and strategy and proactively communicating to its network of strategic partners.

Structure, Diversification, and Expansion

As the strategy and priorities of an organization change over time, so should the structure, as illustrated in Figure 9-13. The two axes in Figure 9-13 represent the degree of **diversification**, which is defined as the number of different industries that a company competes in, and the number of business units a company has. As mentioned before, GM has several business units including Oldsmobile, Saturn, Pontiac, and Chevrolet. As illustrated in Figure 9-13, a simple structure is best suit-

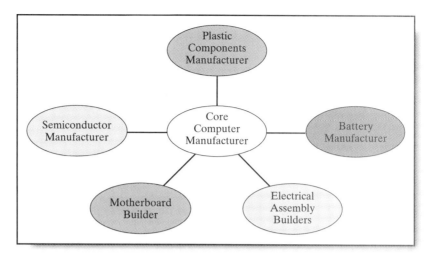

Figure 9-12
Network structure

ed for a company that has a very low degree of diversification and operates a single business unit. As the company diversifies into various industries and adds new business units, the structure changes to support the strategy. In other words, the complexity of the structure matches the increased complexity of the strategy, as shown in Figure 9-13.

Structure Follows Strategy: Some Examples. When Santa Rosa Systems Division (SRSD), formerly of Hewlett Packard (HP) and now part of Agilent Technologies, was formed in 1992, it inherited HP's strategy of standardized products coupled with technical excellence, and a functional organization structure.[30] To succeed, SRSD was to follow a customization strategy to tailor systems to individual customers' needs. When it tried to implement the new strategy with a functional structure—R&D responsible for long-term systems development and a custom systems group to tailor the systems to meet variable customer requests—a cold war developed between the two groups. SRSD could not successfully implement this new strategy without changing the structure from a functional form to a matrix form, whereby cross-functional business teams were made accountable for profitability.

Organizations pursuing a low cost strategy strive to maintain stability and efficiency that can be achieved through task standardization, job specialization, and formalization. A functional structure that puts specialists together minimizes duplication of personnel and equipment and results in economies of scale. Thus, a functional structure is normally best suited to pursue a low cost strategy.

On the other hand, organizations pursuing a differentiation strategy need to maintain their uniqueness. Matrix and network structures are well suited to pursuing a differentiation strategy as these structures can be easily molded to handle changes in the task and environment. The inherent advantages of these structures include flexibility and adaptability.

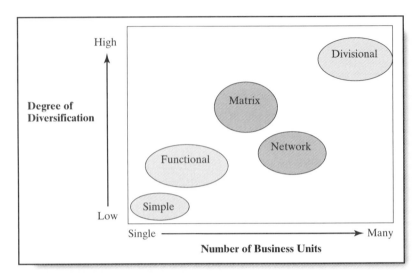

Figure 9-13
Diversification strategy and organizational structure relationship

A simple structure is also suitable for pursuing a differentiation strategy, but is appropriate for smaller businesses. The best form of organization structure for an entrepreneurial firm is often a simple structure.

Organizations pursuing a focused differentiation or focused low cost strategy may want to create autonomous divisions to cater to the needs of a particular market segment. Such needs are met by creating divisions on the basis of products, geographic markets, or customer focus. A divisional structure can accommodate a focused strategy.

INTERNATIONAL ASPECTS OF STRATEGY IMPLEMENTATION

In Chapter 6 we identified several reasons why firms seek global expansion of their operations. Overseas business is central to the continued existence of manufacturing companies. In today's competitive world, companies must search out resources on a global scale, having products designed from a source that offers the best competitive advantage, obtaining technology from the best source, and manufacturing in those countries that offer best access to markets or a favorable cost structure.[31] The declining transportation and communication costs and advances in information technology have made it easier for companies to share resources worldwide. Furthermore, international mergers also afford partners the economies of scale and international reach they need in order to compete globally.

Different strategies to achieve international expansion include: licensing, joint ventures, mergers and acquisitions, and greenfields. From Chapter 3 we know that strategic alliances are cooperative agreements between two or more organizations.

Licensing is a form of strategic alliance where no equity is involved. *Joint ventures* were identified as another kind of strategic alliance with equity contributions from partners. *Mergers and acquisitions* result in one legal entity that emerges when (a) two organizations merge into one, or (b) one acquires another. *Greenfields* are created by the parent company through complete internal development (i.e., without a strategic partner). A greenfield operation is a wholly owned subsidiary of the parent company.

Each of the four strategies for international expansion has different implementation requirements regarding financial, technical, and managerial resources. The *financial factors* include capital requirements, financial risk, and profit potential to the investor. The *technical* or *industrial factors* encompass access to customer feedback, risk of know-how proliferation, and the ability to exploit economies of scale and other cost advantages. The *managerial factors* include the speed of entry and the need for and level of parent company involvement in management affairs. These requirements are compared across the four international expansion strategies in Table 9-4.[32]

As seen in Table 9-4, financial requirements—the need for capital, profit potential, and financial risk—are lowest for a licensing strategy and highest for a greenfield, with joint ventures and mergers and acquisitions falling in between. Two of the three technical or industry factors—access to customer feedback and the ability to exploit economies of scale—also follow the same pattern; the least for licensing and the highest for a greenfield. The risk of know-how proliferation, however, runs in the opposite direction, with the greatest risk being associated with a licensing strategy, and the least risk with a greenfield operation.

Table 9-4 Implementation requirements for different international strategies

| | INTERNATIONAL STRATEGIES | | | |
IMPLEMENTATION REQUIREMENTS	LICENSING	JOINT VENTURE	MERGER AND ACQUISITION	GREENFIELD
Financial				
Need for capital	None	Medium	High	Very high
Profit potential	Low	Medium	High	Very high
Financial risk	Low	Medium	Medium	High
Technical or Industry				
Access to customer feedback	Low	Medium	High	Very high
Risk of know-how proliferation	High	Medium	Low	Very low
Ability to exploit the economies of scale	Low	Medium	Medium	High
Managerial				
Speed of entry	High	High	Medium	Low
Need for and level of parent company's involvement in management affairs	Low	Medium	High	Very high

With regard to managerial factors, licensing affords the greatest speed of entry into a foreign market, with the least requirement for the parent company's involvement in managing the foreign operations. On the other extreme, a greenfield strategy requires greater involvement of the parent company, but the new operation takes a long time to set up and, thus, access to the foreign market is gained slowly.

STRATEGY IMPLEMENTATION: TWO EXAMPLES

To illustrate many of the organizational issues of strategy implementation discussed in this chapter, let's look at two examples—one case of successful implementation and one unsuccessful.

Strategy Implementation at Southwest Airlines: A Success Story

How does Southwest Airlines create value for customers, employees, and owners? Through strategy–systems alignment, and by creating a strong culture that abhors waste, rewards efficiency, and communicates the message that "We care about you" to customers. Southwest has successfully positioned itself as a low-cost, low-fare airline by carefully designing and configuring its organizational systems and structure to support its strategy. Southwest maintains its advantage by keeping costs down and offering on-time arrivals, convenient schedules, and a fun flying experience. These objectives are consistently communicated and supported throughout the organization.

For example, Southwest's operations function helps drive down costs by increasing the utilization of their planes and reducing docking or gate time, as already mentioned in Chapter 4. Specifically, Southwest takes only 20 minutes to load and unload planes as compared to the industry average of about 45 minutes. For quick loading of planes and to keep costs low, Southwest issues reusable boarding passes and does not assign seats or offer baggage transfers. To keep training, maintenance, and inventory costs low, Southwest flies a standardized fleet of aircraft (the Boeing 737). Flight scheduling supports the low cost strategy through point-to-point routes, which also save time for passengers.

In marketing and sales, Southwest utilizes free advertising and promotion through unusual events. Southwest was the first major airline to use the Internet for booking and selling tickets. The cost per booking to Southwest via the Internet is about $1, compared to about $10 per booking through a travel agent. Southwest reported that approximately 30 percent of its 2000 revenue, or $1.7 billion, was generated from online bookings via southwest.com.

The human resources function helps in creating value for customers by hiring people who have a sense of humor and "who know how to have fun." By using its frequent flyers on the recruiting committee, it not only keeps the recruitment costs down but also takes into account customer expectations. Further, it helps create a strong company culture by creating a sense of responsibility and ownership through profit-sharing plans.

Southwest has adopted a functional organization structure[33] as presented in Figure 9-14. It is, however, interesting to note that the company did not have an organizational chart for years.[34] Southwest shuns organizational hierarchy—pilots have been known to assist ground crews and employees often violate the chain of command by going above or around their supervisors to get answers. Not bound by its functional structure, Southwest promotes cross-functional accountability, which diffuses blame and encourages learning.[35] Prior to the early 1990s, Southwest followed the practice of identifying delays and attributing them to a particular crew or a function such as a flight crew or a station. That approach was difficult and expensive to

Figure 9-14
Southwest Airlines' organization structure

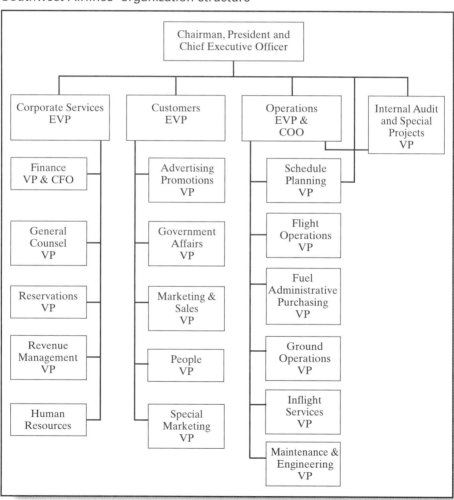

Source: Adapted from Leonard N. Stern School of Business, NYU "The MET Project." www.stern.nyu.edu/MET98/exhibit5.htm, accessed December 4, 2001.

administer and led to arguments between various groups of employees, which did not favor teamwork or the company's strategy of cost leadership. The practice has been stopped.

Southwest's organization is relatively simple compared to its major competitors, such as American Airlines, who are required to manage added complexity due to international operations and strategic alliances with other international carriers. Other major airlines also have to contend with their hub-and-spoke system that increases administrative burdens due to the higher level of coordination required. Southwest's point-to-point system is a simpler configuration that facilitates quick turnaround and supports its overall strategy of low cost.

Xerox: An Example of Unsuccessful Implementation

In contrast to Southwest, Xerox is a company that has struggled of late, due at least partly to unsuccessful implementation of strategy. Xerox had been known for its mastery in continuously revamping and improving the organization through restructuring and repositioning. In fact, Xerox was a leader in developing the *benchmarking technique,* based on the search for best practices that lead to exceptional performance.[36] Xerox was frequently sought as a role model and used as a benchmark itself in various areas, including inbound transportation, materials management, and warehousing.

In recent years, however, Xerox has struggled to implement its strategies. According to a senior Xerox executive, "There was always a huge gap between the visionary aspirations the company nominally was pursuing and what it actually drove employees to do."[37] As a result, Xerox has been losing market share to Japanese rivals in the copier business, such as Canon and Sharp, and is unable to find a profitable place in the Net-centric digital world. Xerox posted a loss of $198 million in the last quarter of 2000, the largest quarterly loss in a decade. The company lost about $38 billion in shareholder wealth in less than 2 years. Figure 9-15 shows a dramatic drop in Xerox's net income in the year 2000 with equally bleak projections for 2001.

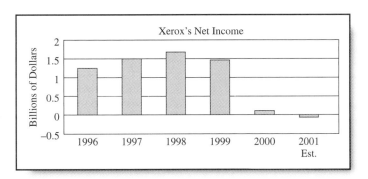

Figure 9-15
Xerox net income

Source: Adapted from Bianco, A., and P. L. Moore, "Downfall X: The Inside Story of the Management Fiasco at Xerox," *Business Week* (March 5, 2001): 85. (Excludes special items.)

Reports suggest that part of the problem at Xerox is its failure to adjust its organizational structure to support a new strategy. Xerox's CEO, Richard Thoman, had the vision to shift the company's emphasis from selling copiers to selling "output management solutions." In retrospect, analysts claim that the new strategy required a reorganization of Xerox's sales force, which traditionally had been designed around geographic areas rather than the industry/customer focus needed to support the new strategy.[38]

CONCLUSION

In this chapter we discussed the role of three organizational factors in successful implementation of strategy—project management, organizational alignment, and organizational design. Blue Cross and Blue Shield of Louisiana (BCBSLA) utilizes project management as a tool for implementing various strategic initiatives. Philip Diab, a project manager of BCBSLA, stated that "project management is specifically used to implement corporate strategic initiatives deemed critical to the corporation and its competitive advantage."[39] By integrating project management techniques with strategic planning and implementation, BCBSLA has witnessed enhanced communications throughout the organization, realized productivity increases, and made better resource allocation decisions.

Two forms of organizational alignment (vertical and horizontal), and ways to achieve them, were also examined in this chapter. Vertical alignment is done to ensure coordination of goals, priorities, action plans, and decisions through various hierarchical levels in the organization. Horizontal alignment refers to efforts to achieve cross-functional and intra-functional integration.

The various types of organizational structure were identified, and the relationship between strategy and structure was emphasized. We also considered the implementation requirements of four different ways to enter an international market. The international entry strategies—licensing, joint ventures, mergers and acquisitions, and greenfields—offer unique opportunities and place different demands on the parent organization in terms of financial, technical, and managerial requirements.

KEY TERMS AND CONCEPTS

After reading this chapter you should understand each of the following terms.

- Action plan
- Chain of command
- Cross-functional integration
- Diversification
- Divisional structure
- Enterprise resource planning
- Functional structure
- Gantt chart
- Horizontal alignment

- Intra-functional integration
- Matrix structure
- Network structure
- Organizational design
- Organizational reconfiguration
- Project management
- Resource allocation
- Span of control
- Vertical alignment

DISCUSSION QUESTIONS

1. How does Southwest Airlines maintain a low-cost operation and high levels of employee and customer satisfaction in the context of a functional organization structure?
2. For an organization of your choice, identify its strategy and structure by visiting its Web site. Evaluate whether the two are in alignment.
3. What is vertical alignment? Horizontal alignment? Explain the steps necessary to achieve vertical and horizontal alignment for a service organization such as an electric company.
4. What is project management? How can it be used to facilitate the implementation of strategy?
5. What is enterprise resources planning (ERP)? How can it help achieve horizontal alignment?
6. What are the different types of strategies available to a firm for entering an international market? Discuss the implementation requirements and organizing principles for the different types of strategies.

EXPERIENTIAL EXERCISE

Develop an action plan for the merger of two hotel chains. See Table 9-1 for guidance. Identify major activities for the project, determine interdependence of activities, estimate activity times, and identify the departments and functions responsible for each activity.

ENDNOTES

1. Shook, D., "Southwest's Lean, Mean Flying Machine," Business Week online. www.businessweek.com:/print/ bwdaily/ dnflash/jan2001/nf20010129_472.htm?mai r . . . January 29, 2001, accessed December 5, 2001.
2. Adams, C., "A Kodak Moment: Advantix Named 1997 International Project of the Year," *PM Network* (January 1998): 21–27.
3. Meredith, J. R., and S. J. Mantel Jr. *Project Management: A Managerial Approach.* 4th ed. New York: John Wiley and Sons, 2000, 195.
4. Stevenson, W. J. *Operations Management.* 5th ed. New York: McGraw-Hill Irwin, 1996, 763.
5. Porter, M. E. *Competitive Advantage.* New York: The Free Press, 1985.
6. Kathuria, R., and F. Y. Partovi, "Aligning Workforce Management Practices with Competitive Priorities and Process Technology: A Conceptual Examination," *The Journal of High Technology Management Research* 11, no. 2, 2000, 215–234.
7. Kathuria, R., and F. Y. Partovi, "Aligning Workforce Management Practices with Competitive Priorities and Process Technology: A Conceptual Examination," *The Journal of High Technology Management Research* 11, no. 2, 2000, 215–234.
8. Schroeder, R. G., J. C. Anderson, and G. Clevelend, "The Content of Manufacturing Strategy: An Empirical Study," *Journal of Operations Management* 6, no. 4 (1986): 405–415.
9. Swamidass, P. M., "Manufacturing Strategy: Its Assessment and Practice," *Journal of Operations Management* 6, no. 4 (1986): 405–415; and Porth, S., R. Kathuria, and M. P. Joshi, "Performance Impact of the Fit Between Manufacturing Priorities of General Managers and Manufacturing

Managers," *Journal of Business and Economic Studies* 4, no. 1 (spring 1998): 13–35.

10. Strahle, W. M., R. L. Spiro, and F. Acito, "Marketing and Sales: Strategic Alignment and Functional Implementation," *Journal of Personal Selling and Sales Management* 16 (1996): 1–20.

11. Kathuria, R., S. Porth, and M. P. Joshi, "Manufacturing Priorities: Do General Managers and Manufacturing Managers Agree?" *International Journal of Production Research* 37, no. 1 (1999): 2077–2092.

12. Kathuria, R., and M. Igbaria, "Aligning IT Applications with Manufacturing Strategy: An Integrated Framework," *International Journal of Operations & Production Management* 17, no. 6 (1997): 611–629.

13. Owen, J., "JM Mold: Small But Agile," *Manufacturing Engineering Magazine,* 116, 6, 1996, 69–73.

14. Owen, J., "JM Mold: Small But Agile," *Manufacturing Engineering Magazine,* 116, 6, 1996, 69–73.

15. Hayes, R. H., and S. C. Wheelwright. *Restoring Our Competitive Edge.* New York: Wiley, 1984.

16. Kathuria, R., and F. Y. Partovi, "Workforce Management Practices for Manufacturing Flexibility," *Journal of Operations Management* 18, no. 1 (1999): 21–39; and Kathuria, R., *Journal of Operations Management,* 18, 6, 2000, 627–641.

17. Kathuria, R., and F. Y. Partovi, *Journal of High Technology Management Research,* 11, 2, 2000, 215–234.

18. Chandler, A. D., Jr. *Strategy and Structure: Chapters in the History of the American Industrial Enterprise.* Cambridge, MA: M.I.T. Press, 1962.

19. Urwick, L. *The Elements of Administration.* New York: Harper & Row, 1944.

20. Bernstein, A., S. Jackson, and J. Byrne, "Jack Cracks the Whip Again," *Business Week* (December 15, 1997): 34–35.

21. Gittell, J. H., "Paradox of Coordination and Control," *California Management Review* 42, no. 3 (2000): 101–116.

22. Mintzberg, H., "Organization Design: Fashion or Fit?" *Harvard Business Review* (January–February 1981): 103–116.

23. Based on the discussion in Chandler, A. D., Jr. *Strategy and Structure: Chapters in the History of American Industrial Enterprise.* Cambridge, MA: M.I.T. Press, 1962.

24. Mintzberg, H., "Organization Design: Fashion or Fit?" *Harvard Business Review* (January–February 1981): 103–116.

25. Mintzberg, H., "Organization Design: Fashion or Fit?" *Harvard Business Review* (January–February 1981): 103–116.

26. Galbraith, J., "Matrix Organization Designs: How to Combine Functional and Project Forms," *Business Horizons* (February 1971): 29–40.

27. Turner, S. G., D. Utley, and J. D. Westbrook, "Project Managers and Functional Managers: A Case Study of Job Satisfaction in a Matrix Organization," *Project Management Journal* (September 1998): 11–19.

28. Morgan, G. "From Bureaucracies to Networks: The Emergence of New Organizational Forms." In *Creative Organizational Theory: A Resource Book,* Newbury Park, CA: Sage, 1989, 64–67.

29. Dell, M., and C. Fredman, *Direct from Dell: Strategies That Revolutionized an Industry.* New York: HarperCollins, 1999.

30. Beer, M., and R. A. Eisenstat, "The Silent Killers of Strategy Implementation and Learning," *Sloan Management Review* (summer 2000): 29–40.

31. Collins, T. M., and T. L. Doorley III. *Teaming Up for the 90s: A Guide to International Joint Ventures and Strategic Alliances.* Homewood, IL: Business One Irwin, 1991.

32. Based on the analysis in Kathuria, R., and M. P. Joshi. "Globalization of Services: Do Service Characteristics Impact the Globalization Process?" Paper presented at the POMS Conference, Orlando, FL, March 2001.

33. Based on the case analysis of Southwest Airlines by NYU Stern at www.stern.nyu.edu/MET98/ structure.htm, accessed December 4, 2001.

34. Matthew, B., "In Herb's Way," *The Boston Sunday Globe,* November 5, 2000, F4.

Chapter 9   Strategy Implementation

35. Gittell, J. H., "Paradox of Coordination and Control," *California Management Review* 42, no. 3 (2000): 101–116.

36. Spendolini, M. J. *The Benchmarking Book.* New York: AMACOM, 1992.

37. Bianco, A., and P. L. Moore, "Downfall X: The Inside Story of the Management Fiasco at Xerox," Business Week (March 5, 2001): 86.

38. Bianco, A., and P. L. Moore, "Downfall X: The Inside Story of the Management Fiasco at Xerox," Business Week (March 5, 2001): 89–90.

39. Diab, P. "Strategic Planning + Project Management = Competitive Advantage," *PM Network* (July 1998): 27.

Chapter 10

Assessing Value Creation

Chapter Outline
Measuring Value Creation: Two Approaches
A Framework for Assessing Value Creation
Conclusion
Key Terms and Concepts
Discussion Questions
Experiential Exercise
Endnotes

*T*he focus of the strategic management process ends where it began—value creation. Just as we set out to create value at the beginning of the process, we conclude by determining the value we were able to create. The purpose of this chapter is to discuss how this is done in the fifth and final major step of the strategic management process—*assessment of value creation.* This step and its relationship with the overall process are shown in Figure 10-1.

The strategic management process begins with a vision, mission, and set of strategies that strategic managers believe will result in value for the organization's customers, employees, owners, and other key stakeholders. As the firm implements these strategies it monitors and measures its success in creating value. In addition to measuring value creation, the firm must manage it by feeding back the results of the measurement process to appropriate functional managers so that corrective actions, if necessary, can be identified and taken.

Consider the example of Hilton Hotels. The Hilton name has become synonymous with the word "hotel," enjoying a brand awareness of 98 percent around the world.[1] Hilton's goal "is to create value for its constituents—customers, owners and shareholders, employees (known as team members), strategic partners, and

Figure 10-1
The strategic management framework

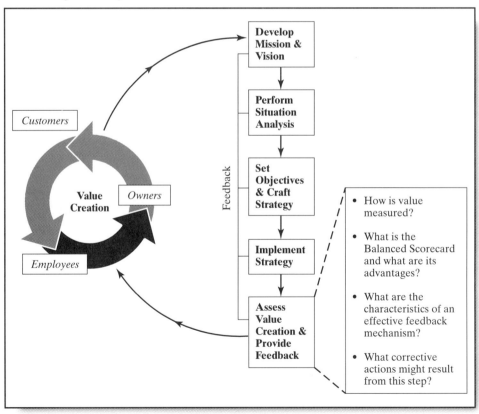

the communities where each hotel is located—by delivering a consistent value proposition."[2] What is a "consistent value proposition?" Hilton's research, conducted during its strategic planning process, determined that the key to delivering value was to ensure a consistent guest experience across all Hilton properties. The research showed that Hilton customers expected, among other things, a clean, quiet, comfortable room, but the quality of the guest experience was inconsistent among Hilton properties, especially between franchised properties and company-owned hotels. This inconsistency undermined Hilton's ability to create value and resulted in less-than-acceptable rates of customer satisfaction.

Hilton's response is a good example of how the *assessment of value creation* step of the strategic management process should work. First, the company set targets of performance in several areas and measured their actual results versus their targets. Next, Hilton pinpointed the areas where performance was inconsistent or substandard and provided feedback to appropriate managers for their review and consideration. Using this information, corrective actions were identified and taken. In time, performance improved and Hilton began to be able to ensure a more consistently positive guest experience across all Hilton properties.

Hilton's approach—measurement, feedback, and corrective action—illustrates the three essential components of the final step of strategic management. Think of the thermostat in your home as an analogy. You set your desired room temperature on the thermostat. The system measures the actual temperature of the room and compares it to your desired temperature. When a significant deviation between actual and desired occurs, that information is fed back to the heating (or air conditioning) unit, which then takes corrective action by generating more hot (or cool) air.

In addition to explaining each of these activities—measurement, feedback, and corrective action—we introduce and discuss approaches or tools for performing them. In particular, the balanced scorecard is emphasized. After reading this chapter you should be able to answer each of the questions about assessing value creation listed in Figure 10-1 and, as an example, be familiar with Hilton's approach to measuring and managing value creation.

MEASURING VALUE CREATION: TWO APPROACHES

Accountability is required in the strategic management process. To achieve accountability, each organization must find ways to translate its mission and strategies into daily operating activities, assign responsibilities for the activities, and measure and evaluate the progress being made. All levels of the organization and each individual employee must understand their roles in carrying out the mission and strategies (recall our discussion of vertical alignment in Chapter 9), and be held responsible for their results. Thus, accountability depends first on establishing clear goals and standards that are communicated and understood throughout the organization. Only then can appropriate measures of progress be identified. As we stated in the first chapter, "If you can't measure it, you can't manage it."[3] Thus, decisions about what will be measured and how are critical. Let's examine alternative approaches for measuring value creation.

The Traditional Approach

Financial measures of value creation, such as those discussed in Chapter 4, have been the tools of the **traditional approach** to strategy evaluation and control. These include different measures of profitability such as return on equity (ROE), earnings per share, and various profit margins (e.g., net, gross, and operating). In addition, analyses of cash flow, the growth rate of sales, and stock price performance are common traditional measures of value creation.

These measures continue to be important barometers of the health of the company and its ability to create value. Their strengths lie in their ability to gauge current organizational performance and in their focus on value for owners and shareholders. On the other hand, the traditional approach has limitations. First, its exclusive focus on financial indicators is overly narrow and owner oriented. Value for customers, employees, and other key stakeholders is not adequately assessed. In addition, financial measures do not necessarily reflect or suggest the future performance of the organization. Today's financial results are primarily the result of business conditions and management decisions made yesterday. These results may not be a reliable indicator of the overall health of the organization and its future prospects for value creation. Let's consider an example.

The Limitations of Financial Measures: An Example.   What would you conclude about the strategic health of a pharmaceutical company that has experienced consistently strong growth in revenues and earnings during the past 5 years? The company has outperformed key competitors as well as the pharmaceutical industry as a whole by achieving an average annual 5-year growth rate in sales of 13.1 percent, as compared to a 10.8 percent industry average. Earnings have grown over the same period by an average of 18.5 percent, versus 13.5 percent for the industry. Furthermore, the company's return on equity was a staggering 53.1 percent, as compared to 34.9 percent for the entire industry.[4]

Based on this information we would most likely conclude that this firm has done well. Its current financial performance is quite strong. Judging from its ROE and profit growth, value has been created for owners, and based on sales growth rates, it appears customer value is also being realized. What can we conclude about the firm's future prospects for value creation? Wouldn't it be safe to assume that this firm's strategic health can be sustained, at least over the next few years? Careful! This is one area where the traditional financial measures are limited.

The example above is real and the numbers are accurate. The company is Schering-Plough, which has indeed achieved an impressive level of financial performance, as the numbers suggest. However, as you might suspect, there is more to this story. Approximately one-third of all Schering-Plough sales comes from one blockbuster drug, Claritin, an allergy/respiratory medication. The challenge: the active chemical found in Claritin, desloratadine, is about to lose its federal patent protection. In the pharmaceutical industry, after a product's patent protection expires and lower priced generic drugs are introduced, it is not unusual for the product to lose 40 to 50 percent of its unit sales within 1 year, and up to 80 percent within 2 years.

Of course, Schering-Plough is aware of this challenge and has been preparing for it by developing a next generation replacement for Claritin, but there is no guarantee that the new drug will achieve Claritin's success.

The implications of this example should be apparent—financial measures of value creation are useful for evaluating current performance but financial measures alone are not enough. The financial perspective emphasizes current performance and value for owners. To be confident in our predictions about the future strategic health of this company, or any company for that matter, we need a more balanced and comprehensive set of assessments and measures.

The Balanced Scorecard

The balanced scorecard concept was developed by Robert Kaplan, an accounting professor at the Harvard Business School, and David Norton, president of the Renaissance Strategy Group. The purpose of the scorecard is to identify and track the key elements of a company's strategy. Organizations that use it have found that it helps them to clarify and translate their vision and strategies into specific operational tasks and activities that must be performed. It becomes the link between strategy and action.

The **balanced scorecard** has important advantages over the traditional financial approach. It is based on the premise that financial measures are necessary but not sufficient for providing a clear and comprehensive focus on all of the critical areas of business. The balanced scorecard includes financial measures that indicate the results of actions already taken but goes beyond this perspective to get a more balanced assessment of value creation. Its advantages include:

- a combination of financial and nonfinancial measures of value creation
- an assessment of current and future indicators of value
- a focus on value for customers, employees, and owners/shareholders
- an internal and external perspective on value creation

As shown in Figure 10-2, the balanced scorecard provides managers with information from four different perspectives. The *financial* perspective focuses on value creation for owners using the financial tools discussed so far in this chapter. This perspective is complemented by three others. The *customer* perspective puts the spotlight on the organization's relationships with its customers and its ability to build and retain satisfied customers. The *internal* perspective focuses on employees and operations and emphasizes the organization's success at developing and keeping qualified and motivated employees. It also examines the internal operations of the organization and seeks to achieve higher levels of efficiency and effectiveness. The *future* perspective assesses the firm's ability to innovate and learn and questions whether it can continue to improve and create value.

The specific measures used to assess performance in the four areas will depend on the company, its strategic objectives, and the nature of its products and services.

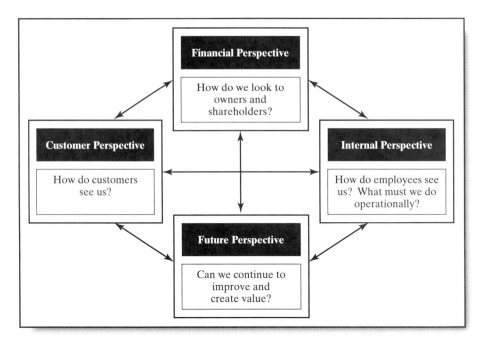

Figure 10-2
The balanced scorecard

Source: Adapted from Kaplan, R. S., and D. P. Norton, "The Balanced Scorecard—Measures That Drive Performance," *Harvard Business Review* (January–February 1992): 72.

The scorecard can be adapted to suit any organization. Some of the common measures for a business organization are listed in Figure 10-3.

Most of the measures in Figure 10-3 have either been explained in a previous chapter (e.g., ROE, asset turnover) or are self-explanatory (e.g., sales to employee, market share). A few need further explanation. **MVA (market value added)** is a measure of change in the stock price of the firm (growth or decline over time). SG&A efficiency is a measure of the firm's ability to control sales, general, and administrative (SG&A) costs. Claritin's patent expiration is an example of **business at risk,** a measure of impending threats to sales. The **freshness index** measures the percentage of total sales from new products. For example, from Chapter 4 we know that 3M places a strong emphasis on innovation. This is reflected in 3M's goal of achieving a freshness index of 30 percent of total revenues each year from products that have been on the market for less than 4 years. **Time to market** is a measure of cycle time, or how long it takes a company to develop a new product concept and introduce it to the market.

This collection of metrics is not meant to be exhaustive. In fact, the possibilities for developing and customizing measures are almost unlimited. For example:

- To assess customer value, a semiconductor company asked each of its major customers to rank the company against its competitors on attributes such as quality, delivery time, and price. When results indicated that the company was ranked in the middle of the pack, managers made changes to move the company to the top of the list.[5]

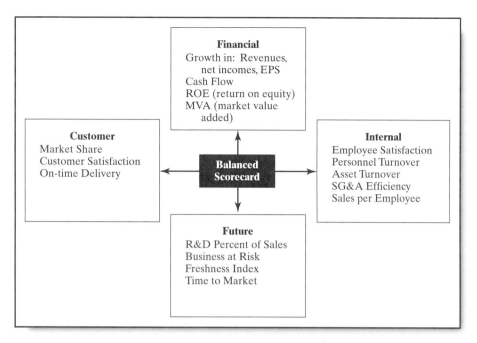

Figure 10-3
Common measures in the balanced scorecard

- When U.S. West, a telecommunications firm based in Denver, undertook an e-commerce initiative, IT managers developed a balanced scorecard for their projects, taking steps to develop measurable goals in each of the four areas of concern. U.S. West surveyed its customers to evaluate the impact of the project on their perception of the firm's performance. Measures were also established to determine the extent to which the project satisfied the need of employees for continual development.[6]

While these examples suggest that strategic managers have many options in establishing the measures to be used in the scorecard, each company is faced with the same challenge—choosing the right measures. Research indicates that an organization's measurement system will strongly affect the behaviors of its managers and employees. What you measure is what you get.[7] In addition to choosing the right measures, managers must not be distracted by the temptation to measure too much. Information overload is counterproductive and overwhelms managers and employees. If the balanced scorecard is to truly drive value creation as it is meant to do, it must focus on a clear and manageable set of relevant factors. Let's consider an example to see how one company used the balanced scorecard to assess and manage value creation.

Hilton Hotels and the Balanced Scorecard.[8] To use the balanced scorecard, Hilton conducts an annual planning process that translates its business strategy into operational activities and corresponding goals in each of the four areas—financial, customer, internal, and future. Goals are stated in SMART format, as we have discussed in Chapter 6. The strategy and operational goals are communicated and reinforced continuously throughout the year. People at all levels of the organization know what is expected of them.

Hilton uses the scorecard concept to provide information on how each individual hotel performs relative to its own historical averages, and to competitors and other Hilton properties. Eight measures are used to provide a balanced view of the hotel's performance. Table 10-1 identifies and briefly defines each measure.

Hilton's measures are a combination of financial and nonfinancial metrics, and address value creation for shareholders, guests, and team members. Once goals and measures are clearly established, performance can be monitored in each of the specified areas. Hilton uses a simple but effective way to communicate performance results. Measures are reported numerically and by color code. There are three color zones: results in the green zone indicate that the hotel meets or exceeds goals for that measure, yellow signifies results slightly below the standard, and red identifies results where the hotel is significantly below the goal.

Results are communicated widely using graphs and charts so that hotel managers and employees can see how well they are doing. The color-coding system draws attention to each hotel's problem areas and clarifies where attention and resources need to be focused. Because results are tracked over time, managers receive feedback on their problem-solving ability as they see the outcomes of their efforts to move performance from the red to green zone.

Table 10-1   Hilton's balanced scorecard measures

MEASURE	DESCRIPTION
Room RevPAR	RevPAR is a standard performance measure in the lodging industry. It measures revenue generated per available room.
RevPAR Index	RevPAR compared to competitors in the local market.
EBITDA	A measure of operational effectiveness based on earnings before interest, taxes, depreciation, and amortization.
Guest Satisfaction	Customers complete guest-comment cards to indicate their overall satisfaction.
Customer Satisfaction Tracking	Telephone interviews of a sample of guests are used to measure satisfaction.
Team Member Satisfaction	All hotel employees are surveyed to determine their overall satisfaction.
Mystery Shopper	Average of scores from random visits by auditors posing as guests.
Standards Compliance	A measure of the hotel's compliance with brand standards such as courteous service, fresh food, clean bathrooms, quiet rooms.

Source: Adapted from Huckestein, D., and R. Duboff, "Hilton Hotels: A Comprehensive Approach to Delivering Value for All Stakeholders," *Hotel and Restaurant Administration Quarterly* (August 1999): 31.

Hilton's reward system is tied directly to results from the balanced scorecard. Hotel-specific goals are linked to bonus programs, merit-pay increases, stock options, and the performance reviews of hotel managers. One example is Hilton's Million-Dollar Team Pride Award. Hotels must score in the green zone on all eight measures to be eligible. An annual pool of up to $1 million of Hilton stock is divided equally among all full-time team members at all eligible hotels.

The end result for Hilton is a tight link between its strategy and the operating activities of individual hotels. Value creation is defined, measured, and managed.

Using the Balanced Scorecard.   The Hilton example provides some helpful insights into how organizations can develop and use the balanced scorecard. These may be summarized as follows:

- Begin with a clear strategy—a lack of clarity at the top (strategy) will also muddle thinking at lower levels (operations). An effective use of the scorecard depends on a clear understanding of the drivers of value.
- Set goals that link strategy and operations—develop realistic and measurable targets and customize them to the operating unit.
- Carefully select measures—employee behavior will be strongly influenced by the measures for which they are held accountable. Measures should give an accurate (i.e., valid and reliable) reading of goal accomplishment and focus on outcomes that employees can control.
- Communicate up front and provide feedback—people need to understand the strategy, goals, and measures and receive prompt feedback on performance results.
- Take corrective action—use performance results to learn where to focus attention and develop solutions to problems.
- Follow through with the reward system—link pay and other rewards to performance. Reward employees for significant accomplishments.

A FRAMEWORK FOR ASSESSING VALUE CREATION

As the discussion above suggests, assessing value creation, the fifth step in strategic management, means more than just measuring value creation. In fact, three activities are needed:

- Measuring value creation
- Feeding back results
- Taking corrective action, if necessary, and striving for continuous improvement

If a Hilton property, for example, determines that it has fallen short of its target in its mystery shopper index (*measurement*), results are communicated to managers and employees (**feedback**) so that the problem can be understood and addressed by new ideas or programs (**corrective action**). Even when there is no problem per se, we look for opportunities to learn and develop (**continuous improvement**).

Let's examine a framework that incorporates the balanced scorecard and may be used to accomplish all three of the activities in assessing value creation. The components of the model include reviewing the situation analysis to examine the underlying bases of strategy, applying the balanced scorecard, feeding back results, and taking corrective actions, if needed. The relationship between the components is shown in Figure 10-4.

Figure 10-4 is a straightforward and practical tool for assessing value creation. It stresses the need to monitor the assumptions underlying our choice of strategy by first revisiting the situation analysis. Have major changes occurred in our internal or external strategic position? That is, do we have a new understanding of our strengths, weaknesses, opportunities, or threats? If so, we may need to take corrective action even if our value creation continues to be strong.

For example, suppose you are a hotel manager in Miami. You just learned that your closest competitor has acquired property less than a mile from you and intends to build and open a new hotel within 2 years. Your current results have not changed; you are still meeting all your value creation goals, but obviously your external opportunities and threats have changed dramatically and you need to consider your strategic response (i.e., corrective action). This example highlights the importance of not relying just on results to trigger corrective actions. If you wait to take corrective action until after you experience some loss of value creation, it may be too late, but by acting now, you may be able to either avert the threat or at least minimize it.

The next part of the framework emphasizes the balanced scorecard. Using the approach described in the previous section, we measure our results in relation to our targets in the four areas—financial, future, customer, and internal. If we have not made satisfactory progress toward stated goals, that feedback is relayed to employees and managers for their analysis and action. On the other hand, if the review of our situation analysis and balanced scorecard do not uncover any significant changes or shortfalls, corrective action may not be necessary. Under these circumstances, the model suggests that a continuation of the current strategy and support-

Figure 10-4
A framework for assessing value creation

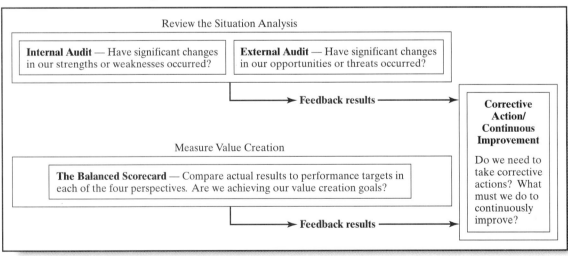

ing operational activities is expected to produce value now and into the future. No corrective action is needed.

At the same time, just because corrective action is not called for, does not mean we should sit back and be comfortable with the status quo. Successful companies look for ways to reinvent themselves through continuous improvement even when things are going well. The search never ends.

Feedback and Corrective Action/Continuous Improvement

We have focused extensively on measuring value creation, but let's further examine the feedback and corrective action/improvement components of the framework. What are the characteristics of an effective feedback mechanism? Think of the Hilton example. The feedback is comprehensive but simple to understand. Hilton's green, yellow, and red color scheme communicates results on eight variables in a clear and direct way. It is supplemented with graphs and charts that track results over time. Furthermore, this information is widely communicated in report form and posted for all employees and managers to see in high-visibility locations such as employee entrances and lunchrooms.

Hilton makes feedback available on a timely basis so that team members may respond quickly to both problems and opportunities. The information helps to build a common understanding among employees and focuses attention on the goals of value creation and continuous improvement. These characteristics are summarized in Table 10-2.

The final component of the framework is corrective action and continuous improvement. What are some examples of actions to correct problems or achieve continuous improvement? The list is very extensive and can range from minor adjustments of operational procedures to a wholesale revamping of the organization's mission. The incremental changes in operations are more common and much easier to implement. At Hilton, for example, this might mean a simple change to the room service menu, having beach towels available at poolside, or changing the way front desk employees greet guests as they arrive for check-in.

At the other end of the spectrum, corrective action may entail a fundamental redirection of the mission, vision, and strategies of the organization. That is why the feedback loop in the strategic management framework connects back to the first step of the process—developing the mission and vision.

Table 10-2 Characteristics of an effective feedback system

- Comprehensive but simple to understand
- Results are disseminated widely (to all team members for whom it is useful)
- Communicated in a variety of formats (e.g., reports, graphs, posters, e-mail)
- Timely
- Fosters a common understanding of issues, challenges, opportunities
- Focuses attention on shared purpose

We saw an example of this fundamental redirection in Chapter 3. Hershey Foods revised its mission statement several times in the last decade as it searched for more effective ways to generate value in the highly competitive food industry. At one point Hershey's mission and strategies emphasized international expansion and becoming "a major diversified food company." Hershey pursued that vision by branching out into the pasta business and making acquisitions outside the United States. Since that time Hershey has refocused again, narrowing its scope and emphasizing its core business of confectionery products and core markets in North America. Similarly, in its search for greater value, Campbell Soup Company expanded and then contracted its business definition, selling off divisions and closing down production facilities. These are all examples of corrective actions taken by firms looking for value creation.

CONCLUSION

Assessing value creation is the fifth step in the strategic management process. The three components of this step—measurement, feedback, and corrective action/continuous improvement—are explained in this chapter. It is important to emphasize that these steps are ongoing throughout the strategy process. The strategic management framework (see Figure 10-1) suggests that this is the final step in the process, and logically this is true. Before we can assess our success in creating value with our strategies, we must first develop and implement those strategies, but as we know, the actual practice of strategic management is not a neat sequence of discrete, nonoverlapping steps. There are lots of things happening simultaneously. While we may be working on developing a new strategy, we are also implementing existing strategies and assessing their results. Feedback is a constant process of communicating the results of ongoing efforts. We don't wait until the end of the process to evaluate results and take corrective actions, if needed. Indeed, as stated previously, we continuously search for new and better ways to achieve the overriding objective of strategic management—to create value for our stakeholders, especially our customers, employees, and owners.

KEY TERMS AND CONCEPTS

After reading this chapter you should understand each of the following terms.

- Balanced scorecard
- Business at risk
- Continuous improvement
- Corrective action
- Feedback

- Freshness index
- MVA (market value added)
- Time to market
- Traditional approach (to measuring value)

DISCUSSION QUESTIONS

1. What are the three activities involved in assessing value creation?
2. What are the advantages of a balanced scorecard for measuring value creation versus the traditional approach?
3. Do you agree or disagree with the following statement: If a firm is meeting its value creation goals and a review of its situation analysis determines that no internal or external strategic changes have occurred, the organization should stay the course. No action is necessary.
4. Can the balanced scorecard be customized to meet the unique needs of any organization? Explain.
5. Check the textbook's Web site to determine Hilton's current corporate-level financial performance. Has it been consistent? Does it look like corrective action is needed? Explain.

EXPERIENTIAL EXERCISE

The Balanced Scorecard. Either in teams or on your own, select a company or organization that you know well. Develop a balanced scorecard for the organization. Identify specific goals in the SMART format for each of the four areas of the scorecard. Describe the measures you would use to assess value creation and the ways you would feed back results within the organization. Be specific.

ENDNOTES

1. Hilton Hotels, "About Hilton Hotels," 2001, www.hilton.com/en/hi/brand/about.jhtml, accessed May 30, 2001.
2. Huckestein, D., and R. Duboff, "Hilton Hotels: A Comprehensive Approach to Delivering Value for All Stakeholders," *Hotel and Restaurant Administration Quarterly* (August 1999): 28.
3. Garvin, D. A., "Building a Learning Organization," *Harvard Business Review* (July–August 1993): 89.
4. PriceWaterhouseCoopers, "EdgarScan Database." http://edgarscan.pwcglobal.com, accessed May 23, 2001.
5. Kaplan, R. S., and D. P. Norton, "The Balanced Scorecard—Measures That Drive Performance," *Harvard Business Review* (January–February 1992): 74.
6. Robinson, R., "Balanced Scorecard," *Computerworld* (January 24, 2000): 52.
7. Kaplan, R. S., and D. P. Norton, "The Balanced Scorecard—Measures That Drive Performance," *Harvard Business Review* (January–February 1992): 71.
8. Hilton's use of the balanced scorecard is explained in detail in an article by Dieter Huckestein, president of hotel operations at Hilton, and Robert Duboff, vice president at Mercer Management Consulting. See Huckestein, D., and R. Duboff, "Hilton Hotels: A Comprehensive Approach to Delivering Value for All Stakeholders," *Hotel and Restaurant Administration Quarterly* (August 1999): 28–38 for more information. The examples of Hilton used throughout this chapter were obtained from this article and from a review of Hilton's Web site.

INDEX

I

IBM (www.ibm.com), 182–183, 186–189
Imitability, 91
Implementing deliberate strategies, role of middle managers, 185
Imprisoned resources, 87
Income statement, 171
   projecting, 172
Individualism, 194
Individualism view (ethical framework), 151
Industrial factors, 229
Industrial Revolution, 34
Industry
   consolidation, 62
   defined, 107
   dimensions of scope
     competitor, 110
     geographical, 110
     horizontal, 110
     vertical, 110
   environment, 100
   norms, 76
   variable in task environment, 107–109
Information Age, 35, 44
Information Resources, Inc., 44
Infrastructural decisions, 218
Innovation, 106
Institutional investors, 17
Integration strategies
   horizontal, 62
   vertical, 61–62
Intel, 33
Intended strategy, 15
Internal audit, 5–7, 72–73
   core competencies (stage 3), 85–87
     3M, 88–89, 90, 91
   defined, 73
   performance assessment (stage 1), 74–76
     3M performance, 78–80
     financial ratio analysis, 77–78

   process, 73–74, 75
   strengths and weaknesses (stage 4), 89, 91–92
   value chain activities and linkages analysis (stage 2), 80
     cross-functional linkages, 82–83
     internal evaluation of the value chain, 83–84
     supply chain management, evaluation of, 84–85
     value chain, 81–82
Internal funding sources, 176–177
Internal growth, 58
Internal perspective of the balanced scorecard, 241
Internal rate of return (IRR), 168–169
International aspects of strategy implementation, 228–230
International Electronic and Electrical Engineers (IEEE), 115
Internet, 14, 43, 44–45, 230
   auto-buying services, 30–31
Interstate Bakeries Corporation, 108
Intra-functional integration, 215–216
Inventions, 106
Investment-ranking device, 169
Irwin, 62

J

Job process, 214
Johnson & Johnson, 5, 56
   credo, 6
Joint ventures, 63, 229
J. Sainsbury plc, 19
Justice view (ethical framework), 151

K

Kaplan, Robert, 241
Kellogg Company, 54

N

Nabisco Brands Ltd., 52
Nabisco Group Holdings Corp., 177
Nabisco Holdings, Co., 108, 109
Nantucket Nectars, 10
NASA, 56
National culture, 193–196
National Rifle Association
        (NRA), 115
Natural environment, 18–19
NBC, 61
NCR (National Cash Register), 189
Nestle, 52, 63
Net investment, 159
Net operating cash inflows, 159
Net present value (NPV), 163–167
Net salvage value, 159
Network structure, 225, 226, 227
Nike (www.nikebiz.com), 1–2, 4, 7, 8, 9,
        11, 14, 19, 31, 33, 56, 60, 64, 67,
        112, 115, 143, 162
  Code of Conduct, 19, 20–21
  Nike.com, 45
Nominal group technique, 119
Nominating committee, 17
Nordstrom's, 33, 68
North American Free Trade Agreement
        (NAFTA), 143
North American Industry
        Classification System
        (NAICS), 108
Norton, David, 241

O

Objectives, 8–9
  See also Strategic objectives
Occupational Safety and Health Act of
        1970, 105
Occupational Safety and Health
        Administration (OSHA),
        104–105

Ocean Spray, 10
Open systems, 99
Operating core, 221
Operational excellence, 31–32
Opinion surveys, 117
Opportunities, 98
Opportunity, 107
Opportunity cost, 161
Oracle, 33
Organizational alignment,
        213–214
  horizontal, 215
    cost leadership and, 216
    differentiation and, 216–217
    enterprise resource planning
        (ERP), 219
    within a function, 218–219
    at JM Mold, 217–218
    weak, consequences of, 218
  vertical, 211
    cost leadership and, 214
    differentiation and, 214
    is it a reality?, 214–215
Organizational change, phases
        of, 199
Organizational context, 148
Organizational culture, 149–150
  in strategy implementation, 189
Organizational design
  components of an organization
        structure, 220–221
  structure, diversification, and
        expansion, 227–228
  structure-strategy
        relationship, 221
  types of organization structure
    divisional, 223–225
    functional, 222–223
    matrix, 225, 226
    network, 225, 226, 227
    simple, 222
Organization of Petroleum
        Exporting Countries
        (OPEC), 113
Organizations, source for
        understanding relevant
        competition, 109

Psychological value for employees, 37–39
Purchasing power, 101
Putting people first, 35–36

Q

Quaker Oats, 108
Qualitative forecasting, 117
Quantitative forecasting, 117
Question marks, 133–134

R

Racial composition of the United States, 103
  (table), 104
Rareness, 91
Rate of return, 160–161
Ratio analysis
  limitations of, 77
  (table), 78
Realized strategy, 15
Recognition, 39
Recycling free cash flows, 176–177
Reebok, 33, 43
Refreezing phase of organizational change, 199
Reinvestment, preceded by divestment, 177
Related diversification, 61
Relative market share, 132
Relevance, 92
Remington Rand Corporation, 209
Research Insight, 108
Resistance phase of change, 197–198
Resource allocation, 211, 212
Resource decisions, 12
Resources, imprisoned, 87
Retrenchment strategies, 177
  cost-cutting strategies, 63–64
  divestiture, 64–65

downsizing, risks of, 64
  liquidation, 64–65
Return on equity (ROE), 77
Return on investment, 161
Ritz-Carlton Hotels, 33, 67
Rivalry among firms, 112–113
R. J. Reynolds Tobacco Holdings, Inc., 177
RJR Nabisco, 109
Roche, 144
Ronzoni Foods, 52
Royal Dutch/Shell, 140

S

Sales forecasts, 172
Santa Rosa Systems Division (SRSD), 227
Satisfaction, 28
Saucony, 43
SBC Communications Inc., 177
Scanning, 116–117, 118
Scenario analysis, 117
Scenario planning, 140–141
Schering-Plough Corporation, 54, 144, 240–241
Schokoladen, 52
Sears, 67–68
SEES (scanning, estimating, evaluating, sharing), 116–120
Senge, Peter, 191
Senior management style (top-down or laissez-faire), 190–193
Senior management team (SMT), 16
  decision-making process, 148
  organizational context, 148
  organizational outcomes, 149
  personal attributes, 147–148
7-Eleven Japan Co., 103–104
SG&A efficiency, 242
Shared purpose, 53
Shareholder social activism, 18
Sharp, 232

U.S. Postal Service, 32
U.S. West, 243
Utilitarian view (ethical framework), 151

V

Value, 91
Value chain
    cross-functional linkages, 82–83
    defined, 80–81
    internal evaluation of, 83–84
    primary activities, 81
    supply chain management,
        evaluation of, 84–85
    support activities, 82
Value creation, 3–4
    assessing, 75–76, 237–239
        balanced scorecard, 241–245
        feedback, 13–14
        framework for, 245–248
        traditional approach, 240–421
    customers and, 27
    customer value, 27
        customer satisfaction, 28–30
        defined, 28
        perceptions of value and usage
            situation, 30
        providing, 29–30
        who is responsible for?, 30–31
    e-business and, 44–45
    emerging technologies and,
        43–44
    employees and, 34
        defined, 36
        financial value, 36–37
        psychological value, 37–39
        putting people first, 35–36
        social value, 37–39
    importance of, 25
        customer-employee-owner
            (C.E.O.) cycle, 25–27
    owners and, 39
        defined, 40–41
        lasting value, 42–43

long-term value, 42
short-term value, 41–42
strategy and financial
    performance, 41
See also Value disciplines
Value disciplines
    customer, achieving, 34
    customer intimacy, 31, 33
    operational excellence, 31–32
    product leadership, 31, 33–34
Value-in-use, 28
*Value Line Investment
    Surveys*, 108
Value system, 83
Veiga, J. F., 35, 39
Verizon Communications Inc.,
    142–143, 178
Vertical alignment
    See Organizational alignment
Vertical integration, 61–62
VerticalNet Inc.
    (www.verticalnet.com), 68
Vertical scope (industry), 110
Very Fine, 10
Visa Card, 68
Vision, 4–5, 55
    lacking clear, 190
    shared, 191
Visionary companies, 49–51
Vision framework, 55–57
    synthesizing and crafting,
        56–57
Vision statement, 55
Visteon, 178
Vlasic Foods International,
    64–65
Voluntary responsibilities, 151
Volvo, 62

W

Wall Street Research Network
    (www.wsrn.com), 108–109
Wal-Mart, 31, 67, 68, 85, 114, 149